Pauline: Napoleon Bonaparte's Scandalous Sister

Pauline: Napoleon Bonaparte's Scandalous Sister

The Exotic and Turbulent Life of an Imperial Princess

Pauline Bonaparte and Her Lovers

Hector Fleischmann

Pauline Bonaparte, a Short Biography

by Joseph Turquan

LEONAUR

Pauline: Napoleon Bonaparte's Scandalous Sister
The Exotic and Turbulent Life of an Imperial Princess
Pauline Bonaparte and Her Lovers
by Hector Fleischmann
Pauline Bonaparte, a Short Biography
by Joseph Turquan

FIRST EDITION IN THIS FORM

First published under the titles
Pauline Bonaparte and Her Lovers
and
The Sisters of Napoleon Elisa, Pauline, and Caroline Bonaparte (Extract)

Leonaur is an imprint of Oakpast Ltd
Copyright in this form © 2025 Oakpast Ltd

ISBN: 978-1-916535-84-8 (hardcover)
ISBN: 978-1-916535-85-5 (softcover)

http://www.leonaur.com

Contents

Pauline Bonaparte

Pauline Bonaparte and Her Lovers

THE VENUS BORGHÈSE

Contents

CHAPTER 1

Her Early Love-Affairs

It was one day in June, 1793, a sultry, sunny, radiant day, that Signora Letizia Bonaparte reached Marseilles, bringing along with her a shabby, cheerful troop of out-at-elbows boys and down-at-heels girls, and took up her abode on the fourth floor of a house in the Rue Pavilion. This is the first lodging they have had for a month which was not more or less of a makeshift. Ever since May 27, the day on which the anti-French *Consulta*, formed by Paoli in Corsica, decreed the banishment of the Bonapartes, the family has been wandering from thicket to thicket, through the bush of the table-land of the island, sleeping on the undergrowth, with next to nothing to eat, living anyhow, an existence without a moment's peace, tracked and hunted day by day, far from their burned house and ravaged fields, pushing on towards the coast, towards Calvi, where Napoleon is waiting with the sailing-boat on which their chance of liberty depends.

On June 11, without money or belongings, the family of fugitives embarked. Just the wind they wanted was blowing, and two days later their boat reached Toulon.

Some means of living, some lodging, must be found, no matter where. To begin with, it is on the outskirts of La Valette, at the house of a woman named Cordeil, that they stay.

After a few days the fugitives take to the road again, stopping a short time at Bandol. Marseilles is stopping-place number three. The town is given over to the Terror; the tumbrils bearing the condemned to their death pass under their windows; but that's nothing; Marseilles is a centre where some help can be had in these days of misery, and whence a look-out can be kept for the turning of the tide.

The older male members find their feet quickly enough. Joseph slips into the army administration, rises to the post of military superintendent of the first class, and gets entrusted with the supervision of the Marseilles hospitals. Lucien, after a spell of enforced idleness, makes up his mind to try his luck further afield. Accordingly, we may find him in the Var, at Saint-Maximin, in charge of a warehouse, orator-in-chief at the Jacobin Club, and favoured suitor for the hand of the daughter of the inn-keeper with whom he lodges.

Uncle Fesch, Signora Letizia's foster-brother, has also made his way. He is with the Alpine division of the army, looking after the stores. Louis has become a lieutenant in the 4th Regiment of Artillery. Jerome will go to school as soon as he has got his first pair of breeches. Such is the introduction to French life of those who one day will be high dignitaries of the Empire, and kings.

Then there are the girls.

The eldest is sixteen; this is Elisa, who is going to be Princess of Lucca and Piombino, and Grand-duchess of Tuscany. At present she is looking after the poverty-stricken housekeeping, and the education of her youngest sister, little Caroline, nine years old and destined to wear the crown of Naples. Between No. 1 and No. 3 comes No. 2, Paulette, that is Pauline, making the most of a butterfly existence, with all the happy-go-lucky zest of thoughtless thirteen. Overshadowing all of them looms the Roman figure of their mother, overworn with cares, a prey to anxiety; day by day and hour by hour on the defensive against the insidious assaults of want. And there, in the distance, hard by beleaguered Toulon, stands the figure of the second brother, Napoleon, beginning his career.

But the whole process is a painful one. What can Joseph do for the family? A little assistance at odd intervals, and that with difficulty. Lucien, too? To meet his bill at the inn he will find himself obliged to marry the daughter. Fesch economises, but that does not yield much! As for Louis, he cannot do much more than keep himself alive. So, too, with Napoleon, nothing happens, and Toulon not yet fallen. But something must be found to eat.

On July 11, 1793, Convention has decided to grant temporary assistance to the Corsicans who have been driven from their island as a result of loyalty to France; something to keep them from dying of hunger. The Bonaparte women-folk are entitled to this. Every month, then, as "needlewomen," they appear before the municipality to claim their dole. So much for necessaries; but nothing beyond: no luxuries, no comforts for the mother, no pretty fripperies for the girls, not so much as a remnant of ribbon. So shabby are their dresses that they are ashamed to go out in daytime. They can but economise and wait;

perhaps one day . . .

Then, suddenly, comes the catastrophe. At Paris the *Thermidor* mob has just overthrown Robespierre. Immediately after, hands still stained with that noble blood are signing revocations, confiscations, arrests. Young Napoleon has been unfortunate enough to win the approval of the *Incorruptible's* brother; so, we see him cashiered, arrested, and though released, sent nevertheless in disgrace to the Vendée Army. Bearing the same name as he, the brothers bear similar burdens. Joseph flies to Genoa, and has to resort to pitiable makeshifts to keep body and soul together; Lucien is put under lock and key; Louis loses his rank and is sent to the school at Châlons. The discreet and crafty Fesch is the only one who, aided in his case by a non-committal name, escapes and continues to thrive, undetected, in various obscure corners.

But then comes the stroke of luck, as unexpectedly as the catastrophe had done. To checkmate the *Vendémiaire* royalist insurrection, Barras has need of a master of men, and, mindful of Toulon, has chosen Bonaparte for the police operations, which end in the "whiff of grapeshot" in the *parvis* St. Roch. Then the wheel of Fortune turns round again. Bundles of paper-money are sent off to Marseilles, Joseph will be appointed consul at Genoa, Lucien military superintendent with the Germany Army, Louis a lieutenant. And the future is under consideration. Everything comes right in a minute. The sisters will have dresses, and feathers in their hats.

To emphasise the suddenness of this *volte-face*—and the need for it—a royalist pamphleteer, Peltier, a refugee in London, invents (during the Consulate) a letter by Pauline, dated from Marseilles at the end of September, 1795. It would be absurd to advance detailed proof of its apocryphal character, but such as it is, it is curious, echoing as it does the wretchedness experienced by the family during this interval of gloom in the early days of the Napoleonidae.

Pauline writes in this note:

Alas I should very much like to have a hat all to myself; Elisa and I have only one between us. It's true that today (which is my turn to wear it) I am making quite a different hat of it by replacing pink ribbon by white ribbon and trimming it with different flowers. But supposing anyone happens to notice that when I am wearing it, my sister goes bareheaded, there are all my tricks discovered! Oh! how red I should get! But patience! Napoleon writes that he has killed lots of Parisians and that he

13

has been promised a fine post in payment for it. Then, I hope, I shall have a hat of my own.

Barring the end, would not this note be worthy of Pauline and of what we know as regards her frivolity when appearance was concerned? But this much is nothing but good-natured jesting; Peltier has other accusations in his sack. It is to him that we owe the earliest tales of Pauline's earliest experiments in dissipation which were to lead up to that career of eroticism in which she was to excel.

According to Peltier, Pauline had her first lover at Marseilles in 1794, that is to say, when she was fourteen. He omits to inform us of his name, but makes up for that by telling us that she bathed stark naked in the harbour. The probability of this is obviously as clear as daylight. It appears that fervent royalists in London accepted them as gospel-truth. Furthermore, Peltier, covered with blushes, states that "widow Bonaparte," at Marseilles, did business openly in the charms of her daughters.

★★★★★★★★★★

Lefebvre Saint-Ogan, *L'Envers de l'Epopée*. These attacks irritated the First Consul considerably. "He was annoyed," says Bourrienne, "by the insults which came forth in plenty in English journals and pamphlets, especially the *Ambigu*, the work of one Peltier, who had been responsible for the *Actes des Apôtres* at Paris. The *Ambigu* was always full of exceedingly violent attacks on the First Consul and on the French nation, a very creditable thing, obviously, to its French author." (*Mémoires de M. de Bourrienne, ministre d'Etat, sur Napoléon, le Directoire, le Consulat, l'Empire, ei la Restauration.*) Bonaparte instituted proceedings, quite unofficially, against Peltier in London, and won the case, which gave the finishing touch to Peltier's defamatory fury.

★★★★★★★★★★

Fourteen years of age! That is the year given by a Russian pamphlet of 1813, likewise, for the beginnings of Pauline's licentiousness. If we may believe this latter, Napoleon's sister began by leaving home to follow her lover, Corporal Cervoni. The next year, *i.e.* 1796, she entered a house of ill-fame at Paris—another of these highly probable suggestions, inasmuch as we know that Pauline came to Paris for the first time towards the end of 1797, after her marriage with Leclerc. Corporal Cervoni, however, with whose name hers is coupled, is not mythological; this is Jean-Baptiste Cervoni, born 1768, "a man of merit, brave and honourable, albeit a Corsican," says Barras concerning him.

★★★★★★★★★★

PAULINE BONAPARTE

Barras, moreover, speaking of Cervoni, recalls the following anecdote which undoubtedly shows him to have been far less intimate with the princess than is affirmed by the Russian pamphlet of 1813. "On her arrival at Aix the princess received the homage of all the old nobility—military and parliamentary. General Cervoni, a companion of her childhood, was received by her on the same cordial footing as of old, and maintained the same attitude himself so naively in fact, as one day to presume to sit down in a chair near her Imperial Highness while a numerous gathering of men and ladies remained standing. One of the princess's chamberlain's considered the general's behaviour so improper that he termed it impertinent and indecent. 'If the princess makes a sign to me,' said the chamberlain, 'I will put this free-and-easy general in his place, that is, out of the door.' When this remark reached Cervoni, which it did through one of his A.D.C.'s, it made him very angry. He is said to have marched up to the group of the princess's officials saying, 'Point out this wag to me so that I can give him a thorough good thrashing.' Cervoni added that the chamberlain took to his heels. Cervoni went back to the princess, who was the first to laugh at the snub to her obsequious chamberlain; and to show how entirely she was on the general's side asked him to arrange a reception and a ball for her at his country-house near Marseilles. Cervoni, when saying goodbye, added, 'I am going to get everything ready, but mind, no chamberlains.'" (*Mémoires de Barras, membre du Directoire.*)

★★★★★★★★★★

It was this same Cervoni who was the first to reconnoitre in Toulon, after its recapture, at the head of 200 men. He was killed on the field of battle at Eckmühl. The list of Pauline's lovers is long enough for there to be no need to lengthen it by adding the name of Cervoni, who had less brilliant adventures in love-affairs and in barracks.

The royalist Peltier, then, is the inventor, or at any rate the earliest propagator, of the myth of Pauline the shameless. He repeated his charges often enough to render it an article of faith among his rivals. Like him, the English Jew, Lewis Goldsmith, gives the age of fourteen years as that of Pauline's introduction to the "honourable profession of courtesan." (Lewis Goldsmith, notary, ex-interpreter at the Courts of Justice and the Council of the Prize Court at Paris.) Given this libellous statement, good Frenchmen of 1815 will have nothing more to do than to amplify in their outrageous pamphlets of the Hundred Days. For example, a personage in a peasant's dialogue holds forth thus with a comic earnestness:

You will know that Pauline, Caroline, and Elisa, Bonaparte's sisters, lived at Marseilles in a way in which we should be sorry for our daughters, or lady friends, to live; that, during the stay that I once made in that town, I have seen them promenade in the evening just as certain girls do in the Rue St. Honore and at the Palais Royal.

(Is there any need to remind the reader that at this date Caroline had not reached her tenth year? But, when endeavouring to overwhelm the fallen Napoleonidae, why consider such details?)

Whereto the local busybody makes a telling reply with her usual absurd knowingness:

Yes, and that's a fact! And how can any respectable woman contain herself when she sees these beggar-girls turned into queens and princesses, and acting their parts with such disgusting impudence? We should have to have no souls, or only be made of mud, not to choke at the idea. Streetwalkers and trulls changed into queens? It's not as if, when they did arrive at high degree, they behaved as queens; not a bit of it; what they were at Marseilles, they still were as queens, the only difference being that then they received money, whereas as 'Their Majesties' they paid it. Fine 'Majesties' those! . . .

What stupid lampoons these were! No doubt, in the course of their reigns, Napoleon's sisters did sometimes, and too carelessly, lay themselves open to such charges, but they can assuredly be acquitted of the wholesale carryings-on that are ascribed to them at Marseilles. The plea in their favour comes from one who was severe enough on them in other respects. General de Ricard, whose controversy with Prince Jerome resulted in his joining the ranks of the pamphleteers under the Empire, and who, moreover, saw much of the Bonaparte girls at Marseilles, admits that "if the behaviour of Napoleon's sisters was irreproachable, in reality it was not so, so far as appearances went." These "appearances" he explains away very plausibly:

I recall certain instances of familiar behaviour, of liberties taken, with young men of Marseilles who were attracted by the charms of these girls. I did not attach any importance to them, but it is possible that these young men may have included in their number some cub who boasted of favours which he had not succeeded in obtaining, or even one who revenged himself for definite refusals by slanders which have clung to the reputation of Letizia's daughters.

Further, "Bonaparte never forgave the Marseillais this." (General de Ricard, formerly A.D.C. to King Jérôme.),

And, indeed, was he likely to thank them for it?

General de Ricard's evidence furnishes the clue to the scandalous myth. It is clear that Napoleon's sisters did not, at this period of their life (nor at any other, for that matter) set an example of a reserve and a virtuousness which were not then in fashion. Young, pretty, mostly without anyone to keep them in order, suddenly emerging out of misery to shine at Marseilles receptions, is there anything strange in their behaviour not always appearing irreproachable? Besides, the thoughtlessness of their demeanour is not lightly to be denied. Paulette's liaison with the handsome Fréron is a living and charming illustration of this.

Stanislas Fréron, born in 1754, was the son of the Fréron whose controversy with the Encyclopaedists led to the most biting and outrageous sarcasms. Fréron senior, having lost his wife Jacqueline Guyomar in 1762, remarried, soon afterwards, Amélie Royou, of Pont-l'Abbé. The bride was sixteen; the husband forty-eight. At this date young Stanislas was just on nine years of age. When he was old enough to go to college his father sent him, in September, 1771, to Louis-le-Grand. The priests welcomed this new pupil, recommended to them as he was by the fame of the sound conservative doctrine preached by his father in the *Année littéraire*, for the maintenance of which same doctrine 3,718 masses were celebrated annually at Louis-le-Grand. (Raoul Arnaud, *Journaliste, sans-culotte, et thermidorien, le Fils de Fréron, 1754-1802*, based on unpublished documents.)

As to the excellence of their methods of educating the minds of youngsters, the future of some of their pupils has illustrated that. It was from Louis-le-Grand that issued some of the chief performers in the Terror: Louvet, the Louvet of Faublas, Maximilien de Robespierre, and Fréron, the Fréron of the awful mission to the Midi of the year II. We may add the name of the Marquis of Sade, celebrated in another way.

Stanislas Fréron remained eight years at the college of the Montagne Sainte-Geneviève, but did not shine at the prize-givings which closed the school year. "Lazy and indolent, all persistent work was repugnant to him, and he could not fall in with the ordinary routine." (Raoul Arnaud.) This was an unfortunate preparation for the editorship of the *Année littéraire*, which the death of his father (March 10, 1776) was going to leave on his hands. To begin with, things went without too many hitches, thanks more particularly to young Stanislas' assistants. But in 1781 an incident occurred which had disastrous results for the young controversialist. In a notice of *Jaloux sans Amour* produced at the *Comédie-Française*, a decidedly mediocre actor in the cast, Denis Deschanet, known as Des Essarts, was roundly slated. (Des Essarts, born at Langres, Nov. 23, 1737, made his first appearance at the *Comédie-Française*, Oct. 4, 1772, and was admitted to membership April 9, 1778. He died at Bagnères-de-Bigorre, Oct. 8, 1793.) The writer of the article, Fréron's assistant Salaün, called Des Essarts the "fat ventriloquist." The comedian thoroughly lost his temper, lodged a complaint, and brought the matter before the *Châtelet*, where, one thing leading to another, Fréron's defence ended in a violent outburst, all the more natural on his part since he was an innocent party.

Things went badly for him. The *Année littéraire* was suspended and, soon after, a royal writ cancelled Fréron's rights in it, transmitting them to his stepmother, who straightway became his enemy. (On July 23, 1791, widow Fréron was imprisoned in the Abbaye prison by order of the municipality of Paris.) Outcries and rages, applications and supplications, all were in vain. Stanislas remained dispossessed of what his father bequeathed him, and was forced to seek some other means of livelihood.

It was not till later that he took his revenge, which was not devoid of cleverness. Collaborating as he did for a while with Camille Desmoulins in the *Révolutions de France et de Brabant,* Fréron made use of his position to pillory his enemy, and belaboured with epigrams the "fat ventriloquist," whose complaint had had such unwelcome success.

That is why, less than ten years after the affair, Camille Desmoulins' readers came across the following short article in his weekly paper, the taunts whereof betray their author:—

IMPORTANT NOTICE TO PREGNANT WOMEN.

Philosophy has not as yet gained sufficient acquaintance with the mysteries of nature as to be able to explain away the mass of facts which bear witness to the curious effects of the imagination of pregnant women. These latter ought therefore to be on their guard against things which might give rise to astonishment, repugnance, or fright. Chance has just brought under my notice a curious birth. A woman who wishes her name to be

19

withheld, while allowing me to quote her case in view of the lesson it will teach, has just been delivered, after a troublesome confinement, of a species of shapeless lump, enormous in size, but possessed of hardly any resemblance to humanity except in having a mouth; the mouth is tremendous.

For a long time, she racked her brains in vain to recall anything that could have exerted so much influence over her in such a way as to produce such an effect. In time, however, she remembered, with a shiver of fear, so keen that the recurrence of the vision threw her into convulsions, how once she had reached the *Comedie-Française* during the fourth act of *Tartuffe*, and had been confronted with the sudden apparition of M. Des Essarts emerging from underneath the table. It is unfortunately beyond doubt that this comedian, whose physique is so lamentably unlike that of any other human being, has struck terror, or aversion, into the hearts of other persons likewise who saw him without being prepared for such a sight, and who had no idea that the French stage could compete with the fairs by having so monstrous a figure to bring forward.

Let us therefore suggest to the company that when, in future, M. Des Essarts is to appear, the public should be forewarned thereof on the posters in very large letters. *Parochel, accoucheur.*" (*Révolutions de France et de Brabant.*)

It was a humorous, if tardy, revenge. In the interval Fréron experienced the miseries of a penurious existence. He seems to have endeavoured to free himself from this by associating with those who had good positions at the Court, for we find him haunting the salons, and, in particular, the dining-room of Bertin, the Comptroller-General of Finance. To keep up appearances there he probably had recourse to money-lenders, of the kind who "accommodate" gentlemen's sons. This is doubtless the explanation of his confession in a little revolutionary pamphlet, "I have long since withdrawn out of the range of my creditors' inquisitiveness." It is said, moreover, that he frequented the worst resorts, Mme. Gourdan's private—very private—house, among others, where frolicsome ways were the usual thing. (Raoul Arnaud.)

He paid a heavy penalty for his wild courses, but whether he was struck by the dart of Venus in the hospitable house in the Rue Saint-Sauveur, or at Bertin's orgies in the little summer-house. No. 11 in the Rue Basse, we cannot say for certain. (The hospitable establishment of Mme. Gourdan, known as the "little Countess," was housed on the site where now is No. 12 of the Rue Saint-Sauveur.) Here, at any rate, we find him, descending into the lowest depths of debauchery and the most disreputable shifts, which will explain his friend Barras' expression of disgust later on, "The acquaintances we pick up in revolutionary times are not such as we should choose."

We may certainly believe Barras here; it certainly was not he—at least so he assures us himself—who selected this utterly vicious Fréron to co-operate with him in his Midi mission, this drunkard who cuts a dash in the least respectable localities, with his finely-chiselled features, attractive in spite of irregularity, (Raoul Arnaud), and his dandified ways, beneath which are already perceptible the *sans-culotte* Don Juan of 1793, and the leader of the gilded youth of 1794. ("The use of spirits, the elation consequent on the use of them, endowed him with an audacity, a fearlessness, which was almost that of a military hero.": *Mémoires de Barras,* 1.)

From the mire into which he dived he escaped in 1784, though not for long. He regained his footing so far as the *Année littéraire* was concerned, his stepmother being still the proprietress, and started collaboration in it once more. But this was only an interval. When the Revolution broke out, Stanislas Fréron has fallen back again into the hell of low-class journalism and doubtful jobs, on the watch for a last chance. When the Bastille fell, he was there. And then, in the avalanche of pamphlets which descends on Paris, comes his contribution, shrieking louder than the average, bitter to the point of frenzy, furious in its rage—*L'Orateur du Peuple.*

I have read practically all this *Orateur du Peuple* and am still in a state of surprise. What a style, what language, what impudent audacity, and what sinister threats for 1790! The throne was as good as overthrown when those who occupied it were being subjected to taunts brimming over with murderous rage, to insults obscene enough for the lowest of low resorts.

And indeed, turning over the pages of Fréron's journal, we find only too much to choose from by way of exemplification. He goes on to declaim that this "queen-criminal combines Messalina's lasciviousness with the Medicis' thirst for blood." (For the rest, Fréron's policy in the *Orateur du Peuple* can be summed up in a single line—two musket-shots to each village: one for the priest, the other for the squire: Raoul Arnaud.)

Yet in his own way he has a bucolic, and lighter, side to his character which comes to light more particularly when we pay attention to his relations with Camille Desmoulins, his schoolfellow at Louis-le-Grand. They had met again at the dawn of the Revolution, and kept together in their participation in all the doings of the mob during 1789. With Danton and Marat, they founded the Cordeliers' Club, and, still together, were to be found again in Danton's room that tragic evening of August 10. Becoming thus intimate with Desmoulins, Stanislas did not remain insensible to the gay and childlike charm of his friend's wife, little Lucile, to whom he addressed sprightly, hasty notes, such as the following:—

> To Lucile Desmoulins, French citizen, at Paris.
>
> Paris, January 21, 1793.
>
> Year II of the Republic.
>
> I beseech the chaste Diana to accept this homage of a quarter of a buck, killed within her domains. Farewell.
>
> Stanislas Lapin.

Stanislas Lapin! That was Fréron's nickname in the Desmoulins circle, at those gay reunions which took place in the little house they owned at Bourg-Egalité, formerly Bourg-la-Reine. There Fréron and Lucile went for long rambles together in the park at night, without any umbrage being taken by Camille, who had entire, and well-justified, confidence in his wife's virtue. Doubtless it was during one of those lazy, misty summer evenings which form one of the charms of the Ile-de-France that the People's spokesman declared his love for the young wife. Henri Michel writes (*Camille et Lucile Desmoulins*):

> In Stanislas Fréron's affection, which remained an irreproachable one—there was a tenderness and an exaltation which makes it approximate to a quite different feeling.

What doubts can we have as to the nature of his feelings when we read the confidences that Lucile entrusted to her diary? Here are some lines which she writes apropos of these days spent thus at Bourg-la-Reine, lines which depict Stanislas as deeply smitten:—

> Only one thing caused me any heart-searching—Fréron. Every day I see things going farther and farther, and I don't know what to do. I spoke to mother about it; she agreed with me that the best way was to make light of it, and treat it all as a joke, and perhaps that is the most sensible course. What else is there to do?

So, I thought I was being very discreet when I received him as a friend and nothing but a friend, just as of old. (Pierre Bliard.)

In August, 1792, Danton sent Fréron to the department of the Moselle to press forward the recruiting. Then follow some tranquil days in Lucile's sentimental existence, but directly recommence:—

Fréron gives me the feeling that he is always sighing; how stupid it is of him! Poor devil! What hopes are you cherishing? Quench this insane love in your heart. No, no, my friend; no, my dear Camille, have no fear; that friendship, that love so pure, will never exist but for you, and those whom I meet will never be dear to me except in so far as they are friends to you. (Pierre Bliard.)

Finally, in another entry, Lucile's feelings get the better of her, and she writes, pithily enough:—

Fréron is always the same, but it makes no difference to me; let him go mad, if he prefers it. (Pierre Bliard.)

It was a kind of madness, wherein Fréron was used to give himself a very free hand all his life. As Lucile's advice was not sufficiently explicit, he did not give up hoping and waiting. He writes from Marseilles, in December, 1793, "Lucile, you are ever present in my thoughts! Camille may complain, he may say anything he pleases; he will only be acting as all proprietors do." And he ends with this advice—rather strange advice considering what is known of the adventure: "Show my letter to Camille, I don't want to make any secret of it."

He was speaking the truth; he made a secret of nothing, not even of his worst misdeeds in the Midi. On September 14, 1792, Paris elected him a member of the National Convention. In the impeachment of the king, he voted for death within twenty-four hours, and the day that Louis XVI's head fell, he went on a shooting expedition in the woods of Bourg-l'Egalité, as his note to Lucile proves. Little more than a month afterwards (March 9) he was commissioned to go with Barras to the Hautes—and Basses—Alpes, and subsequently to the army in Italy. Wherever he passed, horror and dread dogged his footsteps, with the bloody axe rising and falling throughout these departments.

The Conventionalist Maximin Isnard wrote in the year IV:

Each step I take in the Midi, I have found traces of the blood which you have spilt. Every living being there accuses you, the very stones call out upon your cruelties, and wheresoever I meet with a crime, I find Fréron!

To punish Marseilles for its federalist revolt, Fréron caused two hundred persons to be beheaded and requisitioned 12,000 masons to demolish the town, a demand which he thought greatly to his credit, as is clear from his despatch of the *Nivôse* 6 in the year II. On the 19th he appealed for the deportation of all its inhabitants. On *Nivôse* 16 he made up the balancesheet of repressive procedure in Toulon consequent on its having been captured by the English; eight hundred shot; putting the finishing touch to his report on his successes by exclaiming, on *Pluviôse* 6: "The intriguers are falling like hail under the sword of the Law." (Isnard to Fréron.)

"Yes," added Isnard, " I shall terrify France, I shall astound ages to come by my recital of your crimes; you yourself when you look in this trusty mirror will recoil affrighted." The horror of his deeds is summarised in a phrase:

"Go, wretch, the whole world will never have produced a monster like unto thee!"

★★★★★★★★★★

Philodème, *Le dernier coup de tocsin de Fréron*. A few days after the publication of the *Dernier coup de tocsin* the conventionalist Chales wrote: "A pamphlet entitled *Le dernier coup de tocsin de Fréron* is being attributed to me. I am not the author of it, but I am too loyal, too true a republican, not to declare at the same time that the principles set forth in that pamphlet, written as it is with a fiery pen and a soul brimming over with patriotism, are graven on my heart, and that I shall be their defender till I die."

★★★★★★★★★

In the end Robespierre turned his attention to these terrible missionaries of the Terror—Barras and Fréron. In *Ventôse*, year II, they were summoned to Paris, and, on their arrival, lost no time in hastening to the Rue Saint-Honoré to exculpate themselves in the sight of the *Incorruptible*. That striking page of Barras' *Mémoires* which depicts the two men, humble and obsequious, before Robespierre, silent and eyeing them in his glacial way, is well known. Both were well aware, when paying that call, that their hour was come, that the scaffold was already being prepared for them for some morning near at hand.

Then they hide away somewhere in fear and trembling; and in the session of the *Germinal* 11th, in which the Convention delivers Danton and Camille Desmoulins over to the guillotine, Fréron is there, and Fréron keeps silence, and Fréron votes against his old schoolfriend, against the husband of that Lucile who will be a widow tomorrow. That is the sort of man Fréron was.

From *Germinal* to *Thermidor*—four months; four months in which will be planned the ambush in which Robespierre is to be trapped. Fréron assists in that, too; with Barras. The guillotiners of Marseilles, the fusilladers of Toulon, are going to give the *Incorruptible* a lesson in humanity.

With *Thermidor* 9 comes the fight by the brawlers and howlers of the Convention. Two days more, and omnipotence is conferred on the triumvirate of vice-riddled knaves—Barras, Fréron, Tallien—whom Bonaparte's heel will crush one morning in *Brumaire*, as a trio of noxious beasts. For the moment, Fréron shines in the front rank, the "sun of justice, humanity's mirror, majesty all-powerful," as a leaflet puts it in jest. He continues the publication of the *Orateur du Peuple*, he leads the "*jeunesse dorée*," a reactionary rabble "steeped in vice, prostitution, and the lowest scoundrelism." He must always push on, on the lines he has laid down for himself, and forget whatever Jacobin friendships he has made use of in times gone by; otherwise, he will be sharply recalled to order.

Thus we find him calling for the demolition of the *Hôtel de Ville*, "tyrant Robespierre's *Louvre*," whereto Granet, mindful of the demolitions at Marseilles, rejoins, "Punish the guilty and demolish nothing. The stones of Paris are no more guilty than those of Marseilles." Always haunted by that maniac's passion, that lust for destruction, he demands that the suburb of Saint-Antoine, in disgrace on account of the rising of the *Prairial* I, shall be burnt.

But these are the last of his oratorical exhibitions at Paris. Towards the end of *Vendémiaire*, year IV, he leaves Paris on a new Midi mission. This time he bears the olive-branch of peace and reconciliation in his hand, a manifestation which he owes to the departments which had been swept by the blood-and-fire of the royalist reaction, and one that he is willing to fulfil. No longer is there any question of burning, fusillading, plundering "with delirious joy" (Raoul Arnaud); but of calming, appeasing, re-establishing harmony. Accompanied by a dozen individuals, orderlies or secretaries, one of them being Martainville, the ferocious royalist of the Restoration, Fréron sets out, carrying with him two million *livres*, only a trifling portion of which did he bring back. (This second mission of Fréron's in the Midi cost, to be exact, 1,984,099 *livres*.)

Such was Pauline Bonaparte's first lover.

How did she come to know him?

Various versions of their first meeting exist. The most probable states that during his first mission, he had occasion to render some service to Mme. Bonaparte, whom he met two or three times at Bausset, where she was taking refuge during the siege of Toulon, and that he renewed his acquaintance with the family on his return in the year IV. There is no fault to find with these statements, but General Bonaparte's recommendation may be assumed to have carried more weight. For the fact was that Fréron left Paris with the following letter from Napoleon dated *Vendémiaire* 19 (Oct. 11, 1795) addressed to his relation Mme. Clary, (*née* Rose Sonnis, she was the second wife of François Clary, born at Marseilles, Aug. 30, 1737, she died at Paris, Jan. 28, 1815), his brother Joseph's mother-in-law:—

> Fereron (*sic*), who is going on a mission to Marseilles, will hand you this letter; I beg you, *Madame*, to show him all the kindness that you would show to myself. You will find him a man very ready to oblige, loyal, and a good sort; I have told him of the friendly feelings I have for your family, so he will look out for opportunities to make himself useful to you. See that it is due to you that his stay in Marseilles is a pleasant one, and introduce him to Mad. Dejean, (*i.e.* Lejeans) and Pluvinal. (Mme. Lejeans was François Clary's daughter by his first marriage.)
>
> ★★★★★★★★★★

The rest of this curious letter runs as follows. I quote from the original in G. La Caille's collection, published in the *Amateur d'autographes*, 1901:—

> All is going well here; the royalists have been brought under, but there is no need to fear that the Terror will return (cancelled, 'that the Terrorists will return'); we love that no more than you do. If more important occupations did not keep me at Paris, I should be very glad to come to Marseilles, but the Convention has nominated me to the command of the Army of the Interior, subject to the orders of representative Barras. Farewell, *Madame*; my respects to Mme. Pluvinal and to Mme. Sophie, likewise to your niece, and remember me to Clari, assuring him, and the rest of your family, that I shall ever take the same interest in them as I must certainly feel in you.
>
> Yours, Buonaparte.

★★★★★★★★★★

May we not assume that a similar letter was sent by Bonaparte to Fréron for his mother, and that the Conventionalist presented himself to the family under the auspices of that recommendation? If so, was he not likely to have received a welcome? Besides, it was no longer a home over which anguish and misery were casting their shadows that he entered, but a brilliant and gay interior, transformed into an elegant salon by virtue of the general's remittances from Paris. And there, amid such surroundings, are three young girls to smile on their brother's envoy, a form of pleasure which Stanislas never shunned. "He appealed to women, and, even in his most sinister moments, remained a dandy and a libertine." (Raoul Arnaud.) It was a way he had. At the period of his first mission the Jacobins took notice of his conduct in this respect. At the sitting of *Brumaire* 18th, year II (Nov. 8, 1793), presided over by Maribon-Montaut, Hébert ascended the tribune of the club, he said:

> You have heard Fréron denounced, I denounce him to you also. Power has intoxicated him, he has abused it. Fréron is no longer anything but an aristocrat and a fop. At Nice his only compan-ions were aristocratic women, and his expenses were fearful.

Is it surprising that he was struck, immediately, by "*la diva Paolina's*" languid-lively charm? What she has to give him, at the moment and at the age when "he is experiencing a need to give himself up with-out reserve to a deep and lasting affection," (Raoul Arnaud), is all the graces of a new, fresh, youthful beauty. From Mme. Gourdan's "pri-vate" house he has turned to the brothels of Palais-Egalité; Lucile's gay and childlike grace has been denied him; now he abandons himself to this fresh and dazzling mirror of precocious beauty. In his life of fever and fret, of violence and frenzy, here is the peaceful oasis, the blessed resting-place, the haven of love and beatitude, which remain for him to discover in a girl's heart.

He has passed his forty years, and the daily struggles tire him now. Not for his temperament are the contests on the grand scale in which, but a short while before, the austere virtue of Maximilien de Robe-spierre had been triumphant; he remained a child of the light-hearted, sceptical, hedonist eighteenth century, against which his father had levelled such heavy blows. The golden apple of the gay Hesperides is there before him, and is he likely to hold his hand? Out upon these useless self-denials! And Fréron takes his bite at the beautiful fruit.

The fruit, too, is quite willing to be bitten. Pauline is just on her sixteenth birthday, the age of all enthusiasms, all curiosities, all illusions. She comes from a land where the awakening of love is sudden, and, besides, she lives in such a state of over-excitation, in so feverish an atmosphere, that the most level-headed would find it difficult to remain self-possessed. When misery was but just left behind, in the riotous enjoyment of brand-new prosperity, luxury even, Fréron made his appearance wearing the halo of omnipotence.

Of his massacres, of the terror he had struck into departments—what consciousness of this has she? What, except that he has power committed to him? At Marseilles he is the master, the dispenser of pacification by force, the organizer of revolutionary *fêtes* in which he marches amid the thunder of the drums, the sudden unfurling of the banners, the harmonious rhythm of the songs, the roar of the cannon-salutes.

Regally omnipotent, his antechambers are full, his reception-rooms are ablaze with light as no ballroom she has ever seen before; a hundred women press round him, striving to attract his notice, lavish with their smiles, at his beck and call, perhaps, or—who knows?—in love.

And then, to prevent her being deceived by these barren appearances, by these fleeting mirages, is Pauline's mother enlightening her? Whether in ignorance or of choice, she acquiesces. There is no doubt she thinks marriage possible. Fréron is not so negligible a suitor as to be dismissed unceremoniously. What matches, in fact, have her children made? Joseph has married a middle-class girl, Julie Clary; Lucien the daughter of the innkeeper Boyer; and Napoleon has just taken to wife a woman whose only possession is a "past." Fréron is an improvement on this—decidedly so.

He is basking in the sunshine of Fortune's favours. Was he not Bonaparte's benefactor once, under the walls of Toulon? No obstacle then, so far as the mother is concerned, to a liaison between Pauline and Stanislas. She is taken about everywhere, accompanies him to the theatre, "on terms of familiarity far from what even our customs consider proper," observes the austere and virtuous Paul, Vicomte de Barras. In fact, he goes further still and roundly states that the two lovers live as husband and wife. The truth is that Pauline has not yet left her mother's house. Her correspondence with Fréron shows that she even remains without seeing him for days together sometimes.

She whiles away these wearisome intervals with the help of locks of hair which Stanislas sends her. It is a romance *à la Florian* in which naive and puerile little presents are exchanged. "Thank you for thinking to send me some of your hair; I, on my side, send you some of mine. . . ." (Pauline Bonaparte to Stanislas Fréron, Marseilles, *Ventôse* 19, year II.) Later comes a miniature of the leader of the "*jeunesse dorée*": "Your portrait is a great consolation to me; I spend whole days with it, and talk to it as if it was yourself." Burning letters these, studded with protestations of eternal loyalty, according to the prescribed, but rather worn, ritual. "Yes, dear Stanislas, I swear to love but you alone; my heart is not divisible, it gives itself as a perfect whole."

Passionate avowals too: "You know how sensitive I am, and you are not ignorant of the extent to which I idolise you." Puerility, likewise, is not absent from this correspondence, which always adheres to the same fervent and tender note. Pauline has fallen into a brook in the course of a picnic: "The river water which I swallowed has not chilled my heart so far as you are concerned; no doubt it was nectar—if that would increase its warmth." But Fréron was a practical man in love-making, and was not content to play about outside the gate. He formally intimates to Mme. Bonaparte that he wishes to marry Pauline. There is some need, too, for him to hasten. Several times by now the *Directoire* announced his recall; he has been violently attacked in Paris; he will have to leave Marseilles. ("Malice engendered by the mission of the year II pursued the delegate of the year IV.": Barras.)

Leaving Paris on *Ventôse* 21, after his marriage with Josephine, to take up his command with the Italy Army at Nice, Bonaparte stopped at Marseilles a few days, lodging at the *Hôtel Beauvais*. There Fréron met him, and their conversation can be guessed by the Conventionalist's subsequent letter. Far from opposing the match, the commander-in-chief approves of it. He has even settled certain details with Fréron of which the latter reminds him some days later in a despatch which throws light on the previous discussion:—

Marseilles, *Germinal* 4, year IV.
Before we parted, my dear Bonaparte, you promised me a letter to your wife; we arranged that you would inform her of my marriage, so that, in the event of me presenting Pauline to her, she should not be taken by surprise. (Josephine remained behind at Paris. She did not rejoin her husband till more than four months and a half had elapsed. She reached Milan in the middle of *Messidor*, year IV.) I am despatching an orderly to Toulon to receive the letter that I am to take. Your mother is standing in the way of my haste just a little. I still hope that the wedding may take place at Marseilles within four or five days; in fact,

all arrangements have been made to do this; quite apart from the possession of that hand which I burn to join with mine, it is probable that the *Directoire* are going to appoint me to some distant field of action immediately, which will necessitate my prompt departure.

If I am obliged to return here, I shall be losing precious time, and the Government, which, very naturally, pays but little attention to the affairs of the heart, will find fault with an absence which will delay the consummation of the work entrusted to me. I implore you to write to your mother directly to waive all objections; tell her to give me a free hand in deciding what date to fix for the happy moment. I have the full consent, I have the promise, of my young friend; why defer the tying of the knot which so charming a love-story has woven? My dear Bonaparte, help me to overcome this new obstacle; I rely on you.

My friend, I embrace you, and am yours and hers for life.

Farewell.　　　　　　　　　　　　　S. F.

And yet, twenty-one days later, Fréron leaves Marseilles for Paris unmarried. What has happened? Has Bonaparte changed his mind? Or is it a maternal veto this time? No one knows exactly, but we may conjecture that events have introduced a discordant note by means of intervention of Fréron's mistress. Who was this woman? Where did she come from? A mystery. It has been stated that Fréron had married her, a manifest error, in view of Fréron's own official statement.

★★★★★★★★★

By articles IV and V of the decree of *Fructidor* 5, year II, delegates to the Convention were bound to state their age and civil status. Fréron gave his age as 39 years and 3 months; birth-place, Paris; bachelor.

★★★★★★★★★

It had been asserted that she was a dancer at the opera, but this is baseless, and the truth is that we know nothing at all about her. As the latest biographer of the *People's Spokesman* very sensibly puts it:

Nothing is known concerning this liaison except that it existed; the name of the woman who lived with Fréron is unknown to us; unknown, too, the influence which she may have been able to exert over him.

Was she a lady of high degree whom he visited secretly and whom he protected in the evil day, or a woman who had lost her reputation, stirring him up to take vengeance on the world from which she had been expelled? Was she some simple middle-class girl content to love Stanislas for his own sake without asking to share his public life, or a woman of the people in revolt against her former masters, some virago like Marat's mistress, a girl picked up by Fréron in a gin-palace during one of his nights of debauchery?

The most painstaking researches among the archives, careful reading of contemporary journals and of private correspondence, have revealed nothing. It is a gap of some importance in our knowledge of Fréron's career. And yet—does not history depend for its charm on a little mysteriousness, and, were it possible to know all, to learn everything without effort, would it not become as arid and as unpoetic as the sciences in which reasoning reigns supreme? (Raoul Arnaud.)

★★★★★★★★★★

Marat's mistress, Simone Evrard, who was twenty-six years of age at the date of her liaison with the *People's Friend*, had, we know, nothing of the *virago* in her. "Marat's *virago*" is one of the figures in the mythology of the reaction, and is the property of certain ill-informed historians.

★★★★★★★★★★

It is established, however, that this woman had two children by Fréron. She herself informed either Mme. Bonaparte or the general. Stanislas certainly undertook to arrange matters, since in Pauline's letters a reference to this mistress occurs in connexion with the measures that Fréron proposes to take with regard to her. Pauline writes:

I have just received your letter, it has affected me deeply on account of what you say of that woman.

What threats has the forsaken mistress made? Is the fickle lover being terrorised with menaces of vengeance and public exposure? Pauline says further:

I shall be very ill at ease till I know what is going to happen to this woman.

Then comes a pleasing touch of genuine feeling·

I put myself in her place and sympathize with her. (Pauline Bonaparte to Stanislas Fréron, Marseilles, *Floréal* 30, year IV.)

Six weeks later the affair is not yet settled, Pauline writes:

I am not going to say anything more about your mistress, all that you tell me reassures me. I know the uprightness of your heart, and approve of the arrangements you are making with regard to her. (Pauline Bonaparte to Stanislas Fréron, Marseilles, *Messidor* 14, year IV.)

But Bonaparte's attitude towards Fréron became unfavourable. The whole family leagued themselves together against the marriage, even Josephine, who had never seen Pauline and did not know Fréron. The general even wrote to Joseph that he is unwilling to hear anything further about this match. Does he not, in fact, issue orders to Pauline accordingly? But is this to be his final decision? Suppose Pauline writes to him? beseeches him? She suggests the idea to Fréron, but Fréron rejects it—why? Here is her letter, nevertheless, tear-stained and still witness to the heat of the fever which dictated it before it went its way to the Italian battlefield to find the victor of Mondovi:—

I have received your letter; it has caused me the greatest pain; I had not expected this change on your part. You have given your consent to my union with Fréron. After the promises you have made me to overcome all obstacles, my heart gave itself up to those cherished hopes and I thought of him as, the man in whom my fate met its fulfilment. I send you his last letter; you will see that all calumnies with which he is charged are not true.

As for myself, I choose a life of wretchedness rather than marrying without your consent and incurring your curse. You, my dear Napoleon, for whom I have ever had the tenderest of friendly feelings, if you were witness of the tears which your letter caused me to shed, you would be touched; I am sure of it. It is on you that my happiness depends, yet you force me to renounce the only person whom I can love.

Although I am young, there is firmness in my character; I feel that it is impossible for me to give up Fréron after all the promises that I have made never to love any but him; yes, I shall keep them; no one in the world will be able to prevent me shutting my heart to all but him and receiving his letters and answering them and repeating that I shall love none but him. I know my duty too well to set it aside; but I know that I do not know how to change as circumstances bid me.

Farewell, that is what I have to say to you; may you be happy, and, amidst your brilliant victories and every good fortune, think sometimes of a life that is stricken through with grief, and of tears that are shed every day by   Pauline Bonaparte.

Is this letter just such as Fréron would have had her write? What deductions are to be made from it? Pauline will not marry Fréron, but she will remain faithful to him. What does that mean? She will obey, and she will disobey Bonaparte at one and the same time? But quibbles are not in his line, nor is this kind of dialectic one that he cares for. Well then, is the above the letter of a woman hopelessly in love? If so, she would pay no heed to fraternal opposition. What! he to decide her life, her happiness, to cancel *ex cathedrâ* what was going to become the lode-star of her existence, and she acquiesces? She bows to the decision? She consents to the banishment of her sweetest dreams? She is in love, and does not rise swiftly up to cry: Who but I shall decide between my love and me? Yes, but—she is sixteen, she is aware that Napoleon is the dispenser of the family's prosperity, the head of the clan, recognised, accepted; from him comes all: comfort and security today; and tomorrow, who knows?

That is settled, then. Fréron must give way.

A final point remains to be examined. What reasons did Bonaparte give for breaking off the match? Barras does not hesitate to attribute the rupture to the intervention of Fréron's mistress. Not that he blames this intervention, but only the fact of Napoleon's taking notice of it. He exclaims:

> Thus, it is in the name of morality that he commits the revolting immorality of refusing to let his sister marry a man who has been her lover, reserving her for some distinguished general or for some Italian prince who will not deem this sort of thing beneath them. (Barras.)

Yet in view of this virtuous declamation, the question may be put: Which match was, in the year IV, the more brilliant one for Pauline— that with a man without a reputation, the unknown soldier Leclerc, or that with the leader of a victorious and powerful political party, Fréron? The evidence is irresistible; Bonaparte's motive was disinterested. Behind his refusal there was, perhaps, a loftier reason—Fréron's ambiguous celebrity. Could he, in cold blood, receive into the family circle, and bind up with his own future, the man who personified all the atrocities, the guilt, the horror which was associated with the Terror? Was it not in consideration of Fréron's immorality that he preferred the immorality which makes Barras so indignant?

But whatever his reasons may have been, who would not commend them? who would not praise him for keeping at a distance from his own fresh, unstained fame the befouled notoriety of this Don Juan of the Terror? A disreputable, vicious, abandoned man who depended on cynicism for his effectiveness and on low intrigue for his influence?

So ended the love-story of Pauline and handsome Stanislas. "My good friend, I love you more than myself," she wrote to him, *Floréal* 30, year IV. A year later, to the day, she became "Citoyenne Leclerc."

CHAPTER 2

Pauline Married

After Fréron's dismissal, another sighing lover presents himself—Andoche Junot, the future Duc d'Abrantès. At this time, he was the general's *aide-de-camp*, and, as for Pauline, "he loved her passionately, deliriously." Later, he admitted that it was not reciprocated. "She never loved me," he confessed to his wife somewhat pathetically. He made matrimonial overtures to Bonaparte, alleging he was going to inherit 20,000 *francs* upon his father's death. The general answered very wisely that Junot senior was not yet dead and that the net profit at present was nil, concluding, "You have nothing, she has nothing; what is the total? Nothing." And things went no further.

It is curious that Junot subsequently became a member of a family which the general had, at one time, thoughts of marrying into—the Permons. Bonaparte had, in fact, proposed to Mme. Permon that he should marry her; her son, Pauline; and her daughter, either Louis or Jérôme. Mme. Permon had a hearty laugh at his expense. "Really, my dear Napoleon," she told him, "you are quite the high-priest nowadays, marrying off everybody, even the children." Mme. Permon remained a widow, and the proposed bride of Louis or Jérôme became the Duchesse d'Abrantès.

But did Bonaparte entertain the idea of making Marmont do instead, as the latter boldly asserts in his *Memoirs*? ("It is to be desired," wrote Baron Henri Jomini, "that M. de Raguse had been rather less pleased with himself and rather more indulgent towards his colleagues. His *memoirs* would have been more valuable.")

The flattering way in which he speaks of himself will excuse us hesitating to believe him, especially since he boasts he refused Pauline's hand. "I have more reason to congratulate myself thereon than to repent," he says. Indeed!

It is certain that there was no lack of suitors, several of them possible ones. It is as well, however, to begin by striking General Duphot's name off the list, the one who was assassinated at Rome, *Nivôse* 8, year VI. He was betrothed, not to Pauline, but to her sister-in-law Désirée Clary, who became the wife of Marshal Bernadotte. But to replace him, we find M. de La Salcetté, a gentleman of Dauphiné, whose friendship with the Bonapartes dated back to their stay at Marseilles.

> Mlle. Bonaparte's beauty was a great temptation to him, but her deficiencies in the more solid qualities, and the general be-haviour of the Bonaparte family, in which education was more honoured in the breach than in the observance, attracted him less. (Joseph Turquan: *Souverains et grandes dames*.)

More prudent, probably, in his eyes, to be contented with less dain-ty, and more virtuous, a morsel. So, too, with one Mr. Billon, soap-manufacturer, "a rich man who would have married her if her mother had agreed to the match." With all respect to the historian (Gilbert Stenger), who makes this statement, the soap-maker was not so rich as was believed. Here is a contradiction from Napoleon himself, in a letter addressed to Joseph:

> A citizen named Billon, an acquaintance of yours I am told, asks for Paulette's hand. This citizen is not wealthy. I have written to mother to abandon the idea. (Baron Larrey, *Madame Mère*.)

Moreover, he is himself going to make arrangements, having grown tired of this intervention entailed by his sister's caprices or her adorers' claims. Besides, who better fitted than he to choose a husband for Pauline? A few months later all is settled.

Towards the end of *Floréal*, Mme. Bonaparte, Elisa, and Pauline re-joined the general, now victorious over Austrians and Piedmontese, at Milan; it was at the *château* of Montebello, three leagues from Milan on the Como road, that the family took up their quarters. Amidst the new-found luxury of this improvised court, its troop of showily-dressed of-ficers, its crowd of suitors and guests, they could make the most of the astounding freak of fate which had thrust prosperity on them.

Their reunion there offers Bonaparte an opportunity for settling troublesome questions. Elisa's marriage with Bacciochi is an accom-plished fact; but what to do with Pauline is still a problem. The solu-tion is that she shall marry one of the army's excellent soldiers, Leclerc, promoted to be brigadier-general by a decree of the *Directoire*, *Floréal* 7, year V. This is to be his wedding present; fourteen days later, in the chapel of the *château* of Montebello, dedicated to St. Francis in 1744, by Cardinal Puteobonello, Leclerc marries Pauline.

The bridegroom was twenty-five years old at the time, having been born at Pontoise, March 17, 1772; a doorkeeper's son, it is said—and believed—at Paris. But the truth is that the father's status was, although a modest one, somewhat better than that. Connected with the salt warehouse at Pontoise, Jean Paul Leclerc had been a King's Councillor; and brought up six children respectably, whose good fortune is assured, thanks to Pauline's husband, and who are worthy of their name. Emmanuel Leclerc enlisted in 1791, and his profession was thenceforward that of a soldier.

With the help of the entries against his name at the Ministry of War we can trace his career, step by step, though by no means so intimately as could Mr. Lewis Goldsmith, who is grieved to have to state that, during the Revolution, Leclerc picked up an income from the courtesans of the Palais-Egalité. If we believe him, at the time of *Vendémiaire* 13, "this man was a —— of the lowest type." But what was Lewis Goldsmith himself?

★★★★★★★★★★

One of Leclerc's sisters, Louise Aimee Julie, married (Nov. 12, 1801) Louis Nicolas Davout, the future Duke of Auerstaat and Prince of Eckmühl. "The marshal's wife," writes the Countess Potocka concerning her, "was an admirable woman, whose beauty was of the severe type. Educated as she had been at Mme. Campan's, she had acquired refined manners and the conventions of good society, which were lacking in her husband; but she did not know how to make herself beloved, for she had little geniality." (*Mémoires de la Comtesse Potocka* (1794-1820).

★★★★★★★★★★

Physically Leclerc may have pleased Pauline. Appiani's fine portrait of him depicts a narrow bust, a high forehead, a delicate lip, well-shaped nose, eyes somewhat lifeless, but the general impression bears some resemblance to Bonaparte's, only fairer, more youthful, less serious. "Small, slender, lean, with a figure slightly awry, pleasant and straightforward," writes Desaix in his diary. Norvins, Leclerc's secretary at Hayti, completes the picture:

General Leclerc was short but well made, and he combined strength with gracefulness; his features were attractive, his glance keen and quick, his face always lit up by expression and movement. He was a fluent speaker.

The foregoing well explains the phrase habitually used by Pauline in referring to him; she called her husband "my little Leclerc."

For this unexpected marriage, "garrison marriage," Fouché calls it, reasons have naturally been given which do no credit either to Bonaparte or to Leclerc—not to mention Pauline. Baron Mounier is particularly well informed on this point, according to his own account. He declares in his self-satisfied way:

> The Leclerc marriage came about thus. General Bonaparte was working in his room at Milan; Leclerc was on the staff and took advantage of a screen to express his love for Pauline in rather too unceremonious a fashion. General Bonaparte hears a noise, gets up and sees. The marriage was celebrated without losing a moment.

It has been remarked concerning this story that there is "nothing improbable in it." It may as well be asked what there is probable in it. How are we to believe that Bonaparte let himself be befooled and insulted in this way? How are we to admit that Leclerc would have dared to act thus under his chief's nose? We should be attributing a degree of complaisance to the latter which is certainly out of keeping with probability. Furthermore, those who retail these little anecdotes have omitted to make this one harmonise with what we know of Leclerc's character. No doubt he was a very highly-strung man, but to endow him with "a rough and brutal personality" is going a good deal farther.

A final touch is given by a Prussian, though his version really contains nothing but what Peltier, that immaculate royalist, affirmed, which makes out Leclerc to be jealous to a stagy degree. He relates, as fact, that Bonaparte's brother-in-law grew so jealous of Lannes, who was flirting with Paulette, that he actually broke a chair across his back. (Lefebvre Saint-Ogan, *L'Envers de l'Epopée*.)

In that case Fouché was right; Pauline could only have had the deepest, and most thoroughly justified, aversion for her husband.

However, the marriage took place, moreover, all evidence hitherto produced testifies to the affection Pauline felt for the husband Napoleon gave her.

★★★★★★★★★★

Here is the text of Pauline's and Leclerc's marriage-deed, in full:—

Army of Italy
French Republic

Liberty   Equality

Alexandre Berthier

General of Division.   Chief of the General Staff.

This day, *Prairial* I ('*Germinal*' cancelled) year V of the French Republic, 10 a.m.

Before me. General of Division, Chief of the Staff of the Army of Italy,
have presented themselves:—

Emmanuel le Clerc, major, legitimate son of Jean-Paul Le Clerc and
of Marie Louise Musquinet, born at Pontoise, March 17, 1772, Brigadier-General of the Army of the Rhine, on the one part.

And, on the other, *citizeness* Paulette Bonaparte, born at Ajaccio, in
Corsica, Oct. 2, 1780, legitimate daughter of ('the late,' cancelled)
Charles Bonaparte and of Letitia Ramolini, the same being provided
with the papers prescribed by law, and having affirmed that they had
entered into no marriage-contract hitherto, they have declared themselves willing jointly to enter into a marriage-agreement in conformity with the laws of the French Republic, and have signed with us.

Alex. Berthier.   P. Bonaparte.

V. E. Leclerc.

We, Chief of the General Staff of the Army of Italy, certify that the
above declaration has been affixed, in conformity with the law, to the
door of the General Staff office for the period decreed by the law, and
that up to this day, *Prairial* 20, there has been no protest against it."

This piece has been published in the *Carnet historique et littiraire*; 1899,
III. 44, and in the *Intermédiaire*, LIV. Dec. 30, 1906, No. 1 134, col. 958.

★★★★★★★★★★

In fact, after their return from Italy, Paulette and Leclerc received
a visit from the academician Arnault, author of *Marius à Minturnes*, at
their charming house in the *rue de la Ville l'Evêque*. (*Marius à Minturnes*,
tragedy in three acts, staged for the first time at the *Comèdie-Fran-
çaise*, May 19, 1791. Napoleon admired the play so much that he bequeathed the writer 100,000 *francs* in his will.) And of his visit Arnault
has left this significant account:

I found Leclerc at home and intoxicated with happiness; amorous and ambitious, and both with reason. His wife seemed to
me very happy too, not only because she was married to him,
but also just because she was married. Her new position had
not increased her seriousness, as was the case with her husband;
he seemed more serious than usual. But as for her, she was just
as much of a madcap as ever.

Leclerc had not long to enjoy these madcap ways, for, leaving Paulette at Paris, he went back to serve in the Italy Army. This absence

Paulette made some use of, completing her education, so far as she could, both socially and academically. Certain details which were neglected, or even unknown, in Corsica, were of importance at Paris. To acquire this elementary knowledge, "*La diva Paolina*" entered the "*pension*" founded by Mme. Campan at Saint-Germain, then a fashionable one. Little Caroline was staying there at the time; Desirée, Bernadotte's wife, was trying to learn spelling there; Hortense de Beauharnais was winning golden opinions, and not much else. A whole bevy of princesses, duchesses, and marshals' wives, of the Empire, were enjoying themselves there amidst the rustle of skirts and the limpid echoes of youthful laughter. Pauline seems to have been industrious.

Mme. Campan, *Pluviôse* I, year VII, writes to Joseph Bonaparte:

Citizeness Leclerc, has been with us six months. She has made astonishing progress in all respects, and she did not know how to read or write."

Here we must be inclined to suspect Mme. Campan's zeal in defence of the excellence of her teaching. "Neither read nor write"? But what about the love-letters to Fréron in the year IV? The pupil, however, interrupted her studies in order to lie in, giving birth to the child who was named Louis Napoléon Dermide, thus uniting the name of his uncle with that of one of the heroes in the latter's beloved "Ossian." Born in 1798, the child was baptised March 21, 1801, Pauline had only a few months longer to stay in France.

Vendémiaire 16, year X, the First Consul recalled Leclerc, then near the Spanish frontier, to Paris. The reconquest of Hayti, where the revolt of the negroes had been successful, had been decided on, and Leclerc was put in command.

According to Bourrienne, the First Consul's advice to Leclerc, on giving him instructions, were, "Here you have a fine chance to get rich. Go, and don't worry me any more with your everlasting demands for money." The fortune Leclerc left, concerning which we shall have something to say later, was in accordance with this anecdote recorded by Napoleon's former secretary.

Pauline felt no pleasure at hearing the news; "Oh! I shall die before I get there!" she complained. But she was going to give the lie to that gloriously. She would decidedly have preferred to remain at Paris, but Napoleon, already an adherent of the principle that he was to formulate in 1807: "I am accustomed to see wives prefer to be with their husbands," (the Emperor to Joseph, King of Naples; Fontainebleau, Nov. 13, 1807), issued a "pressing invitation" to her to accompany

Leclerc. In the reports of Louis XVIII's secret agents at Paris, during the Consulat, there is a comment on this tale which is worth noting. In it we see, for the first time, the First Consul rebuking his sister for questionable behaviour, and, likewise for the first time, there is a reference to Pauline's lovers. Its date is July 17, 1802, so that the agent is retailing ancient history:—

> When he (*i.e.* Bonaparte) sent General Leclerc to Hayti, Mme. Leclerc, his sister, had no desire to accompany her husband. The First Consul declared that while Leclerc was making war and money at Hayti, it was not his intention that she should remain behind at Paris to play the *coquette* and amuse herself with her lovers. Mme. Leclerc alleged that her health was unequal to it. Bonaparte obtained a certification from his doctor that she was in a condition to make the journey. She objected that, she being pregnant, and the roads of Lower Brittany so bad, an accident might occur. (The agent's memory seems to have played him false here, seeing that Pauline gave birth to Dermide in 1798.) Bonaparte answered that he would provide against that; and, as a matter of fact, had her carried in a litter for more than forty leagues, and in this way compelled her to accompany her husband. (Comte Remacle.)

It is a curious thing that this note is to be found in Fouché's *Memoirs*, briefly summarised but almost identical in its wording:—

> When she was ill and refused to follow Leclerc on his expedition to Hayti, she was carried in a litter, by Napoleon's orders, on board the admiral's ship.

Resistance was ineffectual, then. On *Brumaire* 30, on the ship the *Océan*, the Staff put out to sea from Brest. The fate of Hayti was going to be decided.

This is not the place to tell the story of that ferocious war with savages, that fight against an enemy whose fury extended to cannibalism. It is within narrower limits that our researches must be confined; at a nearer horizon must our investigations come to a halt. What prefaced the contest for the reconquest of this blissful, fertile island which, in 1789, was yielding France a milliard a year, is well known; the manoeuvres of the English to compass the wresting of the colony from the Republic; the fire at the Cape just when the fleet brought its broadside to bear on the roadstead, *Pluviôse* 16, year X.

★★★★★★★★★★

"Towards the end of April (1802) the district seemed pacified, and some months later General Leclerc stored 45,000 muskets in the arsenals, accruing from the disarmament of the negroes; he reckoned to acquire 12,000 to 15,000 more. Almost all were of English make." (A. P. de Forges, *Le Général Leclerc.*)

★★★★★★★★★★

Three months of fierce hand-to-hand fighting reduced the colony once more under French control. To the spell of war succeeded a spell of organisation without delay.

★★★★★★★★★★

"This was a period of quiet, of taking up work once again. Tillage began to make headway and the outlook seemed bright. All this was due to repression by armed force, and also to Leclerc's ingenuity." (Dr. Magnac, *L'Expedition du Général Leclerc à Saint-Domingue.*)

★★★★★★★★★★

Was this a time when Leclerc was racking his brains as to how to ruin the colony by means of exactions? (Comte Remacle, *Bonaparte et les Bourbons*: This report charges Leclerc with stealing sugar from the colonists to sell it for his own advantage.) That was the tale current at Paris in circles which were hostile to the new government. It obtained a very curious, and very persistent, currency.

The German Reichardt on January 11, 1803 writes:

He (Leclerc) appears to have looked after his own affairs very well in the course of a very brief governorship, his widow is supposed to have become the richest member of her family; and the wealth she has inherited from the general, whom she followed very reluctantly, will, it is said, speedily console her.

Far from improving Pauline's position, the "wealth she inherited" according to rumour left her worse off than before. Leclerc at his death left his wife 246,000 *francs* in personalty, and 325,000 *francs* in real estate. Including debts to him, the whole amounted to 700,000 *francs*. It must be admitted that the colony's "ruination" by Leclerc was run on very cheap lines.

The peace which proved so difficult to obtain in 1802 did not last long. The second day after the arrest of Toussaint-Louverture, who was organising a new negro revolt, the insurrection burst out suddenly.

★★★★★★★★★★

Toussaint-Louverture, whose real name was Toussaint Breda, had been a slave belonging to the Comte de Noé, and owed his nickname to

42

the brilliance of his early successes, which had caused the French Commissary Polverel to write, "*Mais cet homme fait ouverture partout!*"

★★★★★★★★★★

So, too, did the yellow fever, as if in co-operation. The hospitals were filled with sufferers; the roads were strewn with corpses. The negro hordes drove the decimated troops from their last trenches. The savage energy of the natives and the epidemic were, together, irresistible. Pauline had to fly from the Cape, where she had taken up her quarters to begin with, and take refuge in the Tortuga islet. How cruel were the disillusions that awaited her! Her mind once reconciled to the idea of departure, she abandoned herself to dreams of a fairy kingdom, imagining herself already queen in a marvellous land, where shone a miraculous sun on landscapes that bordered on the impossible.

On her arrival she found actualities disappointing. The negroes were not of a Paul-and-Virginia type, but cruel, crafty and treacherous, whose idea of war included ambuscades and men-traps; the climate torrid and prostrating; towns reduced to cinders, the bush to ashes; and uninhabited ground ablaze. It was a country in ruins. Where now were the charming dreams of which she had prattled when paying calls on Mme. Permon and on Mme. Junot? Where now were the hours of divine enjoyment in the even swing of the hammock, fanned by the waving, rustling palms? Where now were the miraculous white-and-gold palaces of her daydreams, set in valleys amid springs and gigantic creepers, facing mountains all aglow under a tropical sun?

Instead, there were hospitals to visit, long rows of truckle-beds, lines of dying fever-patients; or lazar-houses to pace through, consoling the sufferers, while the consoler's teeth chattered at the thought of dying as they were dying. Yet from Paris Pauline will receive Napoleon's encouragement: that her loving relations feel her absence keenly, that her name is ever on their lips; what is that compared to the resonant phrases which promise her immortality and fame? Napoleon writes to Leclerc:

> I am very pleased with Paulette's conduct. Well may she have no fear of death, seeing that she would die glorious, dying amidst the army and assisting her husband. All earthly things fade quickly away, save the judgment on us which we leave graven in history."

This might have been meant for Leclerc himself, a prophetic farewell from the First Consul, for, quite suddenly, Pauline's husband is struck down; first yellow fever, then death. During the night of *Brumaire* 10–11, year XI, he is in the grasp of the last agonies. In this torrid climate there is no time to spend in eloquence and meditation. Four hours after the general's death, the doctors arrive to institute a postmortem.

Five of them draw up a report beside the eviscerated body, which lies on the table in the principal hall of the *Palais national* in the island of Tortuga. This mournful, but unavoidable, business has lasted from 6 a.m. to 2 p.m. The body is taken out of the bath of aromatic herbs and spirits-of-wine in which it has been laid for maceration purposes and they proceed to the embalming:

> The body has been enveloped in an infinite number of bindings of two fingers' breadth, strongly impregnated with balm; each finger, each limb separately, right to the top of the head, where the bandaging ends in a little cap, underneath which is some of Mme. Leclerc's hair, placed there at her request as a pledge of conjugal affection, in exchange for some of her husband's, for which she asked.

Now that the corpse has been reduced to the state of a mummy it is wrapped in its cerecloth and sewn up in a shroud; "in which state we laid the body in a lead coffin with tears and lamentations." The empty spaces are filled with cotton and sweet-smelling powders, the leaden cover is soldered on, and this inner coffin is inserted in a double bier. The whole weighs nine hundred *livres*. And outside, the cannon of the island batteries were awakening the seaward echoes with their funeral volleys.

Now, how did Pauline behave at Hayti? In no very edifying way, judging by general report. According to Barras, she subjected Leclerc to an "ostentatious parade of the spectacle of the dishonoured husband." (Barras.) Details of the dishonour are (of course) not lacking, but, observes one of her biographers, "no very exact information is forthcoming regarding Mme. Leclerc's eccentricities at Hayti; only a general statement that she threw herself heart and soul into the business of enjoying herself." (Joseph Turquan.)

This assertion we can contrast with another, a more merciful one. Comte Remacle writes:

> The love-affairs with which Pauline Bonaparte is credited at Hayti are very improbable, she found the climate very trying and, at this date, was in ill-health consequent on her first

confinement, and also by reason of a troublesome sore which did not disappear until after her return to Paris, and then only through drastic remedies.

And it is, indeed, true that authentic information, emanating from the colony at the time, reveals Pauline as suffering. Yet this does not explain everything away. We shall see her in the same state from 1804 to 1815, dragging herself from watering-place to watering-place, a listless hypochondriac, slothfully morbid; yet the fact of her having numerous lovers then is not open to question; we have her letters, we have theirs. Well, then, what was possible in France under the Empire was just as possible in Hayti during this expedition, wasn't it?

Doubtless it is improper for anyone to make definite statements in a case when all the evidence is equally open to suspicion, but, on the other hand, what we do know of Pauline's erotic career does not allow us to dismiss as incredible the whole crowd of tales which were going the round of the foreign newspapers and royalist pamphlets concerning the colonial behaviour of the First Consul's sister. The earliest of these reports, so far as we can trace them, occurs under the date of January 28, 1803, in the records of Louis XVIII's secret police. There is nothing vague about their accusations and the names are spelt in full:—

While her husband was alive (at Hayti), she had given him General de Belle as A.D.C. On the death of the latter during the epidemic at Hayti she replaced him by Boyer, chief of the general staff, concerning whom the newspapers have some pretty things to say. Who is going to fill the places of Boyer and Leclerc? Nobody knows. (Comte Remacle.)

General de Belle was brother-in-law to Hoche, who was Joséphine's lover in the "*des Carmes*" prison during the Terror. This is the only occasion on which his name is mentioned, and there is no possibility of verifying how much truth the tale contains. Fouché, whose information as regards this period of Pauline's life harmonises so curiously with the reports of Louis XVIII's agents, mentions no names here, writing no more than this:

Victimised by the fiery intensity of the tropical climate, she abandoned herself to every variety of sensual enjoyment.

It would appear that what the Duc d'Otrante here insinuates is nothing more nor less than that Pauline showed herself too complaisant towards the natives of the place. Nor need the accusation cause us any excessive degree of amazement when we reflect that away back in the previous century Frenchwomen had been made the object of a similar charge.

A news-sheet of September 11, 1763, refers to a royal proclamation which commands the re-embarkation of negroes domiciled in France, as the favour they had found among the ladies there had become a serious menace to the purity of the French stock. The paper goes on to remark: "At the Foundling Hospital, nearly 1500 *mulattoes* have been counted." At Hayti, likewise, the wives of the French officers were strangely fascinated by these chieftains, who wore silver spurs on their naked heels. Such a scandal was created that a special ordinance was issued by Leclerc to the effect that all white women who had conducted themselves too freely with the natives were to be sent home to France, whatever their rank might be.

Would strict justice have required that this severe decision should take effect on the general's own wife, Pauline? Naturally there comes a chorus of "Yes, yes, yes!" from the pamphleteers without exception; and Barras himself enlists himself in this nasty-minded regiment. According to him, Pauline had adventures "not only in Europe and at Hayti with all the white men in the army, but also with the negroes." (Barras.)

Barras evidently does not worry himself much about numbers! It is noteworthy, however, that a similar charge has been brought by him against Josephine, in reference to the days of her youth at Martinique. In the opinion of this "French knight" (as he terms himself) every woman who went to the colonies was, à priori, likely to be too free with the local natives.

The Englishman Goldsmith does not go so far, contenting himself with the assertion that Pauline reserved "a strong dose of love for Pétion and Christophe." The Pétion here mentioned was a *mulatto* named Alexandre Sabes, thirty-two years old at the time of the expedition, who died, president of Hayti, in 1818. M. Christophe, his rival, was a negro, born on the "plantation" of Limonade. He took an active part in the disturbances in the island, which brought him to the throne.

His consecration, with cocoa-nut oil, took place in 1810, in the church of the Cape, whereby he became Henry I, King of San Domingo, at the hands of a Capuchin, who yielded to the entreaties of the black archbishop. This glorious monarch immediately created a nobility in his own image; princes, dukes, marshals. At his receptions the usher announced the Count Lemonade, Baron Jeremiah, the Duke of Marmalade, the Prince of "Salle-Trone," and other important personages of the same calibre. His Majesty Henry I was represented in London by one with whose name we are familiar:

M. Peltier, a Frenchman, a contributor to the journal called the *Ambigu*, having published several articles which were favourable to this prince, was rewarded by, among other tokens of gratitude, a good-sized cargo of colonial produce; this writer is generally considered as his representative in London.

Colonial produce from Hayti allowed Peltier to utter some supplementary truths directed against Bonaparte and his court.

To conclude, the only lover with whom Pauline is not credited, will never be credited again, was Fréron.

He was there, too, at Hayti, but sadly lacking in the celebrity he formerly enjoyed. Directly after his return from Marseilles, in the year IV, he once again tasted the poverty and the miseries of his early days. He missed re-election to the Five Hundred, and dragged out a pitiable existence, boycotted on all sides, cut by his former friends, condemned to the disgrace and the bitterness of complete neglect. Everything gave way underneath him, while, in the distance, in an interval between two dashing victories, "*la diva Paolina*" married someone else, someone whom Fréron had once met before Toulon—when Leclerc was A.D.C. to his brother-in-law, General La Poype.

Thereupon he turned to the mistress of bygone, happier days. She awaited him, faithful to her fickle lover, still the servant of his desires. Her he married in some hole-and-corner fashion; no one knew anything of it. And he was holding out his hand now, asking help from Joseph, begging alms of Lucien. But what was become of the loot from Toulon? Where were the results of brigandage at Marseilles? Floundering about in his Slough of Despond he was clutching at anything which promised subsistence.

When Lucien came to be Minister of the Interior, he nominated Fréron managing director of the Paris hospitals. In the year X, at the date of the Hayti expedition, someone bethought himself of Fréron, and he was appointed sub-*prefect* at Les Cayes at 18,000 *francs* a year. He was in luck again; and he made haste to embark. *Frimaire* 5, year X, he reached Brest, summoned thither by the head of the colonial administration department, to take his place on board the admiral's ship *Océan*. What feeling kept him on the quay when the anchor was being weighed? He let the ship go without him. (M. Joseph Turquan is in error when he writes that Fréron went by the same vessel as Pauline.) Was he afraid of confronting, in his poverty-stricken, "seen-better-days" state, that effulgent mistress of his—his the day before yesterday? Was it her pity he feared? or her disdain? or her indifference?

This further bitter experience he did not face. But, by way of consolation, had he not with him, next his ravaged heart, the dainty packet of highly-strung, ardent love-letters, posted at Marseilles in the year IV? Four months did he spend at Brest, months of bitter despair, impotent rage, and misery. In time, towards the end of *Ventôse*, he took his place on board the *Zélé*, which was kept at sea by bad weather from *Germinal* to the middle of *Prairial*—seventy-five days. What forlorn recollections must have been those of the exile during the long, vacant hours of that voyage! "Tiger, away to the forests of Tartary to couch with savage beasts!"—thus had Isnard apostrophised him in days gone by. But it was not savage beasts, it was death, that he was going to meet. When he landed at Hayti he had barely a month more to live.

In *Messidor* he was attacked by the yellow fever. He was alone; his wife had not been able to obtain a passage on a Government ship. Alone then, he dragged out his pitiable, short agony. On *Messidor* 26, at four in the afternoon, all was over. Leclerc, informed immediately, wrote to Admiral De Crès:

> Fréron is dead. He dies poor. I recommend his wife and chil-dren to you. He was a good sort and a pleasant fellow, and he went out of his way to assist me when power was his, when he was the representative of the people with the Italy Army.

Thus, brief was the funeral oration over Pauline's first lover, and it reached France signed by her husband. It was in a corner of the cemetery of the Cape, amid the rustling mangroves, that the corpse of the plague-stricken man was thrown, denied the land of his birth for his eternal and unheeded rest. Three months and a half later, it was Leclerc's turn to leave the land of the living. But he, at any rate, came to France to sleep the sleep of the just. The second day after his death a mortuary chapel was installed in state on board the *Swiftsure*. Admiral Touche-Tréville writes to Paulette on *Brumaire* 13:

> I trust that within two days, or, at latest, within three, you will leave behind you this wretched country which must hence-forth be a land of sorrow and weariness for me.

The coffin was taken on board amid the roar of cannon, was hoisted on to the bridge, and there remained, crowned with the dead man's hat and sword. Thus, in solitary state, did he wend his way back to his distant fatherland, guarded by the soldiers who had survived the disasters of the war, majestically cradled on the great billows of the foaming seas. On the ship had been arranged a sombre, warrior's *chapelle ardente,* adorned with trophies and standards; and therein, on a pedestal, stood the great leaden vase which contained the dead man's heart, enclosed in a golden urn, bearing the following votive inscription:—

> Paulette Bonaparte, married to General Leclerc, Prairial 20, year V, has enclosed in this urn her love together with the heart of her husband, whose perils and whose glory she had shared. Her son will not receive this mournful and treasured legacy from his father without receiving that of his virtues.[1]

A sad return home, but twice a triumph! For was not this *Swiftsure* that same English vessel of the line captured by Admiral Ganteaume in a fight (*Messidor* 6, year IX) between Tripoli and Crete, and kept to serve, under the name given it by the enemy, in the French fleet, as a lively and ever-present symbol of victory? (The *Swiftsure* ended by taking part in the Battle of Trafalgar, and, after being dismasted during the battle, was taken to Gibraltar by the English. She was then a vessel of seventy-four guns.)

She arrived at Toulon, *Pluviôse* 7, amid salutes from the guns of the foreign vessels, and transferred the coffin to the Cornelie. The news of Leclerc's death had already reached France, on *Nivôse* 25. Less than one month later the general's remains arrived at Paris, ("January 14, 1803. The news has just come of General Leclerc's death from disease at Hayti": Comte Remacle.) Whence, after the last honours had been paid, they were brought to Villers-Cotterets, and laid from *Ventôse* 5-17 in the church of the little town. The tomb erected by Fontaine in the park of the *château* of Montgobert, which belonged to Leclerc, was soon ready. *Ventôse* 18 the shell of lead was placed beneath the marble monument; the slab over the vault was sealed; all was over.

Pauline's first lover and her first husband, the two witnesses of the happy hours of her youthful love-affairs, have both disappeared. Her heart was about to summon her to destinies both novel and lively.

★★★★★★★★★★

General Leclerc's tomb still exists in the park of the *château* of Mont-gobert, whose present owner is the Duchess of Albuféra. On January 16, 1868, the municipality of Pontoise voted the erection of a statue to Leclerc at the highest point of what was then the *rue Impériale,* level with the church of Saint-Maclou. An Imperial decree of March 18 the same year approved of this proposal. At this date Leclerc's last surviving sister, who had married Marshal Davout, was still alive; she it was who had made the offer of the statue of the general to the town of Pontoise. Lemot was the sculptor.

For a long time, the statue stood in the Panthéon, but when what once had been the church of Sainte-Genevieve was given back into Catholic hands, Louis XVIII ordered the statue to be sent to Marshal Davout, who found a place for it in the park of his *château* of Savigny-sur-Orge. Apart from its artistic value, which is far from being so insignificant as M. Frédéric Masson would have us believe, Leclerc's statue at Pontoise thus presents, as we see it now, a double interest as a curiosity.

★★★★★★★★★★

THE STATUE OF GENERAL LECLERC AT PONTOISE

CHAPTER 3

The Merry Widow

The Consular court went into mourning for ten days from the date of the announcement of Leclerc's death. *Pluviôse* 22 Pauline reached Paris, to take up her quarters at the *Hôtel Marboeuf*, Joseph's home; the *hôtel* which was subsequently handed over to Marshal Suchet. There she rested to tide over the early phases of her sorrow. Besides, she was ill, tired, worn out by the long sea-passage, overcome by all the ritual of the general's funeral ceremonies. Her rest lasted barely a month.

Once back in Paris she was infected by the intoxicating influence of the capital, by the whirl of its luxury and its *fêtes*. Moreover, being domiciled under Joseph's roof—and supervision—probably bored her; she was more or less under restraint there, and she made haste to escape. We find her, therefore, a few weeks after her return, looking round for a mansion to her taste, something magnificent and striking; a shrine for her beauty and a reward for her patience. Her choice fell on the one-time *Hôtel du Charost*, then for sale in the *rue du Faubourg-Saint-Honoré*. (The site of this mansion, is at present occupied by the English embassy, the purchase was effected in 1815. Castlereagh resided there during the Restoration.) The negotiations did not take long.

In *Germinal*, year XI, Pauline moved into her new house, the initial cost of which was 400,000 *francs*. Nobody saw anything surprising in her purchase of this magnificent residence, noble in the lines of its architecture from the spacious *cour d'honneur* to the height of its *façade*. The general opinion was that Pauline had returned from Hayti with colossal wealth. Lewis Goldsmith, in 1814, reckoned her share of the booty at seven millions. He might as well have doubled it; who would have contradicted him? (A pamphlet against Savary, Napoleon's Minister of Police, goes still farther, estimating Pauline's share at 16 or 20 millions of *francs*, not more.) Reichardt, too, asserts that on becoming a widow, Pauline became "the richest of the family," next to

Lucien. Lastly comes Doris of Bourges to give a finishing touch to these charges by means of a characteristic anecdote. With the utmost confidence in his readers' idiotic credulity he writes:—

> General Leclerc's widow, Pauline Bonaparte, returned from Hayti dragging along behind her, Artemisia-fashion, her husband's body, most carefully boxed up and never out of her sight. Some boobies got quite enthusiastic over this touching example of conjugal fidelity; but what would they have said had they known that the general's mortal remains had been consigned to the sewers, and that this coffin, so carefully tended, was filled instead with the diamonds and a portion of the treasure that he and his noble wife had stolen during the expedition.

It is this same Doris of Bourges who, *apropos* of Pauline's mansion, dilates on the scandalous methods she resorted to to enlarge it, to stimulate the wrath of his public of simpletons. If we are to believe him, she had a neighbour whose house she coveted for an annexe to her palace. This neighbour was no willing listener to any of her proposals, and, to avoid listening to them, adopted the course of removing to the country for a month. On his return, what was his astonishment to find all his furniture on the staircase; and, in the house, all the first-floor doors walled-up and, somewhere or other, a slip of paper authorizing Bonaparte's sister's notary to pay over a stated sum as compensation for this summary expropriation. And that is how, under the Restoration, the history of the Napoleonidae was written.

It is curious to note how this same Doris never mentions, in connexion with this topic, Pauline's gay adventures, nor utters a single name. Was he the only one who remained ignorant of what was then the favourite subject of conversation in certain Parisian drawing-rooms?

The fact remains that from 1802 onwards we find Louis XVIII's agents speaking of Pauline's lovers—in the plural, and finding room for the echoes of these pranks in the reports that their master was to read. Sémonville took credit (much to his advantage under the Restoration) for a share in these pranks. The Marquis Charles Louis Huguet de Sémonville was then high in favour at court, having been a stout adherent of the *coup d'État* of *Brumaire* 18. "Short, fat, and jolly"— these were all the charms that he could offer Pauline, with the flower of his forty-three years. There appears to be little doubt as to her having taken pleasure in the homage he paid her. "M. de Sémonville," it has been stated decisively, "had been one of her thousand lovers; he remained on very good terms with her." Well, why should he be otherwise as regards the sister of the man who conferred on him the senatorship of Bourges and the embassy to Holland?

"Sémonville," said Beugnot of him, "is not the kind of man to let himself be forgotten by anyone who can be of use to him." It was a sentiment—the only one, perhaps, to which he remained faithful.

Wasn't it Talleyrand who answered someone who spoke to him of Sémonville being ill, with the remark, "What, Sémonville caught the fever? What use is that to him?" For the rest, he was "an excellent husband." He married Montholon's wife, whose two daughters became, respectively, the wives of Marshal MacDonald and of the Comte de Sparre.

Besides these various characteristics of his, Sémonville had another—garrulousness. To every comer he narrated his adventure, including therein the names of his rivals. To Baron Mounier he asserted that Pauline divided her attentions between five lovers previous to her departure for Hayti. "He did not name them," said Mounier, "but I suppose that he, MacDonald, and Montholon made three of them." Montholon, the Montholon of St. Helena, was Sémonville's son-in-law. (It is a curious thing that Charles de Montholon, whom Sémonville adopted, was legally entitled to bear the name Montholon-Sémonville.) His name is discreetly passed over in silence by his father-in-law, who was more liberal with detail concerning MacDonald.

"He told us"—it is still Mounier who is writing—"that Pauline was very much smitten with him; and that at Saint-Leu they shut themselves up together for three days with provisions *ad hoc* and without opening the door to a living soul."

And, as a matter of fact, we do find some rather obscure lines in the *Memoirs* of the Duchesse d'Abrantès, which refer to MacDonald, Moreau, and Beurnonville, as the protagonists in some mysterious intriguing by Pauline; but the meaning of her words is decidedly vague, almost wholly incomprehensible. We can, however, assume that at the back of Sémonville's garrulous boasting some grains of truth exist, and that MacDonald was one of the numerous angels in Pauline's paradise. Should we likewise include among their number General Jean Joseph Amable Humbert, Ponsard's "*Lion amoureux*"?

At the date of the Hayti expedition, Humbert was barely thirty-five years of age, having been born on August 26, 1767, in the Vosges, at Saint-Nabord-sur-Moselle. He was a handsome libertine, rubicund

MARSHAL MACDONALD

MARSHAL MacDONALD

and powerful; so much of a ladies' man as to have lost two posts for what he did on that account. It was for libertinage that he was dismissed from the merchant's office at Nancy, where he was earning a modest living; for the same reason was he asked to leave the hat factory at Lyons, where he also worked. Thereupon he enlists in the Lyons National Guard and, as soon as he had won his sergeant's stripes, resigns and comes back to live near Remiremont, making the round of the countryside, bartering, trafficking, employing his loquacity to facilitate dealings in rabbit-skins, which were his speciality.

But the taste for soldiering seized him again. It was what he was meant for, to clank his sabre on the field of battle and in public-house, to strike terror into the hearts of battalions and mothers. August 2, 1792, then, he becomes captain in the 13th Regiment of the Vosges volunteers at Epinal, and, thirteen days later, lieutenant-colonel. The following September he is in the army corps, under Custine, which invaded the Palatinate and hoisted the flag of Liberty at Speyer, Mainz, and Frankfort. In October, 1793, he jumps to the other extremity of France—to Vendée, gaining the rank of general in the Brest coast Army. And all the time he serves two deities together—Love and War, Battle and Woman.

At Rennes, accordingly, while the Vendée leaders are protracting the delusive conferences, he is to be found at the theatre, the red-haired giant with the broad shoulders (and proud of them), with his arms round the waists of Mlles. Ninette and Cassin, actresses at the local theatre. Summoned to join the Sambre-et-Meuse Army, he forsakes love adventures for police work. The Directory makes him come to Paris for *Fructidor* 18, despite the law prohibiting armies not summoned by the governmental assemblies approaching within twelve leagues of Paris. Humbert gets out of the difficulty by means of a practical joke. He has the posts which indicate the constitutional radius torn up, and throws them into a cart which he sends on at the head of the army; "a strange way of not overstepping the limit, inasmuch as the latter goes on in front."

After *Fructidor* 18, Humbert obtains a short holiday. Then he sets out with the *Légion des Francs* and directs that descent on Ireland which has made him immortal, thanks to his cool audacity and patriotic gallantry. After seeing service in the Danube Army, and also that of the coasts of Holland, he received a summons to take part in the expedition to Hayti. Such was the man who is said to have been Pauline's lover during the voyage, not only on the way back, but also on the way there. The actuality of these relations between them seems to be equally open to question in both cases. A ship is a small house on such occasions, little secrecy being practicable when the passengers on board are mixing freely with one another.

That the possibility of Pauline having relations with Humbert on the outward voyage is clear, is undeniable; but that is a different thing from affirming that they happened. It would be necessary first to postulate Leclerc being an imbecile or complaisant. We can acquit him both of the ridicule implied by the first hypothesis, and of the insult implied by the second.

As to what may have taken place at Hayti itself is not a case where we can speak so decidedly. A widespread belief did exist in a liaison between Paulette and the ex-rabbit-skin-merchant. a Restoration biographer wrote:

> Humbert, was a poor courtier and never obtained any favours from the Emperor Napoleon, but it is stated that he succeeded much better at Hayti with regard to that sovereign's sister.

This statement has led to a deduction being made that Leclerc cashiered Humbert as an "act of revenge" under pretext of malversations by him. The obscurity in which certain episodes of the reconquest of the colony are enveloped do not admit of a definite decision on this point. But, guilty or not guilty, Humbert re-embarked for France. It has been said, and printed, and repeated, that this return of his took place on the *Swiftsure* when that vessel was bringing back Pauline and her husband's remains.

But in reality, it was not so at all. Humbert was already back in France by the time that Pauline was completing her quarantine at the Nozarettes at Toulon. This authentic evidence strikes hard at the root of the legend, but what completes its overthrow is the discovery of the name of the *Swiftsure's* captain, which was Huber. From this information M. Frédéric Masson has drawn a strictly logical inference, and has thus been enabled to demand, with entire confidence in his conclusions, "Is it not from the fact of these names being almost identical that the pamphleteers have woven their anecdote?" There is no question that this is the right view.

The case of Humbert may therefore be summarised thus—moral impossibility of relations with Pauline on the outward voyage; physical impossibility on the homeward voyage; possibility during their stay there. But since on this last point we have no information whatever, all that we read about it is merely inspired by the more or less fertile imagination of the anecdote-mongers. We are far from having undertaken to re-edit their effusions.

★★★★★★★★★★

Twenty days after his arrival in France Humbert was deprived of his rank. He retired to Crevy, near Ploërmel, without pay, where he turned farmer and horse-dealer. On Nov. 17, 1806, the emperor granted him a pension, and, Aug. 8, 1809, gave him employment again as brigadier-general in the Flanders Army. Sept. 26 following, Humbert was transferred to the Northern Army, with which he only remained a few months, for he was discharged on March 7, 1810, with 3000 *francs* pension. Fully convinced that a return to the army was henceforth out of the question for him, he adopted the course of passing over to America (1812) to offer his assistance in the revolt against the Spaniards. He took part in almost all the battles of the war, and ended his varied career on Jan. 3, 1823, at New Orleans.

★★★★★★★★★★

On her return from Hayti did Pauline find Sémonville, MacDonald, and Montholon still in Paris? Did she resume her former relations with them? Information on these points is somewhat scanty. If we are to believe Sémonville's confidences, the answer is—Yes. It is possible. "*La diva Paolina*" never turned a wholly deaf ear to a tender "Don't say goodbye." In any case, she welcomed back one admirer and one lover. The admirer was by no means unworthy of her: this was Denis De Crès, the admiral, Minister of Marine. She certainly encouraged him, for she almost sent him off his head. "He very nearly got thin in consequence," remarks M. Masson incidentally.

It was not Pauline, however, who profited by the admiral's improved figure, but Rosine de Saint-Joseph," whom he married at Paris, November 15, 1813.

★★★★★★★★★★

Here is the letter, in our possession and unpublished, in which the new Duchesse De Crès informed her uncle, Nicolas Clary, the husband of Malcy Anne Jeanne Rouyer, of her marriage:—

Paris, Nov. 20, 1813.

I like to assure myself, my dear uncle, that both Malcy and yourself will be pleased to hear of my marriage. I have greatly regretted your not being here when it happened; I should have asked you to act as witness. I had not the courage to write to you for fear of putting you to inconvenience. I should very much have liked to have had you here today to dine with my relations, and I feel disappointed at not having had that pleasure. I hope that I shall soon see you and Malcy (whom I embrace) again.

I have seen grandmamma today; she is just the same as usual. M. De Crès is anxious to make your acquaintance. Both of them and Moina (her daughter by her first marriage) send you their love.   Duchesse De Crès.

★★★★★★★★★★

If Pauline ever had any regrets at having used her heedless, fascinating ways to make game of De Cres, she might have consoled herself with the thought that she had escaped a second, and speedy, widowhood. In 1813 the admiral had only seven years to live.

★★★★★★★★★★

Nov. 2, 1820, an occurrence which has remained a mystery came to hasten his end; M. De Crès was burnt in his bed through the explosion of several packets of gunpowder which had been placed underneath the mattress. At the same moment his valet threw himself from a window 40 feet high. The suspicion fell wholly on this wretched man, who died the next day without being induced to say anything more than that, persons unknown to him had seized him and thrown him out of that window. Missing money and promissory notes have left no doubt as to the contriver of this murder. M. De Crès died of his injuries on the 7th of the following December. (*Biographie de tous les ministres depuis la constitution de 1791 jusqu'à nos jours.*)

★★★★★★★★★★

As for the lover, if he had the best of it, so far as personal appearances went, he was not quite such a success. He was Mr. Pierre Rapenouille, known as Lafon, actor at the *Comédie Française,* who played romantic "heroes" and ended by aspiring to transfer to real life the adventures in which he took part on the stage in the evenings.

He "shone to as great advantage on the stage as in society," says a Consulate pamphlet of him, although the same author denies him even physical charm. While admitting he was tall, he reproaches him with having doctored his slender figure; and as for his head, says that it was totally lacking in nobility of character. But the ladies thought exactly the reverse. Mlle. George, who was, it is true, very fond of him, said:

He may be termed a pretty man, his features were very delicate, nose slightly tip-tilted, small black eyes but very keen and brilliant; immaculately elegant, an excellent voice, excellent, too, at making love, at tears, at enthusiasm; his fervency most contagious, his by-play most striking, but no depth and little 'composition'; like fireworks which dazzle and compel the most enthusiastic applause.

★★★★★★★★★★

And also excellent at making meals. A letter from him is extant, dated Feb. 5, 1807, to Grimod de la Reynière, the famous epicure, and author of the *Almanach des Gourmands,* wherein, after asking for information *anent* certain stage-parts, he continues, "You do not forget. *Monsieur* (I dare hope you do not, at least), that I have the greatest faith in your traditions, in your good taste, and in the enlightenment emanating from your understanding and from your long experience." But, he adds, spiritual nourishment is not all that he expects of him, and he has high hopes that Grimod de la Reynière will answer his letter with provisions of excellent quality.

★★★★★★★★★★

The fireworks had dazzled Mlle. George herself. Did not Lafon propose to her, swearing faithfulness by Ariadne's rock? At the mention of Ariadne, Mlle. George timidly reminded him of Theseus' desertion, whereto Lafon peremptorily retorted, "My dear little girl, you can't compare the two. Theseus was a libertine and Lafon highly respectable." His respectability, however, took the form, later, of unblushingly cuckolding Camillo, Prince Borghèse. But then, he "was very attractive to women," and "his gifts were of a kind whose business it is to be seductive." Moreover, "love he expressed to perfection." In this blissful and unexacting profession Mr. Rapenouille-Lafon had made his debut at school.

At seventeen years of age, he had written a *Death of Hercules,* in five acts, in consequence of which his parents had promptly sent him to study the elements of the Pharmacopoeia at Montpellier University. In 1800 he definitely forsook the art of the scalpel to put on the tragic buskin, being then twenty-seven, with a marked southern-provincial accent. That was why one of his comrades at the *Comédie* familiarly knew him as "*l'Orosmane du Midi*." (He was born at Lalinde, in Périgord, Sept. 1, 1773. His debut at the *Comédie Française* took place May 8, 1800, and he was admitted to membership in the September following.)

Where did Pauline make his acquaintance? Probably at Lucien's house; Lucien patronised Lafon. At Plessis-Chamant this paragon of romantic "heroes" stage-managed the tragedies and comedies in which Lucien, Elisa, and sometimes Pauline acted with the retinues of the First Consul's relations. The realism of some of these performances annoyed Bonaparte. Says a contemporary:

> The ardour of the declarations, the energy and expressiveness of the gestures, the too nude accuracy of the costumes, made a bad impression on the audience. Lucien was rebuked by the First Consul.

It was, perhaps, in the course of one of these mild tragedy-courses that Pauline acquired the taste for tragedy and tragedians which made her leave the arms of Lafon only to fall into those of Palma. What seems to be a moral certainty is that she was the redoubtable Rapenouille's mistress before setting out for Hayti. That is the inference to be gathered from an anecdote which is to be found in several *Memoirs* by contemporaries, and is certainly far less apocryphal than it has sometimes been represented as being:

> When Mlle. Duchesnois heard that General Leclerc was taking his wife with him, she thoughtlessly blurted out before a lot of people, 'Oh, my God, I *am* sorry, it's enough to kill Lafon; the poor boy does *so* dote on her!'
>
> ★★★★★★★★★★
>
> Catherine Joséphine Rafuin, known as Duchesnois, born at Saint-Saulves, near Valenciennes, June 5, 1777, made her first appearance at the *Comédie-Française*, August 3, 1802, was admitted to membership March 17, 1804, was pensioned off Nov. 1, 1829, and died at Paris, January 8, 1835. Georges Monval, *Liste alphabétique des sociiétaires*. The sentence probably comes from one of Lafon's other fellow-members. In any case, it is hardly one to throw doubt on.
>
> ★★★★★★★★★★

It was no use making signs to her to stop her unfortunate expressions of sympathy; she went on for several minutes lamenting the sad fate of her "unlucky comrade." Lafon subsequently got even with her by declaring that he really couldn't act with that "monster." He was only half right.

Pauline's relations with the tragedian were not so much of a secret as to pass unobserved. In 1814 a pamphlet said: "The celebrated Lafond (*sic*) is the 'favoured lover,'" an assertion which was far from having the merit of being unpublished or new.

The lovers' meetings took place not, probably, at Lafon's house, but rather at Pauline's.

Was it not these meetings that the author of Fouché's *Memoirs* had in mind when he exclaimed, in lyrical wise:

Voluptuous *château de* Neuilly! magnificent mansion of the Faubourg-St.-Honoré! If your walls revealed the truth, as did those of the kings of Babylon, what licentious scenes would you not delineate in unmistakable characters!

But the walls, at any rate, had the merit of discretion. And it is true that Lafon cannot be accused of babbling in this respect. If he took anyone into his confidence he did so with exceptional reticence. Nobody's reminiscences contain echoes of the affair; no letters have come to light to give a clue. His silence was, then, exemplary and he never dreamt, as did Blangini, one of his successors, for example, of making money out of his recollections of his amours. This cautiousness renders it quite impossible to settle the date when the lovers broke off their relations. Probably the end came in the early days of the Empire, since we do not find Lafon attending on the princess or crossing her path between 1805 and 1815. But he was punished for his sin; one day there fell on him the fate which he inflicted on Borghèse.

"Domestic troubles in conjunction with some special incidents have decided M. Lafon to apply for his pension," writes a Restoration biographer. He did not, however, take his pension till seven years after this announcement—on April 1, 1830, to be exact. Retiring to Bordeaux, "*l'Orosmane du Midi*" died there May 10, 1846. The name of a town, a date, that is all we know of the closing years of that lover of divine Pauline in those halcyon days of the Consulate.

CHAPTER 4

Pathology of a "Light-o'-Love"

Before dealing with the latter half of Pauline's sentimental-erotic career, it will not be out of place to bring together a few specimens of the evidence which defines her influence and her attractiveness, if only to explain how easy it was for her to make conquests. The unanimity of the praise which her contemporaries accord her beauty reveals the extent of her seductive charm, the royal ascendency which "this wayward, florentine, creature, half jewel, half siren," established over those nearest her, and even over those whom etiquette compelled to keep their distance. Napoleon himself did not escape this ascendency of hers. "He has admitted," notes Las Cases, "that she was beyond dispute, the prettiest woman in Paris."

Here lies the explanation of the emperor's indulgence at times, of his incomprehensible pardonings, and of his tolerance; strange in one who prescribed respectability, and watched, or appointed others to watch, as if under martial law, to see that it was observed. Sometimes indeed he was forced to remind Pauline of the respect which she owed to the name, and to the fame, in which she had a share; but it seems to have cost him an effort to do so. He was almost afraid, it would seem, of being thought to tyrannise over so charming a woman who was said to be an invalid, and, in fact, was one, though solely in the intervals between an adventure and an assignation.

The emperor gave way, tacitly consented, shut his eyes. That is why, for one or two lovers sent away under surveillance to the provinces, ten others were left alone to please themselves—and the princess. At St. Helena, the exile affected scepticism as regards these dissolute ways of hers; he was endeavouring to divert spiteful gossip from the facts of the case. Later on, we shall have occasion to show that, as a matter of fact, nothing, or at any rate very little, escaped him. That Pauline's charm achieved this victory over Napoleon makes it perfectly easy to understand her less startling successes. Everyone around her joined in a chorus of sustained, fervent, enthusiastic admiration; women especially, far as they are, as everyone knows, from erring on the side of leniency.

Jealous they doubtless were of her dazzling and faultless beauty, but how were they to give expression to it without making themselves ridiculous? Will they even be found minimising the magic of the picture by pointing out some half-concealed defect? Here and there, perhaps, a note is struck which suggests enmity, but it is always the lightest of touches, and the picture survives them unimpaired. Listen to Mme. d'Abrantès:

> It is impossible to form an idea of the perfection of the beauty of this truly extraordinary woman.

There is but one hesitation in the eulogies; the princess's ears were somewhat large, flat, and without hems: the merest trifle, in fact. Did not Her Highness wear her hair in a fillet? The cloven hoof is still less in evidence with the Polish Countess Potocka:

> Princess Pauline Borghèse presented the type of classic beauty, such as is to be seen in Greek statues. In spite of all she has done to hasten on the effects of time, that evening, with a little artificial assistance, she still bore off the palm in everyone's opinion; not a woman would have dared to contend with her for the apple which Canova adjudged to her after he had seen her—if tales be true—unveiled. In addition to the most delicate, and also the most regular, of features imaginable, she possessed a figure whose lines were admirable—admired, indeed, too frequently"

Finally, the completest, although the briefest, eulogy is this, from a third, (Georgette Ducrest): "Mme. Leclerc is beyond dispute the prettiest woman I have seen."

As for the men, they are no less unanimous and enthusiastic. For General Desaix, a sober diarist, reserved in his enthusiasms, she is simply "a very beautiful woman." Arnault calls her "the prettiest at this period so plentiful in pretty women." Beugnot is more eloquent still in his terse note: "This princess is the type of French beauty, that is to say, of lissom beauty lit up with vivaciousness."

The more diffuse Thiébault gives vent to his admiration thus, characterized as it is by a naive soldierly surprise:

A most magnificently made creature, with the most seductive ways, and the prettiest figure that nature has ever made, and one that, with a god-like liberality, is no stingier in displaying its charms than Heaven had been in endowing it.

Finally, the pamphleteers themselves add their quota. The Jew Goldsmith admitted that in spite of her youthful irregularities Pauline still remained "very beautiful and fairly fresh," thus contradicting Mme. d'Abrantès, who declares her "already faded, even withered," on her return from Hayti, a contradiction which is certainly quite disinterested.

Unfortunately, the same agreement is to be found again in relation to Pauline's moral qualities and psychical attractions. The pages devoted by the Duchesse d'Abrantès to her schoolgirl pranks and to irresponsibilities worthy of a bird without a brain, are well known. To these there is nothing to add, unless it be from Arnault's word-picture of that famous dinner at Montebello to which he had been invited by Bonaparte, where he found the youthful conqueror surrounded by his relations and by the companions of his newly-won glory. It is Arnault's only portrait of Pauline, yet it suffices; it is complete, and his analysis is most intimate:—

At dinner I was placed beside Paulette, who remembered having seen me at Marseilles, and, further, knew that I must be well informed about her, since I was a confidential friend of her future husband. She therefore treated me as an old acquaintance. What a curious mixture she was of everything that goes to the making of physical perfection combined with all that is, from a moral point of view, grotesque. While she was the prettiest woman that anyone could set eyes on, she was also the most irrational that anyone could imagine. As deficient in equilibrium as a schoolgirl, talking at random, laughing *apropos* of everything and also of nothing at all, mimicking the most dignified personages, putting out her tongue at her sister-in-law when the latter's eye was not on her.

★★★★★★★★★

Some while back M. Arnault was asked what pleasure he could find in a conversation with a very pretty woman who talked a great deal and hadn't an atom of intelligence. He answered that the conversation would afford him any amount of pleasure. I should love to *see* her talk.

★★★★★★★★★★

Prodding me with her knees when I did not pay enough attention to her tomfooleries, and every now and then bringing down on herself one of those terrible glances with which her brother recalled to order the most refractory of men. But they had hardly any effect on her; the next moment she was off again; and the authority of the commander of the army in Italy got the worst of the contest with a scatter-brained chit of a girl. Yet she was a good sort of girl, by nature rather than of set purpose, for she had no principles; and was capable of kind action, if only as a mode of eccentricity.

All that remains to be done, then, is to enquire what this lack of moral discipline led to in connexion with "*la diva Paolina's*" erotic psychology.

"A most curious person to study," Mme. Junot said of her. The study is particularly "curious" when it is pursued in the light of contemporary evidence.

There is no doubt that Pauline was one of the most remarkable, and one of the most energetic, of wooers of the Imperial epoch, far outstripping her sister Caroline, who cannot be credited with more than four or five lovers; or Elisa, the "Semiramis of Lucca," who, so far as is known, did not exceed the former number. Pauline "always preferred pleasure to greatness," says Méneval (formerly private secretary to Napoleon as First Consul and as Emperor, and also the Empress-Regent); which is not hard to understand, psychologically and pathologically.

In referring specially to Pauline, Chancellor Pasquier says:

"Perhaps no woman since Messalina has surpassed her in the use to which she has dared to put her attractions."

But was Pauline, after all, morally responsible for her actions? For whatever may be said about the "specific" disorder which she is alleged to have contracted, it is abundantly clear, though it would be inappropriate here to discuss the evidence in detail, that she was a victim to some form of erotic hysteria, and that under the influence of this complaint she gave way to irregularities which undermined her health and occasioned her medical advisers and her relatives the gravest anxiety. Hallé, physician-in-ordinary to the Imperial household, in a letter to Peyre, the princess's own doctor says:

"It is clear, that if she is not prompt (*i.e.* in battling with her disease) it will soon be too late. . . . We certainly must rescue this young and attractive woman from her doom. And if there is someone who is encouraging her failings, and is her accomplice, that person, whoever it may be, would not be blamed, whereas we should be blamed for having noticed nothing or permitted everything. I am not inclined to allow myself to pass for a fool, nor to let myself be accused of base and cowardly complaisance; but quite apart from this, this excellent but unhappy woman must be saved. Her condition is a personal grief to me, but fortunately I cannot say I have no hopes. Be quick, therefore, my dear colleague, for there is no time to lose. Make use of my letter as you think fit, and enable me to speak frankly and freely. If we can only speak academically, we must leave the matter alone.

All this makes it evident that Pauline's aberrations are to be attributed to a physical rather than to a moral cause; she was, in short, an invalid—and her palace a hospital. Let us therefore now proceed to examine, as pathological phenomena, the various paroxysms of her malady.

CHAPTER 5

The Dummy Husband

Some good people imagine that a prince is under consideration as a husband for the First Consul's sister.

Thus, as early as the beginning of 1803, did the royalist agents write in their reports. Leclerc's body had not yet reached Paris, and yet Pauline's next wedding was being discussed. The royalist agents, however, made reassuring statements in advance concerning the check that was to be called against the combinations that Bonaparte was supposed to be devising. "It cannot be seriously believed that any prince would accept the alliance," is the conclusion they arrive at with placid self-confidence. The irony of it was that six months later they were giving themselves the lie.

Soon after going to reside at the *Hôtel Charost*, Pauline had become acquainted, at Lucien's house, with Prince Camillo Borghèse, introduced by Angiolini di Serra Verra, the Grand Duke of Tuscany's Paris agent. Borghèse had only been at Paris a few days; his address was *Hôtel d'Oigny, rue Grange-Batelière;* and he had begun his stay, according to some pamphleteers, by being a frequent visitor at the porter's lodge. "The first friends he made in the capital were the *concierge* of the house and his family."

Borghèse has been exculpated on account of these modest visits by means of eloquence as brilliant as it is futile; he was hardly in need of it. Being rich, (though, it is true, avaricious, he possessed an immense fortune in landed estate), his name and relations might easily have opened other doors for him than that of the lodge of the rue Grange-Batelière. The princes of those days did not all belong to the Papal nobility.

Pauline seems to have been attracted from the very beginning. Borghèse could well hold his own as a suitor; a good presence, curly hair; elegant, despite incipient stoutness; nothing to say, but a lively way of saying it; in his general bearing something attractive, something of the vivid Italian ardour. He was young, twenty-eight years old; a fine name and a great ancestry; great-nephew of Pope Paul V; and, lastly, Prince of Sulmona and of Rossano, a wedding-present likely to meet with the approval of a young woman belonging to a family which had not hitherto succeeded in attaining such a distinction. ("Borghèse was a handsome youngster who brought her a very large fortune, diamonds which eclipsed all others in Paris, and, finally, the title of princess, hitherto unknown for excellent reasons, in the First Consul's family circle.": Arther Levy *Napoléon* intime.)

Was not all this well calculated to favour Borghèse's pretensions? To decide matters, he, too, was surprisingly anxious to be included in the all-powerful family, and perhaps, also, quite eager to possess so radiant a *fiancée*. To compass the same ends, she also brings to bear all the ardour of naive vanity, of youthful pride, and—who knows?—perhaps affection likewise; for her, for the moment:—

"*Quels meilleurs fruits que ceux dont on n'a point goûté?*"
"What better fruits than those of which we have not tasted?"

There was no long delay. From Lille, *Messidor* 20, year XI, Josephine, then on a journey with Bonaparte, writes to Hortense:—

You doubtless know that Mme. Leclerc is going to marry; Prince Borghèse is to be the husband. Two days ago, Bonaparte heard from her, saying she wanted him for her husband, and that she felt she would be very happy with him. She asks Bonaparte's permission for Prince Borghèse to write to him to ask her hand. Joseph and M. Angelini (*i.e.* Angiolini) seem to have been the match-makers. Supposing that no one in your household has mentioned this to you, say nothing about it.

The news did not long remain a secret. It filtered through to the public about the middle of *Thermidor*, the royalist agents notifying it under the date of the 22nd. (Comte Remacle.) And, immediately after, Peltier bursts out into guffaws in the *Ambigu*, in London, and into congratulations to Bonaparte in an open letter.

I present you with my sincere felicitations, on widow Leclerc's forthcoming marriage to Prince Camillo Borghèse. When I read the details of her grief I straightway became sorely afraid of her wanting to play the Malabar widow. . . . I do not despair

PRINCE CAMILLO BORGHÈSE

of seeing her become a Lady-Pope someday, judging by the pace you are taking the world at now."

Peltier had not come to the end of his maddening surprises.

The First Consul opposed no obstacle to the marriage, consenting to its celebration with the sole stipulation that Pauline must first allow the ordinary term of mourning to expire. As sister of the Head of the State, ought she not to be the first to adhere to the article concerning *"Customs in use at Paris as regards mourning,"* which deals with cases such as hers, and which had been published in the *Almanach national*? Mourning for a husband was to be one year and six weeks.

★★★★★★★★★★

Here is the article relating to mourning for a husband: "The first three months, a dress of woollen material; for the first six weeks, head-dress and *fichu* of black crepe; during the following six weeks, head-dress and *fichu* of white crepe. The six succeeding months in black silk; in winter in paduasoy, in summer in Tours taffeta. The head-dress of white crepe, trimmed. The three other months in black and white, and the six last weeks in white altogether." (*Almanach national de France*, year XII *of the Republic*.)

★★★★★★★★★★

Now, it was barely eight months since Leclerc's death. Pauline must wait, therefore, from *Messidor* to *Brumaire*. But four months was a long wait, and Pauline not the kind of person to put up with it. As early as *Fructidor* 5 she signs the contract of marriage with Borghèse at her house, wherein she owns to possessing 800,000 *francs*, 500,000 of which were Napoleon's gift, 300,000 being in diamonds. (Frédéric Masson, *Napoléon et sa famille*, II., asserts that these 300,000 *francs'* worth of diamonds in the marriage-contract only masked a personal gift to her from Napoleon in the year XI.)

The following week she gave the First Consul the slip and promptly hurried to Joseph's house at Mortfontaine, and there married. Not till two months later, in *Brumaire*, was the official wedding celebrated; thus saving appearances and making out Pauline's mourning to have lasted the year.

★★★★★★★★★★

Mortfontaine (or Mortefontaine) was famous before Joseph Bonaparte stayed there. In the eighteenth century the domain was nothing but untilled land, barren rock, and marsh-land. It was a rich *dilettante*, M. Le Pelletier, known as *de* Mortefontaine, president of the Paris Parliament, who, in 1770, turned this wilderness into a charming park. In 1790, M. Dumey, Court banker, developed the rich estate anew. Joseph completed his predecessor's work and spent enormous sums on extensive improvements; a Naiads' Grotto, an ice-house, an orangery, a theatre, an artificial mountain; taking such interest in Mortefontaine that he was often to be seen there in the middle of the workmen encouraging them and urging them on. It was his favourite residence; thither he came to rest from the labours of the Concordat, and of the treaties of Lunéville and Amiens.

At Mortefontaine were received the ambassadors of the United States, who came to France in Oct., 1800, to draw up and sign the treaty regulating maritime commerce and the rights of neutrals. Joseph seems never to have left this favourite residence of his without regret; even on the throne of Naples, and still more so on the throne of Spain, his thoughts went back of their own accord to that charming estate where he spent the last years of the Empire. After Napoleon's fall it was offered for sale, and leased to a rich Prussian gentleman, named Schikler. In 1827 it was bought by the Prince de Condé, and, in 1850, passed to Mme. de Feuchères (his mistress) and subsequently to her niece, Mme. Corbin. (Maurice Vitrac.)

★★★★★★★★★★

The First Consul, however, by this secret marriage of *Fructidor* 13 had been befooled and deceived. He refused to sanction, by being present, this sham marriage ceremony, and, in order not to have any hand in this mockery of the proprieties, in this breach of the rules of a custom which he was just re-establishing, he left Paris before the ceremony and went to Boulogne.

Thither Pauline sent a letter after him, announcing her departure for Rome, to which city she was going to meet Borghèse's mother, the grand lady who, in her letters of invitation for her son's marriage, had ignored the marriage with Leclerc. The First Consul informs Joseph:

Paulette writes to me, that her marriage has been notified publicly and that she is setting out for Rome tomorrow. It is desirable that you or mother should write a letter of introduction for her to Borghèse's mother. I likewise request you to inform her that I shall be willing to receive Borghèse's brother as an officer under me if he desires to be a soldier.

★★★★★★★★★★

Francesco, Prince Aldobrandini-Borghèse, born June 9, 1776, Brigadier-General in the French Army, married, April 11, 1809, Adèle Marie Constance Françoise de la Rochefoucauld, born at Paris, Sept. 16, 1793, died at Magliarino, Nov. 2, 1873. Prince Francesco Aldobran-

Princess Pauline Borghèse, 1808

dini-Borghèse died at Rome, May 29, 1839. A letter which Pauline wrote to him once occurred in a catalogue of autographs. "I am told, my dear little brother, that my letters give you pleasure," the princess wrote, "I have no need of that encouragement before sending you news of myself." She declared her health had become excellent, and "the good news which we receive from the army contributes towards its improvement in no small degree."

★★★★★★★★★★

And, by the courier of *Brumaire* 19, he urges his sister to set out. He wishes to avoid the pain that he must give himself in making the remonstrances with her that are forced on him. This letter of Napoleon's is singularly eloquent and noble. It lays down for Pauline a programme of behaviour both strict and creditable. If she follows it, no protest will ever be lodged against her claim to be a charming paragon of beauty and of goodness. "And especially, see that your house is a happy one; and above all, no levity or caprices!" Good advice for a week and a day—but afterwards? As for the rest, here is the letter:—

Madame la Princesse Borghèse—I shall be away a few days more; in the meantime, the bad weather is coming, the Alps are getting covered with ice; set out for Rome, then. Render yourself remarkable for sweetness, for kindliness towards everyone, and for the utmost consideration for the ladies (whether relatives or friends) at your mother's house. More will be expected from you than from anyone else; in particular, conform to the customs of the country; never despise anything; express yourself pleased with everything, and do not say, 'We are better off in that way at Paris.'
Show yourself very much attached to, and very respectful towards, the Holy Father, whom I love very much, and who, by reason of the simplicity of his habits, is worthy of the post he fills. Of all that will be told me of your doings, what I shall be most pleased to learn will be that you are good. The only nation which you are never to receive at your house is the English, so long as we are at war with them; and you are never to allow any of them to become acquaintances of yours. Love your husband, see that your house is a happy one; and above all, no levity or caprices. You are twenty-four years old, and you ought to be grown up now, and sensible. I love you and shall always hear with pleasure that you are happy.

Your dear brother,   Bonaparte.

Happy? Doubtless she will be so for a few weeks, for the time it will take to be initiated into the pleasures peculiar to her new title, to taste the monotonous splendours which fill the palace whither her husband leads her. But what about when the honeymoon is waning, always the same pictures on the same walls, always the same icy immobility in the ancient marbles, the same views seen, as the same tastefully dignified pictures, from the same windows? And then, the palace is unhealthy.

★★★★★★★★★★

King Charles IV complained that when he took up his residence at the Borghèse palace the whole of it was not put at his disposal. He was forced to lodge part of his suite in houses nearby. The villa Borghèse, which was put at their disposal, not being healthy, the king inspected the former Papal palace (Castel-Gandolpho) which has not met with his approval.(Report of the Prefect of Rome, July 12, 1812.)

★★★★★★★★★★

And Borghèse. . . . Six months had not elapsed before Pauline set out on a journey, alone, already seized by the first symptoms of that peripatetic mania which was to retain its hold on her to the very end of her life.

★★★★★★★★★★

I have just learnt from Madame la Princesse Borghèse that she is coming to Florence in two months' time; I beg you, citizen minister, to acquaint me in what manner the First Consul wishes her to be treated at Florence, and whether it is his intention that I should give fetes on her behalf. If so, I beg you to be kind enough to provide the expenses."(G. Clarke, minister-plenipotentiary of the French Republic in Tuscany, to Talleyrand, minister for Foreign Affairs; Florence, *Floreal* 7, year XII (April 27, 1803.)

★★★★★★★★★★

From that date onward, it became a rooted, insatiable habit. From bathing-places to watering-places will she ramble at the bidding of her longing for movement and change, a wandering Jewess with imaginary sufferings, everlastingly a thirst for adventures, finding solace in intrigues and her recompense in eroticisms. But, suddenly, in the middle of these lonely ramblings comes a bolt from the blue to afflict her; on August 14, 1804, at Frascati, Leclerc's child, little Dermide, died. (Frascati belonged to Lucien Bonaparte, who sold it, in 1808, to his brother Louis, for 200,000 *francs*.)

"No one has ever spoken of her sorrow for her son's death," someone has written; which implies, to say the least of it, a charge against

Pauline. Yet—"nothing equals the grief of this unfortunate mother," is the information sent from Lucca, *Fructidor* 9, year XII, by Derville-Maléchart, France's representative with the Republic of Lucca, to Tassoni, the Italian republic's minister at Florence. Subsequent despatches, furthermore, show us that Pauline's health suffered severely through the loss of her child.

★★★★★★★★★★

Her Imperial Highness is intending to leave tomorrow for France. Her health has been very unsatisfactory ever since her son's death, and for that reason she can only make the journey by easy stages. She is thinking of going to her estate at Montgobert. (Siméon, first secretary of the French embassy in Tuscany, to Talleyrand, minister for Foreign Affairs, Florence, *Vendémiaire* 6, year XII (Sept. 29, 1804).

★★★★★★★★★★

But it was with her grief as with her love-affairs—neither lasted for ever. A year later all will be over and done with, and her attention will be absorbed by thoughts by no means so bitter. She will be inaugurating her double life of princess and "light-o'-love" and will be struggling to reconcile the demands of that dual existence. For of Borghèse there is no further question by this time; as to his good points, incidental and personal, Pauline lost no time in coming to conclusions—uncomplimentary ones. If her early impressions of this lover with "an Adonis-like head, but with no brain inside, smiling but insipid," were favourable, she soon had to undergo a grievous disillusionment; Borghèse was far from being what Pauline had imagined and hoped. He had, it is true, "the appearance of possessing a constitution," but it was nothing more than appearances.

When he was put to the test there was only one conclusion to come to; Pauline had been "let in." And what, for her, could be a more disappointing, a more distressing position? How could she retain any respect for such a poor specimen of a husband? "To give herself to him was to give herself to nobody!" exclaimed Thiébault, which is probably the echo of certain indiscreet confidential remarks of Pauline's that had reached his ears.

She was perfectly open in her expressions of resentment, distress, and regret when she was imparting information to her lady friends, such as the Duchess d'Abrantès, or entertaining her lovers, such as Blangini. It was a brilliant reputation that she built up for Borghèse's amative potentialities! "She discussed the matter aloud with the most incredible freedom," says one of these most intimate friends of hers, thereby lifting the veil from a corner of Pauline's lack of the moral sense, of her innate impulsive freedom from second thoughts.

Inasmuch as love was the end and aim of life to her, she saw nothing extraordinary in parading its secrets before everyone's eyes, and being as far from shamefaced in her words as in her acts. And these little anecdotes that she retailed concerning Borghèse to all and sundry, do they not incidentally suggest excuses for what she allows to be guessed of her life of dissipation and amorous intrigue? Married as she was to a cold and listless husband, was it not strict justice that she should seek some degree of compensation amongst more ardent lovers? There was something of strict equity in it, especially of equity as seen in the light of her temperament, her tastes, her needs, and her caprices.

Borghèse, on his side, offered no serious opposition. "He looked on, or seemed to look on, with indifference," affirms Mme. de Rémusat. Sometimes, however, albeit very rarely, he played the part of the jealous husband. Thus, about 1806, he took umbrage at the frequency of one Comte de L——'s visits to Pauline; a sudden blaze, but a short one! Borghèse went off and consoled himself with her ladies-in-waiting. That is why, no doubt, someone has written, with a candour that borders on the sublime: "Pauline endured her husband's neglect of her with resignation." (Félix Wouters.)

But when we are discussing Pauline is it not really beside the point to lay all the blame on Borghèse? His share of it consists in not belonging to the level that Pauline expects and insists on. What may charm some of her ladies-in-waiting is not good enough for her. Hence the above mistake. Borghèse understood immediately and was not obstinate; he retired to the background, taking it for granted that he is too mediocre an Hippolytus for this Phaedra. Little drinking-parties—with developments later—do occur; but anything fiery or overwhelming in its energy he does not want. And so, when all was said, he did not aspire to be the hero of the piece; he rests content with the role that Pauline allots him, and, "super" as he was in the Imperial theatre, he accepts, in his married life likewise, the part of dummy husband.

Book 2: The Imperial Venus

CHAPTER 6

Napoleon and His Sister

What attitude did the emperor adopt towards Pauline subsequently to the date when he made his family a factor in the political organisation of the Empire, when it became his wish that it should take an active part in the realisation of the Napoleonic system? What measure of toleration did he extend to his sister's transgressions? How did he keep within limits the scandal whose mire shot up, in consequence of the behaviour of some of her lovers, to sully his own great name? We have already touched on the subject, but here it is desirable to produce the evidence furnished by Napoleon himself. (We shall not pay any attention here or elsewhere in this book to the charge of incest brought against Napoleon and Pauline by Restoration pamphleteers and their successors. C.f *Napoléon adultère*.)

From the earliest days of the Empire, Pauline remained more or less outside the Napoleonic system. Caroline becomes a queen; Elisa almost omnipotent in Tuscany; Pauline will have nothing, except, one day, the little principality of Guastalla, a miserable market-town peopled with lepers, beggars, and a poverty-stricken middle-class. The truth is, then, that the emperor was alive to the fact that she was incapable of presiding over the destinies of a feudatory province of the Empire, for at Naples, it was not the ever-absent Murat who reigned, but rather Caroline; and what was Bacciochi at Lucca?

This creature of pleasure Napoleon left to her pleasures, on condition that she kept within bounds and respected conventions. Evasion of this obligation brings with it an immediate recall to order from the emperor, wherever he may be. No doubt, her charm, her looks, her natural, or at any rate well assumed, unselfishness, (at Elba the emperor said of her, "She is the member of the family who has given me the least trouble,") the friendly accommodating attitude she sometimes adopted towards Josephine; all this encouraged Napoleon to prefer her to the importunate, self-seeking Caroline who sometimes rebelled against the Imperial will, or to Elisa, undignified whenever she was grateful, and so shrewish! (Pauline was "the one of whom he was most fond, without, however, ever letting his affection get the upper hand.")

But this preference was never allowed as a plea for relaxation in the rules governing Pauline's behaviour. Or if they relaxed sometimes, it was never past breaking-point; but if, now and again, her brother's anger did thunder down on her, it was not for want of repeated warnings. We have already seen how, in the above-quoted letter of *Brumaire* 19, year XII, he requires of Pauline, with very wise tact and moderation, that she shall conform to the conventions of Roman life, of the world into which her new marriage was introducing her.

The advice remained a dead letter so far as the Princess Borghèse was concerned, and complaints reached the emperor's ears which resulted in the despatch of further orders. Fesch is the intermediary through whom Napoleon transmits this restatement, and what he says, by way of explanation, to her uncle is not devoid of sting.

> Tell her then from me that she is now no longer beautiful, that soon she will be still farther from it, and that she ought to be good and respected throughout her life. (Paris, April 10, 1806.)

Such qualities are those of the heart only, the only ones that Napoleon requires of this sister of his, perfectly well aware as he is that it would be waste of time to require of her those of the head. To be good, to be respected, that also is to contribute towards her brother's political system. The latter, therefore, will not tire of speaking and writing to her on that subject, and the letter which he asks Fesch to deliver to Pauline is significant from that point of view.

> *Madame et chère Soeur,*—I learn to my sorrow that you have not had the good sense to conform to the manners and customs of the town of Rome; that you exhibit contempt for the inhabitants, and that your eyes are persistently fixed on Paris. Preoccupied as I am with important business, I am nevertheless desirous that you should be acquainted with my intentions, in the hope that you will act in conformity with them. Love your husband and your relations, be obliging, accommodate yourself to the customs of the town of Rome, and be quite clear about this, that, if, at the age at which you have now arrived, you allow yourself to be governed by bad advice, you can no longer reckon on me. As for Paris, you may be sure that you will

find no encouragement there, and that I shall never receive you there otherwise than with your husband. If you quarrel with him, the fault will be yours, and then France will be forbidden you. You will lose your happiness and my friendship. (Paris, April 6, 1806.)

Except for being more definite in the threat concerning his sanction, it is a repetition of his letter from the camp at Boulogne, and a type of those Pauline will continue to receive, from Bayonne, for instance, in 1808, wherein she is once more counselled to "be affectionate; be affable towards everyone; cultivate an even temperament"; and, truly a piece of unseasonable advice: "make the prince happy." (The emperor to Princess Pauline Borghèse, Bayonne, May 26, 1808.)

We see how, after two years' interval, the emperor's patience is not worn out, never will be worn out. And if—and even this much is open to question—Pauline ceases to be on comfortable terms with Borghèse, she will, at all events, never have a break in her friendship with Napoleon. Did she not grow more and more accommodating to keep and to strengthen it? Why, if not with that in view, did she carry this so far as to subserve her brother's amours in the choice of her ladies-in-waiting? "I note with gratification that you are pleased with your lady-in-waiting, (Comtesse de Cavour) and with your Piedmontese ladies," wrote Napoleon to her. May 26, 1808. It was just on one of these ladies-in-waiting, Mlle, de Mathis, (Mme. la Baronne de Mathis), that his choice had fallen. Small and fair, and a trifle fat, nobody, generally speaking, saw anything out of the common in her. Pauline assisted these transient amours with discreet zeal.

"The princess, like a good little sister, gives introductions to His Imperial and Royal Majesty," is a contemporary jest. But, in this respect, was not Pauline but a successor to Caroline, who had, so to speak, covered with the mantle of her forethoughtfulness the emperor's relations with one of her ladies, Eléonore Denulele de la Plaigue? This considerate behaviour, however, was not a thing on which either party could plume himself or herself, subsequently, at will. Proof of this, as regards Pauline, is to be found, when, in 1810, she gave currency to a certain joke at the expense of Marie-Louise, as we may read in Fouché's *Memoirs*:

Seeing her pass by in a *salon*, she allowed herself to make a certain sign behind her back with two fingers, tittering as she did it; a sign that people only use in moments of vulgar ridicule of over-trustful and deceived husbands.

And did not Lewis Goldsmith say, earlier still, in 1814:

> She is very bright and has plenty of wit; in her sallies, home-truths and sarcasms sometimes escape her directed against the Imperial Holy Family at whom she laughs all day.

Really, the emperor has not to tolerate either sarcasms or ridicule. For the family, Pauline has "the feelings that she ought to have." (The Emperor to Prince Eugène, vice-king of Italy, Rambouillet, Aug. 23, 1806.) If she had any feelings that required hiding, the emperor would know of them nevertheless; there were couriers acting under instructions from the Minister of Police. (General Savary, duc de Rovigo, Minister of the General Police.) No more childish pranks now, liable to create public scandals. No more is heard of "Paulette," the name which "suggests Italy," a "pretty, charming, uncommon name," but "somewhat childish" and "suitable for a little girl." Now it is "Pauline" that she is to be known as, for that is "different, being noble and suggestive of Corneille." (Frédéric Masson.) But did she herself ever trouble her head about Corneille?

One question remains to be examined, that of the emperor's knowledge concerning her lovers. Generally speaking, and so long as their behaviour did not include conceited advertisement of their luck, they received only silent contempt and indifference from him. What sanction, then, for M. de Montbreton, the princess's riding-master? None; M. de Montbreton's amorous admiration for Pauline dated back to the Directory period, to the evening of that famous ball given by Mme. Permon, whereat Pauline appeared so divinely perfect in her radiant and dazzling beauty.

With a *coiffure* of little strips of tiger-skin surmounted by a golden bunch of grapes, enveloped in a transparent cloud of muslin encrusted with golden vine-branches, and her arms bare, "*la diva Paolina*" that evening achieved the most complete, and the most exquisite, of her victories. And, just as she had subdued to her service M. de Montbreton's ardour, she had roused the passions of an overbearing, enterprising man who was celebrated for his luck, M. de Montrond. He, too, was present at the ball.

Montrond was a personality of the period. Philippe François Casimir, as his Christian names ran, was born at Besançon, on February 10, 1769, the son of an officer in the French Guards, and of a fiery royalist mother who subsequently returned from her voluntary exile pitted by smallpox, and deaf. At nineteen years of age Montrond was a lieutenant in the Mestre-de-Camp Cavalry, and he took part in the early fights of the 1792 campaign, as A.D.C., successively, to Mathieu Dumas, Théodore de Lameth, and La Tour-Manbourg. His dandified ways were famous. "What scent will *M. le Comte* use this campaign?" his valet used to ask before each departure. M. de Montrond avoided taking part in those that savoured of Jacobinism. In August, 1792, he resigned, which ultimately led to his being put under lock and key at Saint-Lazare. There he came to know that frivolous, amorous, Aimée de Coigny, a fellow-prisoner, whose dainty charms André Chénier was to sing:—

La grace décorait son front et ses discours.

We know how M. de Montrond married her, to abandon her soon afterwards, flitting from bedroom to bedroom, from Mme. Récamier's to Mme. Hamelin's, from the sentimental surrender of Lady Yarmouth, who gave him a son, Lord Seymour, to Pauline's voluptuous frenzies. As alert with men as with women, it is to him that we owe that repartee to a former regicide-Conventionalist who was winning from him at cards: "You fellows have got into the habit of 'cutting' kings (*couper des rois*), haven't you?"

His, too, the impertinent reply to a lady whose dance with him he had taken the liberty of ignoring: "You are acquainted with history, M. de Montrond?"

"Certainly."

"Well, Louis XIV was right when he maintained that punctuality is king's civility."

"Yes, *Madame*, but (with a glance at his cross-examiner's ample bosom) he was quite wrong when he said that there were no longer any Pyrenees." (Alfred Marquiset *Une merveilleuse: Mme. Hamelin.*)

Besides, to these attractions of ready and caustic repartee, he added others, more substantial ones. He was:

Suave, fair, and rosy, with a Faublas figure, Hercules' shoulders, and the gracefulness of Adonis; a sword and spirit which commanded the respect of men, an eye and an energy which promised protection to women.

To this kind of protection Pauline was never averse. The period, however, was unfortunately not one when she was wholly free to make the most of it. M. de Montrond belonged to little cliques in which devotion to the emperor was not regarded as essential. He was implicated in certain intrigues which were not unknown to the police, and he let fall epigrams and witticisms which did not pass unheeded. Napoleon took advantage of these facts to relieve Pauline of a lover who was inclined to boast.

"She was tenderly loved by her brother," says Méneval, "in spite of some minor annoyances which she occasionally gave rise to."

Was M. de Montrond one of these "minor annoyances"? No exact information is available, but the police requested him to take a rest after his amorous exertions, in the department of Deux-Nèthes at Antwerp, where he was thoughtfully recommended to the special care of the prefect, M. le Chevalier de Voyer d'Argenson. There he took up his quarters, in 1811, at the time Pauline was staying at the watering-place of Spa. From Antwerp to Spa was put a few posts. M. de Montrond promptly covered them, and came to reside in the same house as his Imperial mistress.

> The result of this stay was, it is said, a request for a pardon for him transmitted by the princess to her illustrious brother, but the request did not meet with the hoped-for result. (Alfred Marquiset.)

It succeeded, nevertheless, thus far, that the exile was allowed nearer the capital, being authorised to stay at Ham, in Picardy, and subsequently at Châtillon-sur-Seine. By this date it seems fairly clear that he had broken off all relations with Princess Borghèse who, on the other hand, we know to have been fully occupied with M. de Canouville. It was, therefore, without leaving regrets behind him that M. de Montrond suddenly escaped from this last dwelling-place, July 12, 1812. He passed over into England, where he remained till 1814.

On returning from Elba, the emperor, knowing him to be Talleyrand's "damned soul," entrusted to him that mysterious mission to Vienna which is still but half understood. There he failed brilliantly. M. de Montrond's end was worthy of his early days. A guest at the Prince of Benevento's table, this high patronage opened many doors to him. He does not seem to have had any desire to induce Pauline's to open for him again.

"He was received everywhere, but without much respect," writes Mme. Gabrielle Delessert, *née* Laborde, of him on the back of a pastel she made of him in 1832. After Talleyrand's death, being without resources, he opened a secret gambling-hell. The police shut their eyes, which allowed him to die (Oct. 18, 1843) without having become acquainted with the hard measure meted out by the tribunal for misdemeanours.

If the emperor thought nothing of the attentions paid to Pauline by Marie-Louise's uncle, the Prince of Würzburg, if he shut his eyes to an undoubted intrigue with Maxime de Villemarest, Borghèse's secretary, and subsequently hack-writer-reviser to the publisher Ladvocat, it was not the same with regard to M. Jules de Canouville who, somewhere about 1810, made the utmost of one of the princess's amorous caprices. Canouville was termed by Marbot, who knew him, "one of the army dandies," belonged to Berthier's famous general-staff, fit, according to Thiébault, "to rank as a *harem* equal to satisfying the whims of ten *sultanas*." This same Thiébault adds that Napoleon's sisters made the most of them.

"People talked of nothing but Pauline's intrigues," writes Countess Potocka, "and they certainly did provide material for lengthy discussion."

Canouville's bragging, moreover, was of great use in maintaining the interest. "His intimate relations with her soon acquired a scandalous publicity."

It is due to him to observe that Pauline co-operated actively in this open declaration of these liaisons. She "gave herself a free hand in the extent of her control over her favourites, and took a kind of pride in making her preferences public property." (Georgette Ducrest.)

Two occurrences, at least, substantiate this. The first was made known, quite innocently, we may believe, by the dentist Bousquet, who was summoned one day for a consultation at Princess Borghèse's house. There he found a young man in a dressing-gown lying at his ease on a sofa. The princess was in the same room. It was on her account that Bousquet had been called to render his services. The charming young man said to him:

Sir, be careful, I implore you, in what you are going to do. I am most particular about my Paulette's teeth, and I shall hold you responsible for any misadventure.

Whereto Bousquet made answer with deference and respect:

Be calm, my prince; I take all responsibility on Your Imperial Highness's account; there is no ill effect of any kind to fear.

Bousquet skilfully performed the operation to a running accom-

M. Jules de Canouville

paniment of instructions from the "charming young man," and then, on his way out, after hastening to reassure the ladies-and gentlemen-in-waiting with good news as to the princess's health, went on to add, with the candour of amiable ignorance:

> Her Imperial Highness is very well, and ought to be well contented with the tender devotion of her august husband. He has just given most touching proof of it in my presence by his extreme solicitude. His anxiety was extreme; it was only with difficulty that I could reassure him concerning the results of the little operation. It will be a pleasure to me to repeat at Paris what I have just witnessed, a true pleasure to have such instances of conjugal devotion to quote, seeing how rare such a quality is in persons of such high degree. I am indeed touched. (Georgette Ducrest.)

They had self-control enough not to burst out laughing in his face; the "charming young man" was no other than M. de Canouville.

Such disdain for discretion, and taking such liberties with conventionalities, naturally brought their love-affair to a bad end. As long as they went their way at a distance from the emperor's eye there was nothing to fear but his brief and stinging recalls to order; but things took a different turn directly unruly manifestations took place under his very nose. From Erfurt he had brought back, among the presents from Alexander I, three sable *pelisses*, exceptional in quality and chosen for their flawlessness.

From one the emperor had made the famous *pelisse* referred to in *memoirs* dealing with the 1812 campaign; the second went to Bernadotte's wife; the third to Pauline. She did not keep it long; on de Canouville's happening to mention that a bordering of that description would set off his uniform well, his mistress compelled him to accept the emperor's present. To a review which was held soon after de Canouville went, wearing his gorgeous Imperial furs for everyone to admire; but, quite against his will, he attracted the admiration of one who knew them only too well.

It so happened that his horse, took to prancing backwards suddenly towards the group of marshals who surrounded the emperor, and, in spite of all the efforts that de Canouville could make, nothing could prevent the unruly beast's hindquarters from barging into the flank of the emperor's mare. Napoleon turned round, recognised the *pelisse*, and guessed who it was that wore it; Canouville got his beast away and regained his position among the Prince of Wagram's staff-officers. It was not till he returned from the review that the emperor's wrath burst on Berthier. The matter was settled in a few words, and that very evening de Canouville received orders to take the minister's despatches to Massena, then busy with the war in Spain.

While M. de Canouville was risking his life in the ambuscades of the Salamanca road, Pauline was giving prompt attention to the task of finding his successor. Said Beugnot of her in 1809:

She is rapidly running through all the pleasures which belong to her age, her beauty, and her fortunate independence.

M. de Canouville found this out by experience. Pauline had se-lected as his rival a comrade-in-arms. Captain Achille Tourteau de Septeuil, son of a former *valet-de-chambre* to Louis XVI. But the young man was in love, and his affection caused him to be so little of a courtier that he refused the august proposals; he was above dividing his attentions. Pauline's disappointment straightway sought, and found, a revenge. The War Minister sent M. de Septeuil to Spain to rejoin his regiment of dragoons. On the way he met M. de Canouville who had been sent to the Peninsula a second time. As they rode side by side, therefore, they personified the extremities of favour and disgrace. One had gone too far, the other not far enough.

This campaign was fatal to M. de Septeuil. On May 5, 1811, as he was charging into the fray at Fuentes-de-Onoro at the head of his dra-goons, a bullet from the enemy tore off his thigh, thus setting him free to return, a cripple and an invalid, to his virtuous love-affair, and to philosophise on the unjust and spiteful devices of the little blind god. Canouville's experience of them was likewise bitter in the extreme. After sending him back to Spain four times, they ended by getting tired of making him carry despatches. In 1812 he was ordered to join the *Grand-Armée* against Russia, "which occasioned deep distress, it would seem, to Pauline and to his numerous creditors."

In spite of her manoeuvres round M. de Septeuil, she seems nev-ertheless to have returned to Canouville at this date. Every fortnight she commissioned a courier to find her lover in Russia and speak to him, "as a letter did not reassure her sufficiently." (Georgette Ducrest.) This courier had but few journeys to accomplish. On September 27, 1812, Pauline being then at Aix-les-Bains, she learnt simultaneously of the red and white victory of the Moskowa and of Canouville's death. (Frédéric Masson.) A bullet had carried away his head. When he was lifted out of the purple blood that streamed from him, a miniature of Pauline was found on him, under his uniform; this was taken to Murat, who sent it back to his sister-in-law. (Georgette Ducrest.)

Thus, tragically did two of the Princess Borghèse's love-affairs terminate, two in which we may observe what it was that compelled the emperor to use severity. In Montrond's case he was punishing bragging and suspicious intrigue; in Canouville's, scandalous ostentation in connexion with youthful indiscretion. In the one instance he was freeing his sister from entanglement in equivocal and compromising political schemes; in the second from a fatal and final scandal. But, with all this, it would be rash to maintain that he rescued Pauline from Cupid.

CHAPTER 7

A Gentleman of the Old School and the Modest Musician

M. De Forbin undoubtedly belonged to the nobility. Born at La Rogue, in the Bouches-du-Rhône, he was in the pink of his twenty-seven years when he met Pauline at Plombières, in 1806. At that date he had not yet attracted the notice of the public by means of literary and artistic qualities out of the common. He only shone as a brilliant maker of couplets which he set to rhyme by the dozen. *Sterne, ou le voyage sentimental*, a vaudeville comedy, which appeared in 1800 in a neat *octavo* form, formed practically his only claim on the attention of the *Académie des Beaux-Arts* of which the Restoration, in its anxiety to reward all deserving cases, was going to make him a member.

His pictorial abilities, likewise, had not as yet revolutionised the arts and forced the doors of the Louvre to open to him, the Louvre, which he was one day going to manage with a careful incompetence which became notorious. The unveiled charms of her from whom Canova modelled his Imperial and immortal Venus, may have developed his artistic tastes, but he was so extremely modest that he only gave the smallest indication of them, as in the "Death of Pliny during the Eruption of Vesuvius" for example.

He was, in short, one of those brilliant amateurs, wholly superficial, nothing but a talker, a fine figure of a man, a lady-killer, scornfully elegant—a quality which always impresses women—in his demeanour. He found favour directly, no niggardly favour either; on October 5 following he was appointed chamberlain to the princess. And so, he remained within his fair wooer's reach, if we may so describe it.

From start to finish this romance was not a lengthy one; it barely lasted out the year. Whether it was deception, or whether it was weariness, no one knows, but M. de Forbin did get out of hand—if we

Comte de Forbin

may drop into the metaphor once more. Souvenirs of this one of Pauline's adventures only survive in the shape of one love-letter, so far as he was concerned, and, in her case, debts; for "Forbin proved expensive."! (Frédéric Masson.) This gentleman's sensitiveness was of an easy-going, accommodating description in relation to his mistress's liberality—a custom which points to illustrious precedents in the Great Century.

We know what it cost Mme. de Polignac to have a Vaudreuil on her hands. It was not without reason that Pauline begged her agent to call in her income from her estates, lamenting, "I am decidedly poor." M. de Forbin had contributed materially to worries of this kind. But there is something better than figures to bear witness to the character of his influence over Pauline. This is the long love-letter which she sends him during a separation which she is prolonging through the departments of Var, Hautes-Alpes, and Bouches-du-Rhône, testing the ineffectual virtues of the waters of Gréoulx.

This loving epistle is long enough, but that is not a serious matter, for Pauline's amorous correspondence is so rare that we may well be pardoned for quoting it here in full. Except for her letters to Fréron, it is the only love-letter of hers known, and it is well calculated to make us regret those that it has been thought advisable to destroy. In her illegible, nervy handwriting on the green-bordered paper which she was in the habit of using, she scribbles to her absent lover as follows:—

Gréoulx, June 10, 1 o'clock a.m.

Beloved—No letters from you this morning. I am most anxiously awaiting one, considering you said in your last that you were feverish. I hope that nothing will come of it and that my A. (*amant? adoré? aimé?*) will be perfectly well. This morning I took my bath and drank four glasses of water, which went down well enough, but on coming out of my bath I find myself very weak, but I am assured that it does me good. Little Marie (?) is going on well; she is nearly cured. You have written to Ma . . . that you will soon be coming to Aix, and that you have been ill, but that Mme. Derville's very careful tending, and that *you have been so well coddled*, that you feel much better for it. (To retain Pauline's way of expressing herself necessitates throwing over English conventions to the same extent as the original departs from French ones.)

Mme. Derville is a lucky person! To take care of you, to see you, to confess her feelings towards you openly; her lot is an enviable one. As for myself who am forced to put a check on myself, to be reserved, but who love you, cherish you, have given you already so many proofs and who can only be happy through you; oh, are you not my husband? Has mine deserved that title, so sweet, so sacred? No; he has not deserved it, for, if so, *you would not be mine*. And so, it is necessary to return me love for love, trust for trust . . . to believe that all I do is for our good, for the good of our love. I have thoroughly considered matters, and I am more sure than ever that all around us are fully persuaded that all is over between us and that we can feel at ease. Otherwise, what will happen?

The doctor has quite made up his mind to raise hell and go away. It was he who revealed everything to M. Mo . . . not through malice, but through fear, through stupidity. Mother and my uncle know everything, for you have no idea of what I went through at Lyons, the tears that I shed on seeing we were discovered. Mme. de B—— (Bréhan; La Baronne Louis de Bréhan, lady-in-waiting), took advantage of the moment to tell me that the way you behaved in her presence was awful, that she was not the kind of person to put up with our forgetting ourselves before her as we had done at Paris.

You understand how I was likely to suffer, considering that I am kind-hearted and that I had taken her into my confidence without reserve. M. de Mon . . . (Montbreton), you know better than anybody how he has behaved. He has been the cause of our separation and of a deal of trouble. (Having been Pauline's lover, it may be queried whether his behaviour as regards Forbin was not dictated by jealousy.) He has betrayed my trust in him in a way that is very hard on a . . . (?). Little Mi . . . (Millo) has shown herself unworthy of being a confidante, and so I may be sorry for her and kind to her, but no more of trusting her; Mlle. D—— (Dormy; lady-in-waiting to Princess Borghèse), is a good girl, but there is no reason to trust her; she is very fond of the little one.

Mme. Du . . . (Ducluzel; housekeeper says M. Frédéric Masson), does not love you; she is afraid of that compromising her. Ad . . . (Adele; chamber-maid) is a tattler; Mme. de Ba . . . (Barral; La Baronne de Barral, lady-in-waiting) is neither a good friend nor a bad enemy. She did not wish to be useful to us. M. and

Mme. de St. Ma . . . (Maur; Dupre Saint-Maur, private secretary to the princess), don't count. So, I only see Minette, Emilie, Nini. (All three chambermaids.) To impose on everybody the greatest caution will be necessary; sacrifices, self-denial will be needed, too, if you want to keep me. I will let you know in writing how you are to behave; you will have to put up with it, and believe that I suffer more than you from restrictions which will save us from much annoyance and even from losing each other altogether.

Besides, if my husband is coming it would certainly be necessary to resign ourselves to that. Accordingly, I am only providing against what will happen. Goodbye, I am going to try to have a rest, for I have never written for so long straight off, but you know well I perform impossibilities for you. This evening I will write again.

★★★★★★★★★★

The majority of the persons here reviewed by the princess, are mentioned as belonging to the personnel of her establishment in various Imperial almanacs.

★★★★★★★★★★

And in the evening, up in her room again, she continues her letter. It may well serve to call to mind her tender phrases of the year IV, and, just as she did in her letters to Fréron, she scatters caressing Italian phrases in this letter to the new lover, aware that their promises are more suggestive in their languishing way than the words which she finds by trying to think of them.

9.30 p.m.

I have been out; the weather is charming; a carriage road is being made. We went there. The breadth was enough for two four-horse carriages; but I felt sad. Neither occupations nor amusements can take your place for an instant, not even in my recollections. Madame —— has fever, so that I am alone with the doctor and Isoard, who has come to stay here at my uncle's request; he wrote to him. He is a good boy, but awfully stupid. I am making arrangements which will let you come to my bath and stop there all the time that I am there; but Mme. Du . . . (Ducluzel) will be there too, likewise the gentlemen who are here, but don't let that frighten you; it will only be the doctor and M. Isoard, and I have arranged it in that way entirely so that my dear one can come; but I am afraid that the heat will make it uncomfortable for you.

For myself, in spite of the other people there, I shall see no one but you. How pleasant will it be to be alone like that with you there. Though it cannot last for ever, yet we will never say goodbye, never! If we are cautious, we shall always be happy. I am impatiently waiting for news of your fever. Tell me what you are doing. And bring what you need for painting, to make pretty things for me. My cottage is being set straight now. I am making flowers grow everywhere. I am having things made as nice as possible so that my dear one may find it comfortable.

By the way, I forgot to tell you my husband has been appointed Gé . . . (Général). He writes me charming letters full of affection; where it all comes from, I don't know. But I am going to stop because so much writing tires me. The waters are pulling me down rather. *Addio, caro, sempre caro amíco, amante caro, si ti amo ti amaro sempre; carcado veni ma mando.* Tomorrow I will write down how you are to manage here, I will give my very best attention to arrange things well. I am going to try to sleep, but I am always dreaming of you, especially lately. *Si ti amo di più, caro idolo mio. Ti mando dei fiori che sono stati nel mio sino, le ho coprati di bacci. Ti amo ci io sola.*

For ten years she has been using all the resources of this kind of literature: she has not modernised nor varied the formulae. The lovers, apparently, had always possessed the same tendencies, had always belonged to the sentimental variety, on a par with the novel *Charles Barimore*, which Forbin published in 1810 in two *octavo* volumes. It was by no means the sentimental only that it impressed. Beugnot sighs:

It dealt with the subject with charming lightness of touch, reminding me of Atalanta, who runs over flowers without leaving a trace of her footsteps upon them. I looked at it, and said to myself with bitter regret, 'Happy beings those who still abide in this beautiful phase of life in which it is permitted them to offer up votive offerings on such altars!'

It was likewise the Blangini phase; Blangini almost immediately succeeded Forbin in the favour of this capricious princess. He had, indeed, one advantage over the count, for he had not been born till 1781, at Turin. Having taken refuge at Paris towards the close of the Directory, he worked at setting songs to music, of which a kind critic said that it was characterized by "smooth and sweet melody, and harmony light of touch and well arranged."

For the rest, he gave recitals at a little hall in the rue Basse-du-Rempart. There he gave first performances of his numerous compositions, which were sung as far away as Siberia—we have it on his own authority, though doubtless the tale lost nothing on that account. One of them (his own tale again) brought one of his publishers 20,000 *francs*. Meanwhile the musician himself was running through the gamut of misery. Far from foolish, and most adaptable, he took to dedicating his songs to persons of high degree.

To Caroline he proffered a set of nocturnes, nothing in it but music, it is true, but he naively confesses, "nobody did anything for the princes and princesses of the Empire without receiving a reward immediately." From Caroline he received a diamond pin, which seems to have gratified him inordinately. Destiny took him from Caroline to Pauline, who thenceforth became the beautiful Muse who inspired his music. "Perhaps it would have been better for my happiness had it gone no further; but who can escape his fate?"

Not Blangini, certainly. It naturally fell out that since Pauline "loved the Arts and Letters, and they found in her a powerful protectress," our musician was not long in experiencing all the forms of protection vouchsafed by the Imperial Venus. He resisted at first, being by nature a modest man. Thus, when the inspection of conscripts took place at the *Hôtel de Ville* at Paris he was quite overcome by the idea of having to strip. "I should not know how to describe the feeling of shame that came over me when I had to show myself to these gentlemen." The latter reformed him, however, and our Blangini gambolled about joyously almost as far as the street, forgetting to adjust his braces, which nearly involved the loss of his breeches.

In the end he grew less modest still, joining forces as he did with another of Pauline's lovers, his friend Maxime de Villemarest, with the object of turning an honest penny over his gay adventure. He apologised, it is true, explaining that his relations with her had given rise to too much scandal "in society, for me to believe that I am bound to a reticence which would serve no purpose."

1808 was his lucky year. He entered Pauline's household as concert master at a salary of 750 *francs* a month. (Frédéric Masson.) He had got his sister included, too, as a reader, but really for musical purposes. We do not dare to believe, however, that he carried a brother's love so far as to make her a partner in his duets with Pauline.

★★★★★★★★★★

Blangini

The following extract from the Almanack Imperial de 1808, shows the composition of Pauline's household at the time when Blangini entered it:—

Pauline was fond of duets, Blangini assures us. On his arrival at Nice, in January, 1808, during the princess's stay there, he was called upon to assist every day.

> The princess was so fond of singing and I of hearing her and of accompanying her that hours flew by as if they had been minutes; but all throats are not made of iron, and sometimes I lost my voice.

We know how lovers cure that species of loss. But Blangini overdid it. Mme. de Laplace wrote to Elisa that same year, 1808:

> Mme. la Princesse Borghèse is receiving no one, she is suffering from nervous trouble which renders her state of health troublesome, though not dangerous.

Thanks to Blangini we know that her doors were sometimes shut for other reasons. Thus, one day at Nice the Princess's High Almoner asked to see Pauline. Labour lost! Cardinal Spina remained, Peri-like, outside a closed Paradise.

> It is true that at the moment we had reached the climax of a duet.

In the end they occurred so often that the violinist got unstrung. Pauline commandeered him to continual attendance, forbade him to dine in the town, kept a watch over him, overworked him. "If my slavery was a pleasant one," sighs Blangini, "I was none the less a slave." Pauline's demands on him went farther still. Despite the musician's reluctance, she took him for public promenades in her carriage, a fine carriage with panels proudly parading the Imperial arms. Blangini took fright. Supposing the emperor got to know? And, in anticipation, he pondered on the fate that was then awaiting a less fortunate lover, M. de Canouville.

> I was not at all anxious to receive promotion in the shape of a subaltern's commission and be ordered off to sing my nocturnes in Spain, to an *obbligato* accompaniment of bombs and bullets.

Blangini a subaltern! The violinist is laughing at us! His turn of mind was of a more peaceful kind. But on the heels of fear of the emperor comes fear of the husband.

Prince Borghèse was, in fact, about to rejoin his wife. Having been nominated Governor-General of the Departments-beyond-the-Alps by a decree of the Senate of February 2, 1808, a post which had been raised to the status of "Grand Dignity" of the Empire, Borghèse started for Paris on the following April 4. Some days later he reached Nice, and the married couple took the road to Turin, where they arrived on April 22, with Blangini in tow, a lean, sore, whiny Blangini, testing all the tones of the chromatic scale with the modulations of his grief.

Now that he was forced to abandon the princess to her husband, he regretted her bitterly. He no longer found any opportunity for making an appointment with her, of seeing her again at a lover' s meeting. Summoned to Jérôme' s court in Westphalia, the new king' s subterfuges went far towards consoling him. The Empire having fallen, in 1816, he married. Shortly afterwards a letter from Pauline summoned him to Italy, probably to his former occupations. But——Fallen princesses, what place have they in a musician's *clientèle?* To Italy, too! And "the proprieties"? It was a trifle late for him to think about the proprieties.

Moreover, his fame was at its zenith. *La Lyre des Dames* which he compiled, won for him the most flattering success, success that he enjoyed to the end of his career, which terminated in 1841. He had become the *Chevalier* Félix de Blangini—nothing higher.

CHAPTER 8

The Sybaritic Princess

Between two liaisons, however, the princess incessantly complains, and bewails her state. Her disease, whether imaginary or otherwise, provides her with plenty of excuses for abandoning herself to the despair which she wears like a new dress. Compelled to put herself in doctors' hands, to listen to their advice, and to let them experiment on her with their remedies, she does nothing but wander from town to town, sampling the waters here, taking the baths there, yet a rebellious patient, in revolt against finality in the medicine-mongers' efforts, and for ever in carriages, in litters, in sedan-chairs—on the road in search of a cure.

When the Imperial will condemns her to go and play her part at Turin in Borghèse's province, she has but one aim: to escape at the earliest moment, to allege new crises, to act the part of a victim overwhelmed by a fresh attack of the malady, in order to regain, as she wrote to Murat, "that dear France on which one's thoughts dwell in spite of oneself."

★★★★★★★★★★

The letter has since been published in full by Baron Albert Lumbroso, in his *Miscellanea Napoleonica;* Rome, 1898; it runs as follows: "I have received your letter, my dear Murat. It was time it arrived. I accused you some time ago of being very quick to forget your little sister, and I find it very comforting to know I was wrong. You really are settled at Paris? I do hope that that event is giving you all the happiness that you deserve, what with your goodness and your devotion to my brother. You have said goodbye, then, to beautiful Italy? I too should like to leave it for a while to see all my relations again and that dear France on which one's thoughts dwell in spite of oneself! I don't know, but I think that the air of Rome does not suit me very well. I am always catching colds.

My little Camille has just been obliged to journey to Naples on una-

99

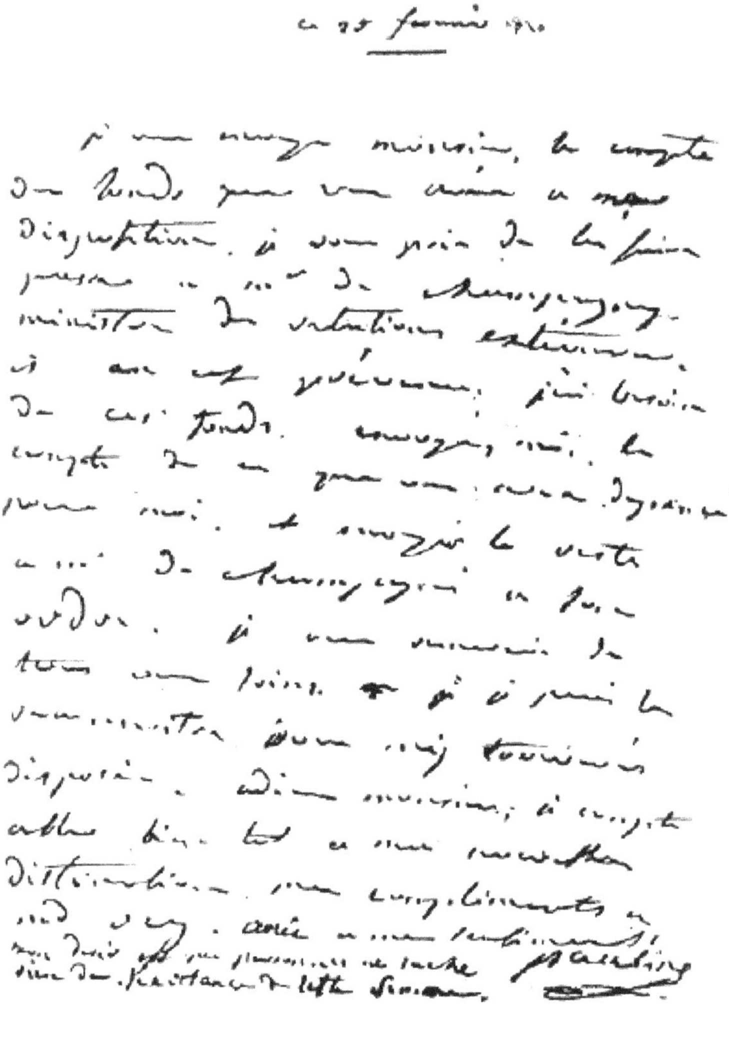

Autograph letter of Pauline Bonaparte

voidable business; he has given me thousands of messages for you. When he comes back, he will answer your nice letter: I am delighted to find that kind Caroline does not forget her sister. Please give her an affectionate kiss on my account. I have received a letter from her, too. I hope that we shall all meet again in France soon, all together, and happy, and congratulating ourselves on things in general. Goodbye, my dear Murat, a thousand kisses for your little children. A kiss for my dear Caroline likewise, and I beg you both to be assured of my fond love. Take care not to forget your sister.—Bonaparte-Borghèse.—A thousand remembrances, please, to all my relations."

★★★★★★★★★★

We know that it was not merely the beauty of the French landscape that attracted her. Nor was Napoleon misinformed on that point, either; for which reason it sometimes happened that he was opposed to the princess's journeyings. In December, 1807, for instance, he makes use of the badness of Italian roads as a pretext to oblige her to wait at Nice. Moreover, had not Pauline drawn on all the resources of her acute and feline diplomacy to get as far as she had done? The whole faculty, she said, prescribed her stay at Nice. Not long after Cambacérès undeceived the emperor. "Had I received your letter earlier I certainly should not have authorised it," answered Napoleon.

He compelled her therefore to stop at Nice. But why should we be surprised to find the brother sceptical, from this time onward, concerning his sister's illnesses? In the island of Elba "the emperor often took pleasure in saying that 'her illnesses were imagination.'" And had he not written, as early as 1808, with good-natured irony:

> I regret to learn that your health is bad. I suppose you are being sensible, and that it is not your own doing?

What happened was that certain rumours had reached him from Nice concerning Blangini's occupations and his variety of chamber-music.

And, in truth, it was a curious life that went on at M. Vinaille's villa facing the sea, where the princess had taken up her quarters with her household. Its personnel took the greatest liberties and indulged in the most extraordinary etiquette. Not one of them but combined the most diverse duties. Thus, Pauline's physician-in-ordinary. Doctor Peyre, who also passed for one of her lovers, (Barras), undertook, in addition to his medical functions, those of steward to the Household. (Blangini.) He was a kind of *maître Jacques*, standing fiercely on guard in front of the cashbox. The cook likewise played more than one part;

he let the joints burn, but he played the guitar. (Blangini.)

Here we gain a glimpse of the distractions of Pauline's idle existence. Around her, extravagance on the part of the under-servants was rampant; higher up, "kleptomaniac" ladies-in-waiting; general systematic exploitation of her acquiescent indolence. It was unusual for her to rouse herself. The Duchesse d'Abrantès writes:

> It has been stated that she was spiteful, and this rumour has even been spread by persons of her own household,

This rumour could only have come from a chambermaid who, at Elba, received a smack from the princess on account of her clumsiness. And even then, she begged her pardon directly afterwards, Pauline remained the capricious, impetuous, creature, always liable to sudden outbursts, to affectionate liberality, or the childish avarice of her young days, who consulted fortune-tellers on the success of her amorous intrigues, swore undying love to Fréron, and, the next day, married Leclerc. She issued regulations about the amount of sugar in her household's coffee, and arranged for a daily supply of news by courier as to the latest Parisian fashions. The emperor said at St. Helena:

> Had I known that, it would not have lasted long; she would have had a thorough good scolding. But there it is, when you are emperor, you never find out these things.

Yet he was not quite so ignorant as he made out. Had he forgotten that, as early as 1806, he had notified Fesch of Pauline's "unfortunate habits"?—"those unfortunate habits which good taste checks even in the most frivolous circles of the metropolis." (The emperor to Cardinal Fesch, Paris, April 10, 1806.) And what of the thousand other details of Pauline's private life—did nothing ever reach Napoleon's ears? Did Hallé, to whose edifying diagnosis we have already referred, who was still attending her in 1808, (Letter from Mme. Laplace to Elisa, Paris, Aug. 5, 1808), never say anything, and go on incurring a responsibility of the consequences of which he was fully aware?

This is barely credible, the more so, inasmuch as Caroline, not to mention others, had made an excellent guess at the causes of the state Pauline was in. She was doubtless informed of her sister's stratagems, in concert with Forbin, to deceive the doctors, but she understood that no improvement was to be looked for, since the Princess Borghèse had acquired a habit of disdaining the advice of her husband, her relations, her friends, her most devoted attendants. The Queen of Naples asked Lucien:

> What are we to do, then? What are we to do? Love her and leave her alone as she is, and not oppose her or worry her with useless advice, since she has made up her mind not to follow it.

And she goes on to allude to other reasons still, hesitating to write them, but reserving them to speak to Lucien about at their forthcoming interview. (Autograph signed letter from Caroline to Lucien, July 30.) What these motives were we may make a shrewd guess; they were concerned with her lovers. Deprivation of those was a remedy to which Pauline would never submit.

So, she continued to wander about to watering-places with that strange retinue and that series of lovers, some of whose portraits we have already sketched. It was in the course of one of these journeys, that to Gréoulx, that Barras met her, in the following extraordinary circumstances. It is a curious picture he has left in outline in his *Memoirs*; let it serve to illustrate Pauline's neurotic ramblings through France considered as a collection of bathing-resorts.

> The princess was going to take the waters at Gréoulx; she accepted the kind offers of her bathing-master, M. Gravier, proprietor of the baths. Passing by Aulps on her way to Nice, Her Highness became really very ill. Being in the state of health that she was, she had to be carried in men's arms. She halted on some rising ground, in a meadow, near an estate belonging to M. César Roubaud, at whose house she was to spend the night. Some courtly gentlemen respectfully undressed in order to lay their clothes on the grass, so that the princess might sit down without risking anything through the dampness of the ground. M. Desbains, sub-*prefect* of Grasse, with hair *à l'oiseau royal*, offered his back to support the princess's, while General Guyot lay down at right angles and placed the princess's two feet on his stomach, the three forming a grotesque group which highly amused passers-by and idlers. Roubaud had prepared a magnificent dinner; the thrushes which the princess loved had been procured regardless of cost. Dinner was served, and the guests took their places; it was only those of the greatest importance who were admitted. Roubaud, who was giving the dinner, made his appearance to do the honours; a chamberlain turned him away, saying, 'The princess has not invited you at all,' and the host was not received at his own table.

Barras goes on to make his readers' mouth water with:—

> The itinerary of the journeys of this incredible establishment would be extremely curious.

The tale of Pauline's own, indeed, would possess a rare piquancy. Nevertheless, we cannot contemplate the idea of making this the place for collecting the scattered anecdotes. M. Frédéric Masson has briefly dwelt on them with a light hand; and to set them forth in order would add nothing to our knowledge of Pauline's private life. Moreover, some other characteristics of hers remain to be reviewed which are of greater assistance to us in defining her psychology, and in forming an idea of her hysterical neuroticism—her willingness to receive men when she was taking her baths, for one. We have found her writing to Forbin:

"I am making arrangements which will let you come to my bath and stop there all the time that I am there," which confirms Blangini's account of her holding a reception when in her bath. She had herself carried to her milk-baths (which cost 10 *francs* each) by a negro in her service, Paul by name, or Rode, it is not clear which. This means of conveyance, it seems, caused gossip, for, to put a stop to malicious tittle-tattle, Pauline married her negro off to one of her chambermaids, thinking that, after that, nothing remained for scandal to say about her negro's duties, which gives a good idea of her logic.

Women's praise, too, was a thing that she did not despise. Says Fouché: "She loved magnificence, dissipation, and every variety of homage." That was why, when her toilet was in progress, she condescended to promenade naked before her women-attendants. Yet never, to our knowledge, have any scandalous anecdotes of the Lesbian type been current about her.

Her motive, then, must have been that of the most *naïve* and childlike vanity. Nevertheless, according to Constant in his *Memoirs*, "concerning her toilet details are told that seem incredible."

These details Constant passes over in modest silence, but some trifles have reached our knowledge all the same, thanks to a woman, the Baronne du Montet. Her budget of picturesque souvenirs includes a little sketch of Pauline at her toilet which may be hung in this gallery of pen-portraits. It is more than a bust, and truth to nature obliges us to present it with the others. Once again is light thrown on Pauline's psychology, as we read through the plain statement of fact which Mme. du Montet entitles:—

Un tableau de genre.

You are well aware that our reminiscences fall like leaves of spring, summer, or autumn. Some come from the heart, some from I know not where. The imagination has no system; thus, I am thinking, I know not why, of the beautiful Princess Pauline Borghèse, Napoleon's sister. Our dear Wilhelmina Hoehenegg, lady-in-waiting to the Empress (of Austria) was telling us one evening how, when at Rome with Princess Ruspoli who had given her a home after the death of her mother, the conversation turned on pretty feminine feet. Princess Ruspoli knew how frivolously vain the Imperial princess was, and did not forget to go into raptures over her foot. 'Would you like to see it?' said Princess Borghèse quietly. 'Come tomorrow at twelve.' Great was Princess Ruspoli's astonishment, but there was no means of escaping this peculiar invitation.

She presented herself at the Palazzo Borghèse with Mme. de Hoehenegg, and was ushered into an exquisite *boudoir*. The princess was reclining at her ease in an invalid's chair, her little feet well in view; but that was not the treat in store. A page, pretty as a Cupid, and dressed as pages are in mediaeval pictures, entered, bearing a costly ewer, a silver-gilt basin, a napkin of fine cambric, perfumes, and other cosmetics. He drew a velvet hassock up to the chair, the princess graciously put forth one of her legs, the little page took off the stocking, the garter, too, I think, and began to massage, to rub, to wipe, to perfume this beautiful foot, which really was incomparable.

★★★★★★★★★★

The page's name is not given by the Baronne du Montet, and it would seem that no document can furnish it. By way of a clue, however, here follows Prince Borghèse's *Maison des Pages* as it appears in the *Almanack impérial* for 1813, the last in which it figures:—

MAISON DES PAGES DE S.M. (*sic*)

M. le baron Provana del Sabbione, *Chamberlain and head-master.*

M. le capitaine Merlin, *Superintendent and instructor in behaviour.*

Teachers.

MM.			MM.		
Bidone	.	Mathematics	Merlin	.	Drawing and Fortification.
Deperret	.	History and			
	·	Geography	Guaretti	.	Fencing.
Marenco	.	Latin and French	Savant	.	Writing.

MM.	MM.
Caissotti de Chiusano	Coardi de Carpenetto.
Armand de Gros.	Galliani d'Agliano.
Bruco de Sordevalo.	Berton de Sambuy.
De la Chiesa de Cinsan.	Nomis de Pollon.
Ferrero de la Marmora.	Giustiniani.

★★★★★★★★★★

The operation was a lengthy one, and the astonishment of the lookers-on so great that they lost the faculty of enthusiastic praise which was doubtless expected of them. I told Mme. Hoehenegg that that would be a pretty subject for a *genre* picture; she was delightfully gifted in that way. We laughingly reproached her for having neglected a completely new subject. While the little page drew off, and drew on, her stockings, perfumed her beautiful feet, filed and refined the nails, she was chatting and, to all appearances, quite devoid of self-consciousness as regards her toilet.

Was it not that same lack of self-consciousness, of the moral sense, which induced her to grant the sculptor Canova those famous, much-discussed sittings for the Venus which has immortalised both artist and model?

"The audacious caprice which led Pauline to pose in the sculptor's studio in this far from chaste, albeit highly classical, fashion, is an all-sufficing clue to her character," is the comment of a fair judge. (Arthur Lévy.) Her only pre-occupation, in fact, on that occasion, was concerning herself; Canova, "with more to recommend him in the way of talents than of character," is relegated to the background. This sculptor, who first came into notice by modelling a lion out of a lump of butter at the table of the lord of the manor, has not struck the pamphleteers as objectionable; he has not been accused of abusing the "altogether" which his Imperial model conceded him. (Henri de Latouche assures us, however, that Pauline only sat for the head of Canova's statue.) Was the idea of this statue his own?

It seems rather to have been Pauline's. Did she not have before her, by way of a stimulant, the gallery of the Palazzo Borghèse, filled with Venuses of all sizes and all varieties of beauty? Kotzebue, who had the opportunity of paying it a visit, says:

It was a charming idea to reserve a whole room to Venus alone, it is pleasant to see and compare the various conceptions that so many celebrated painters have formed of beauty. For instance, there are two of them, one by Rubens, who would have found it difficult to get a place as governess in a bishop's household.

The probability is, therefore, that it had occurred to Pauline to have executed a pendant to the Venus de' Medici; what we know of her innate vanity leaves us but little room for doubt on that point. Besides, could not her beauty stand the comparison well? Canova made the attempt. We know his work. In it he reached the highest point of his art, combining grace with dignity, and elegance with robustness. The statue which he carved out of the marble is worthy of a tomb or a triumphal arch. It was finished by 1805, for, in a letter of February 19, Artand, secretary to the minister Cacault, mentions it among the completed works in Canova's studio.

No. 7, Her Imperial Highness, Mme. la princesse Borghèse, almost naked, reclining on an antique couch. (Quoted by Lieutenant-Colonel Th. Jung.)

It appealed to Borghèse's taste only to a moderate degree. He shared Kotzebue's opinion—"I should not like to expose my wife to the public gaze in this way"—and acted on it. He put the indecent statue under lock and key in a private apartment, and a special authorisation was necessary to those students who wished to admire it. The lyrical Beugnot was very wide of the mark when he exclaimed:

I wish that Canova had been commissioned to execute a statue of her, and that, once completed by his admirable chisel, it should have been reproduced in a thousand different places that it might take the place for modern times of the recognised model which antiquity found in the Florentine Venus.

It is clear that Borghèse in no wise favoured this flattering multiplication. After his death in 1832 it was supposed that the statue passed to London. Nothing of the kind happened. It still adorns the Villa Borghèse, perpetuating, amid the damp silence of that necropolis of marbles, the Imperial beauty of her who personified in that age, and will continue to do so through the eternity of harmony and of the fitness of things, Venus in France.

CHAPTER 9

A Hitherto Unknown Liaison of Pauline's

In 1812 we find Pauline with four lovers! Lieutenant de Brack, a brilliant soldier, who seems to have been well fitted to become an intimate acquaintance of the princess's without any waste of time; Commander Duchand, whom we shall meet again about 1814; Canouville, who is far away amidst the snows of Russia; and, lastly, Talma.

★★★★★★★★★★

Talma's letters to Pauline Bonaparte, which are drawn on in this chapter, are all unpublished, and come from the Lebrun collection in the *Bibliothèque Mazarine*. We shall not indicate the source of each quotation, but refer the reader to *Lettres inédites de Talma à la Princesse Pauline Bonaparte*; Fasquelle, 1911. All other sources of our evidence are indicated.

It was to this de Brack, by that time a colonel, that Queen Hortense addressed the following curious letter, in 1832, concerning the Duke of Reichstadt's death: "My dear Friends—I am answering without delay the letter which I received from you. I am feeling very keenly the grief which you share. Some fatal influence seems to cling to the name I bear, and we must apparently pay for the glories of the past with the loss of what constitutes our present glory and our happiness. This son of the emperor, so worthy of him, has only been made to pass away from our earth. Everybody agrees in saying that he was the most distinguished young man to be met with; though brought up in strict seclusion, he matured rapidly, and adopted a military career with passionate enthusiasm as soon as he was allowed to choose. He wished to pass through all ranks, wore himself out as a commanding officer, and his chest was attacked almost before anyone thought of his being ill. May France, at any rate, regain once more her strength and her tranquillity; he did not repine at the thought of probably having to pass his life far from her, especially if that life would only

Queen Hortense

have served as a source of unrest. My son has been deeply distressed; I am expecting my cousin. Yes, a settled gloom will ever surround us. May God guard us against further misfortunes and still leave us, as all our happiness, a quiet life and the sympathy of our friends. I embrace my dear Stephanie and assure both of you of my affectionate remembrance.—Hortense." (Carnet *historique et littéraire*. III.)

★★★★★★★★★★

Such is the lovers' four-in-hand that she sets herself to drive; God knows how and with what attention at awkward moments! Each one of the favourites is, of course, to believe he is the only one of his kind. For the time being three were at Aix, whither, from Lyons, the never-cured invalid has come early in June.

Three of these liaisons became known. Nobody has ever suspected the fourth, the hero of which was the tragedian Talma. And now, suddenly, we come upon a dusty bundle which has lain forgotten in a garret, from which falls a packet of letters which enlightens us as to this new adventure of Pauline's. To tell the truth, some contemporaries had guessed as much; some, indeed, knew, and knew full details; but they were discreet. Talma's wife, (Charlotte Vanhove) in a book about her husband, is the only one to drop a hint concerning the romance which today is placed beyond doubt, she writes:

> Talma became a lucky man all of a sudden. Being pursued by women of the highest position, challenged by them, in fact, the idea occurred to him of achieving celebrity in this direction, damaging as that is to domestic happiness.

Furthermore, a letter from Talma himself, addressed to his brother-in-law Ducis, allows us to guess what gossip was saying at Paris concerning his liaison with Princess Borghèse. Writing from Lyons, August 2, 1812, he enquires:

> What are people saying at Paris? Any scandal-mongering? For myself, I don't suppose anybody is making any remarks, and I expect that the absence from Paris of the two persons, one in one direction, one in another (nominally), will have caused all comment to cease. My wife has been writing to me on the subject, and makes out that it is still being discussed, but that I don't believe.

What we may be sure of is this: that any such comment ran a very quiet course, inasmuch as none of it crops up in *memoirs* or private correspondence known to us.

At this period Talma was by no means a conquest to be ashamed of. If Pauline could have owned to having a lover, he would have been the one. He had by now reached the zenith of his great reputation as a tragedian, victor in the struggles which he had had to wage against his comrades at the *Comédie* in days gone by, at the dawn of the Revolution. Of the Rue de Richelieu company he is the greatest, the noblest, crowned with the crown of laurel which the brilliance of his genius had earned him. He then personified the splendour of French tragic art, the victory of live, passionate tragedy over the dismal, pompous, icy spectacles of the dead past.

He was the incarnation of the heroes—and of the hero, the ideal, noble, hero of the tragedy as Corneille understood it, the tragedy that the emperor loved and welcomed. Thus, appreciated by the brother, what difficulty is there in imagining him appreciated more keenly still by the sister, considering the universality of his expressiveness, gesture, movement, accents speaking to eye, heart, and senses? Is it not so that we can explain Pauline's passion?—and the shortness of its duration, too? for, the "boards" once left behind, the purple falls from the shoulders, the laurel from the forehead; Talma becomes—Talma; no more a lover—as other lovers are, the others who come, and love, and go. Beyond doubt, it was the magic of his genius alone that conquered Pauline. That spell broken, all was over. The circumstances and the incidents of the liaison supply all-sufficient evidence of this. We have but to set them forth.

Under pretext of taking the waters the tragedian arrived at Aix, but he confesses to his brother-in-law, they "have done me a great deal of harm." According to the Duchesse d'Abrantès he had only come to "drink hot water and improve his health." For visiting Pauline, he had a good excuse—that of taking the invalid out of herself by reading Molière to her, the "*Malade imaginaire*," perhaps. (Frédéric Masson.) Mme. d'Abrantès was a guest at these little gatherings, or, at any rate, at some of them. In her *Memoirs* she laughs at Talma on account of the efforts he made to work himself down to his subject. "The poor man got out of his depth a little; or rather more than a little." Before Mme. d'Abrantès wrote about it she probably took a malicious pleasure in holding forth on the subject in the society of the queens and princesses at Aix. Pauline got wind of this, and bewailed it by letter to Talma. From her epistle to Forbin we can gauge the kind of missive that the subject would occasion. The lover's sympathetic reply is:

My friend, what you tell me of that duchess grieves and annoys me! These are things that I did not dream of; I did not dream that all who came near you, all who knew you, had any thought of you but loving ones! Oh! what a soul is that which remains insensible to your sufferings, to your sweetness, to your goodness!

Talma, we see, was in complete agreement with that candid historian who, with blindfold generosity, conceded Pauline "all the virtues that we love to discover in women." It remains to be ascertained if fickleness enters into the category, fairly comprehensive though it be, of feminine virtues. Really, we cannot help being astonished at the suddenness with which Pauline has passed from de Canouville to Duchand, from Duchand to de Brack, to fall on the neck of the bewitched, dumbfounded Talma. M. Frédéric Masson, in his ignorance, has written that for the moment "her occupations were quite respectable," and that, among them, "her health was the chief." The correspondence with Talma shows that, as in Forbin's case, some compromise was arrived at in matters of health. He writes to Ducis:

No one has been received, save one person only, and that in such a way that no one has been let into the secret. I tell you this for yourself alone; there is no need for me to remind you of all the unfortunate consequences which would ensue if anyone knew of it.

Ducis will keep quiet; no one will know anything. But Talma, at least, will inform us, in a letter to Pauline, that the Chevaley mansion, where she is staying, "is not to be approached by me"—except at night. For the rest, all would have remained a mystery to us had not Talma, at intervals in his impassioned correspondence, marshalled his reminiscences of his amours. Who would have said that as late as this Pauline was still lavish with oaths on the head of little Dermide, Leclerc's child, who was at rest far away beneath Tuscany yews? To her promises she had added the gift of some ringlets of her hair. Talma put them in one of her handkerchiefs and carried the keepsake next his heart. Who would have guessed that, if he had not reminded his mistress of it at the hour of the final parting, when she was far away and lost to him?

It was nearly three months that this liaison lasted at Aix between the Imperial Princess and him who at this period remained the last hope of the tragedy to which his genius had imparted fresh life.

On September 13 he leaves, to begin the series of performances which he was under contract to give. His first halt was at Geneva. There he arrived in the depths of despair, and overwhelmed by burning memories.

> On getting out of the carriage I found a crowd of people waiting to see me. These tributes of the curiosity and of the esteem of the public of which I once was so proud hardly move me now, and if they still retain any value in my eyes, it is merely that they may serve to render me more worthy of your affection.

That very day a brisk correspondence springs up between the two lovers. Talma's letters are addressed to "Mlle. Sophie," *poste-restante*, Aix, and it will be Ferrand, Pauline's *major-domo*, who will go to enquire for them. What a degree of carefulness does Talma bring into play in his correspondence! He drafts one rough copy after another; of one letter, dated October 25, 1812, from Lyons, there are four! He polishes his phrases, dovetails them with scrupulous care, takes thought for the turn of the phrase, the niceties of wording, that they may make their mark, may strike the imagination, may make "the tears flow from his dear one's eyes."

He succeeded in this at times, if we may believe Pauline. But we know that harmless little knaveries do occur in such connexions, which will never bind the unbound. What the tragedian seems to have especially at heart in this affair is not to lose touch with Pauline. He writes to her:

> Link me with your existence in every possible way. You have promised me that.

Verily, verily, Pauline was not stingy with promises! But she was reckoning without Talma's excellent memory, as we shall discover later on. For the moment he is intent on maintaining the relations which they entered into at Aix; moreover, he seems deeply smitten. He offers to carry out all commissions that shall be entrusted to him. The princess requires watches, it appears. The courier brings prompt and most disinterested offers of his services:

> I have seen some very good ones set with fine pearls and enamels for seven *louis*; really very cheap.

And then the invalid is probably at a loss what to do; what shall he send her? Books? He has hardly any, barring theatrical pamphlets, and not many of those. He will send those.

I have sent you by the courier the books which Ferrand asked for on your behalf.

Perhaps that is why Pauline's library included a considerable number of dramatic works.

★★★★★★★★★★

This library, long ago dispersed, is that of Napoleon's favourite sister, Princess Pauline Bonaparte; we have before us the manuscript catalogue. It is a volume of thirty-seven pages containing 250 entries. The writing is pretty enough, but that is certainly its only merit; for the compiler, whether male, or, which is more probable, female, may have been very charming, but his or her strong point was not bibliography, nor literature, nor even orthography. He or she had adopted a sort of rudimentary alphabetical order, basing it on the simple principle of taking the initial letters of the titles on the backs of the books, classing, with child-like simplicity, all those entitled '*Oeuvres*' under 'O' without distinction and without taking into account either variety of subject or authors' names.

Hence a confusion in which discords abound, and also some very quaint juxtapositions. Under the letter V, for instance, side by side with *Vie de Xénophon* (the *Cyropaedeia*?) and the *Vies de Cornelius Népos* occurs the *Vie de . . . Faublas*! The beautiful owner of this collection was not exactly strait-laced, if we may judge of her by certain well-known anecdotes, such as that of her posing to Canova. Nevertheless, we ought to say that Louvel's novel, *Les liaisons dangereuses,* and *Jacques le fataliste*, are the only books of that description which figure, in isolation, in that library, which is, as a whole, astoundingly serious, as we shall see.

The princess's predilection for plays is obvious. Not only did she possess the majority of first-rate and second-rate dramatic works by French writers, but also Shakespeare and Le Tourneur." (Baron Ernouf)

★★★★★★★★★★

But Talma was thinking of consolations for himself likewise. At a dinner to which he was invited at Geneva he resumed his acquaintance with Dr. Buttini, who, not long before, had been in attendance on Pauline. (Frédéric Masson.) Talma monopolised him, for, "I could talk about you to him." Now and then some light clouds cast shadows over the height of his passion. Why does Pauline no longer treat him with that friendly freedom which used to give him so much pleasure but a few days ago?

> My dear friend, for goodness' sake, don't always say '*vous*.' Let your hand write the '*tu*' which your mouth has so often spoken to me.

His lady-love had some excuse; at Aix had just arrived the news of Canouville's death, of the terrible and glorious end of the elegant and beloved lover, perhaps the most ardently beloved of all. If she has any desire at all to hear—and what curiosity could be more legitimate?—Pauline can learn how he died on the banks of the Moskowa; what piteous, terrifying remains they were that they threw on the ambulance straw. No consolation, no mitigation, could have been the lot of that bloody agony. There lies the corpse in a strange land, amid the bones of his enemies. For ever, for ever, and for ever, all is finished for that fascinating, fair-haired phantom lover.

At least she will weep for him? An hour or a day? We know now. Let us note the dates. It was on September 27 that de Canouville's death became known at Aix. From Aix to Geneva is a day's journey for couriers. On the morning of September 29, or the evening of the 28th, Pauline wrote to Talma, a "charming, tender letter" for which the tragedian thanks her effusively, he cries:

> Oh, my dear one! what horrible anxiety have you dispelled; all day yesterday I was beside myself, and then—your letter arrived at 8 p.m. My dear one, how your charming, tender letter touched me to the heart! Yes, my dear one, yes, I shall obey you; yes, I respect the weakness and the sufferings that you are still experiencing. It is a horrible sacrifice that I make for you, but it is enough for me that such is your will—I submit uncomplainingly to the frightful torment that you inflict on me. I leave in an hour's time, Pauline. I turn my last look towards you, accept my 'farewell'; as I say it my eyes fill with tears. I can scarcely write . . .

What is it she has asked of Talma? to give herself up, for some days at any rate, to the grief which has entered into her life? Not to write to her anymore? to wait? Hardly; seeing that on October 2 a further letter from the tragedian leaves Lyons addressed to "Mlle. Sophie, '*poste-restante*.'" If her tears had been shed for Canouville, they soon dried. The next day but one, in fact, after the tragic news arrived, she wrote to Talma, whom, later, when she has grown decidedly tired of him, she will leave without news of her for several months together.

It is at this later period that we find the tragedian's correspondence recalling, again and again, the memories of lost happiness. "Pauline, Pauline, my heart is riven!" he declaims; but adds:

> "Ah, tell me, do you remember those delirious moments of intoxication into which you plunged me before my last journey to Grenoble? Do you remember the caresses which you, you alone, inspired (which none but you have ever received from me); you called them forth, and I was lavish with them, moistening my face with your tears?"

Similar ardent expressions of sensibility were still his wont subsequently to his return to Geneva, when he stopped before the Chevaley house.

> "Oh, my dear one, what a storm is this that has come over me; all the circumstances of our liaison have risen up in my memory as one thing, all my limbs grew weak; I spoke some words to you, called you by your name, as if you had been there; and my tears gushed forth—oh, my dear one, to what pain have you condemned me!"

Pauline is still in the phase of her passion in which such, means can call forth some evanescent sentiment. How blithe is Talma when he learns that she has wept to read one of these vehement, voluble, declamatory letters! He cries in ecstasy:

> "My dear one, my Pauline, for I feel a need to call you by so sweet a name, I prostrate myself at your feet, I embrace them in my transports of gratitude; your soul is ever revealing itself as kinder to me than I had believed, and your good deeds are always surpassing my hopes." (This last phrase is reminiscent of the part of Orestes, in *Andromaque*, one of Talma's best parts.)

On this kindness he was always making demands, month by month, throughout the liaison. He deals gently with her, prudently, avoiding the shocks of sudden demands. At first his requests are for little souvenirs, of small value. From Geneva, during his stay there in September, he asks:

> "Be so kind to me, my dear one, as to send me some *Madras*, but only such as you have often worn. I want to wear it round my head, and, in the morning, round my neck."

Pauline Bonaparte

How could Pauline refuse to grant this prayer for a little sentimental present? Probably she sent the *Madras* as requested, through her *major-domo*, for we do not find it cropping up again in the tragedian's letters. But this is not the case with regard to a certain bust she has promised him. Oh! this bust! It becomes a nightmare! Talma presses for it unceasingly, unremittingly, untiringly.

And that bust? And your bust? And my bust?

He wants it. Is he going to have it? As early as September 21, 1812, he is reminding Pauline of her promise:

And your bust, my dear one, do not forget to give orders for it to be sent me. Make arrangements with Ferrand to that effect. Above all other things do I want that bust, I long for it infinitely! I shall leave you no peace till it is sent me. Realise that you have promised it to me.

A month passes, and he returns to the attack; he has not received his bust yet. Pauline once more puts off sending it.

You say you will not be able to give me the bust on which I was counting until one of your people comes to Paris. There I am all at once deprived of it altogether; but it is your will, I make no protest at all.

He resigns himself, therefore, and his resignation lasts five months. Not one of Pauline's attendants has come to Paris as yet. Tired of the struggle, and in despair at remaining without news. Talma writes direct to Ferrand, charging him to go on his knees to Pauline. The *major-domo* on his knees before the princess! That is all very well on the stage, but at a Napoleonic court? The lover's instructions runs:

Impress upon her, all my grieving over her absence and her sufferings!

A journey spares the willing Ferrand the execution of this delicate commission. On March 19, 1813, he suddenly makes his appearance before Talma. Ah, with what anxiety is he cross-examined! How detail after detail is wrested from him! How minute is the tragedian's amorous curiosity! And what ecstasy is his after listening to the story!

And my ring—what, my dear one, you are wearing it, wearing it as a memento of me! And that sign that you made to Ferrand at the moment of his departure, when so many were standing round, pointing to the ring to remind him of the orders you had given him! My dear one, so many touching marks of your perfect sweetness make me lose my reason.

But the bust? His bust! Talma did not lose his reason so far as to forget to think about that. Ferrand has no orders to deliver it, but the princess will have it sent later.

And your bust, my dear one, which I am so troubled to be without, which I have seen at Cor(visart)'s house, (the emperor's doctor, in August he had been summoned from Paris to Aix to attend Pauline), and which I thought so much like you! which occasioned such violent emotion in me when I looked at it! Ferrand assures me that you will give me one when you return.

Return! Pauline was hardly thinking of that! It was at Nice she was living now, ever since February 8, the second day after she received permission from her brother:—

The Emperor to Princess Pauline Borghèse.

Fontainebleau, January 27, 1813.

I have your letter of January 20. I note with regret the bad state of your health. You would have done better to have come to Paris than to have let yourself be transported to one place after another through the hopefulness of doctors. You would have done better to go to Nice rather than to Hyères; I do not see what there is to prevent you going to that town.

That is what Talma has already written to Pauline, word for word; and afterwards to Ferrand. But now arrangements are made. The princess is condemned, for long weeks to come, to a depressing *sojourn* at Hyères, where mournful surroundings and solitude come near to killing her.

During this time, at Paris, Talma goes on begging for little presents, trifling souvenirs. While waiting for the bust which is so long in coming, he will remain contented with a little boat, one of those charming light skiffs which, tied to white posts, are swaying at the will of the wave on the pools of Pauline's country estate, the Château de Neuilly. We should not have expected to find the tragedian on the water. He says to the princess:

You will authorise me, to take one of your boats. As I am going to shut myself up in my country house, it would give me a great deal of pleasure to have this boat, which will be a present from you.

The unfortunate part for Pauline was that he did not rest content with means of conveyance on the water, but aimed at more important presents. On December 23, 1812, the lover ventures to make a handsome request. He leads up to it with great skill, making a pretext of his quarrel with Geoffroy, the *Journal de l'Empire's* dramatic critic, whom he had recently struck in his box at the *Comédie-Française*. He is thinking of retiring from the stage, and it is here that Pauline's protection can avail him. He writes to her about it with a weariness and a humility very creditable to a man of his ability:—

> . . .I cannot and will not remain for long in a profession in which the respect and favour of the public cannot protect a man from such insults, from diatribes hawked about all over Europe by the newspapers. People who live far away from Paris cannot be enlightened respecting all these shameful intrigues. You are my only haven, my dear one. I rely on your tender friendship for my escape from an intolerable situation. As things stand it would be assuming too much to believe that my annual salary will be secured to me. If it was cancelled, I should find myself in considerable difficulties by reason of the contracts I have undertaken for the ensuing year.
>
> One of my friends affords me, at this juncture, an opportunity of not merely making his loss good, if the worst comes to the worst, but also of making a start to assure my independence. He offers me a considerable share in one of those licences which the Government grants for the exportation of goods to England. He has just lodged an application for one of them (they are continually being granted) with M. le comte Sussy, Minister of Commerce and Manufactures; but it is needful that his application, which is already well backed, should be still more so, if possible, in order to render success certain.
>
> It has occurred to me that you would not refuse to assist me in an important matter like this. The thing to do, then, is for you to be so extremely kind as to write to M. le comte de Sussy, Minister of Commerce, strongly recommending to his notice M. Marguerie, jr., merchant, of Havre, saying that you take a special interest in the success of his application. You will send the letter to me for me to forward it to the departmental office

through M. Mazurié, or you will address it direct to the minister, just as you think fit. That would decide the minister in his favour immediately.

But, my dear one, there is no time to be lost, for the affair is in hand, and the time for presentation for signature is very near. Perhaps it is decidedly indiscreet, my dear one, to ask this assistance of you at a moment when you are not equal to taking thought for others' troubles, but, dear and loving friend, to whom shall I turn if not to her who has shown herself so kind to me, to whom it will be so sweet to owe all?

And, delicately, on the last page of the letter. Talma slips a "little ring" over Pauline's finger, bearing a discreet inscription. On second thoughts, he decides against leaving the *Comédie-Française*, and thenceforth this business of the licence does not come up again in the correspondence.

On the other hand, he does not cease to offer his services to Pauline, just as he had done, some months earlier, at Geneva. He discovers that she is thinking of purchasing the *château* de Petit-Bourg, and straightway makes a proposal.

I have obtained information, and think that it will suit you to perfection. Would you like me to go and see it and report on it?

It was at the moment when Pauline was realising 750,000 *francs* on certain estates of hers in Westphalia, that she thought of acquiring this estate near Paris, which had the advantage of Neuilly in several respects. The idea caught her fancy sufficiently for her to set the business part of her household to work and to send her confidential businessman, Decazes, thither. (Decazes, Louis XVIII's future minister, was entrusted with Pauline's most important business.) But Talma was there too, and he addresses a detailed report to Pauline, full of all he saw when visiting his mistress's future residence. Between two passionate outbursts he abruptly interposes a eulogy of the *château* as follows:—

If you buy it you will have to repair it. I think it will suit you perfectly; its situation is, as you know, very beautiful, very dry, very healthy. The principal suite on the ground floor, which is well raised and suitable in every way, consists of a hall, an antechamber, a very large dining-room, a very fine drawing-room, and a large bedroom, with the requisite smaller apartments. The first floor is divided by a very long, very broad corridor, and the rooms are well arranged on either side. Twenty-two visitors could be accommodated there.

The style of architecture of the *château* would not, I fear, allow of wings being added, or other buildings, but they could be erected in the courtyards, where there is plenty of room. There would be repairs to be done and I certainly think that to do it up and to furnish it according to modem ideas of luxury, the outlay would have to mount up to two or three hundred thousand *francs*; as for the farms that go with the estate, they are in the best condition possible and have just been overhauled anew. The income is nearly 25,000 *livres*. The park is very beautiful, and will lend itself to further improvements. That, dear friend, is all I can tell you, and all that I think needful, to allow you to form an opinion as to whether it will suit you.

And then the undercurrent of enthusiasm on his own account comes to the surface:—

For myself, I desire it from the bottom of my heart, inasmuch as I might hope to pass a good part of my life not far from you.

But the day of hope is nearly over! Tomorrow (1814) will come the Eagles' first fall; then 1815 and their overthrow. Besides, what could Talma hope for? Could he think of being able to renew a liaison which had certainly run its course and on which judgment had been passed early in 1813? In fact, on March 25, we find him writing to Pauline:

I was ardently awaiting the arrival of the moment when I should see you once again as a dear friend, seeing that other sweeter ties must be renounced.

This beautiful affection, then, outlasted the amours of Forbin, of Montrond, of ten others. Death alone touched it with irony—it was Lafon who uttered the farewell in the name of the *Comedie-Frangaise* on the brink of Talma's grave. The lover of 1802 eulogising the lover of 1812! But then is it not Love who is Death's playfellow?

CHAPTER 10

A Beauty to the Last

It was a mournful year, this year 1813, for Pauline. Far from every-body, she was pining away, sinking under the burden of her disillusions. The four months, February to May, that she passed at Nice, passed to the mournful accompaniment of boredom, boredom, boredom. Talma was back at Paris and nothing more was heard of him, apart from the echoes of his quarrels and striking successes, but letters which she got tired of receiving and to which she did not reply. Lieutenant de Brack was quite forgotten. Among the caprices of this queen of caprices he had been the most evanescent.

As for Commander Duchand who, at Aix, had escorted her during her promenades, cased in his uniform and raising on high the plume of his monumental busby—Duchand had, in January, 1813, received orders to rejoin the *Grande Armée*. Blangini was creating melodies in Westphalia; Forbin was out of favour; Montrond in England. In her exile there only remained to her fading spectres of faded lovers, "ships that had passed in the night"—and the nights had passed, too; here to-day and gone tomorrow. Weariness born of so many sentimental erotic experiences weighed on her, beyond doubt; even on her by this time.

The last resources of a vitality sapped and ruined to its core had been drawn upon, and now it began to drag along, irremediably over-tired by reason of the amours that were no more. At this period, we no longer find her occupied with her favourite distractions. Around her is nothing but her household, quite a modest household, now that all the brilliant followers have set out for the armies which, far away in Germany, are winning the Eagles' last victories. Peyre, the pharmaceu-tical *maître Jacques*, has likewise taken his leave, on the second day after a dispute with Pauline. No one waits on her now but her ladies-and women-in-waiting, complaisant assistants in her amorous intrigues.

Long, monotonous, empty evenings, whose end is so long in com-

PAULINE BONAPARTE

ing; which they try to foreshorten with childish games, and which leave the drawing-room deserted by 10 o'clock. And the nights! the dreary nights, lonely ones too; when the hand of insomnia lies heavy on the heart, when wide-open eyes see phantoms galore in darkness which gapes and terrifies. What dreams then for the radiant Paulette of the year IV? What dead lovers does she wrap in memory's shrouds? What slow and silent tears fall from her eyes as their disconsolate shades pass stealthily by? What tenderly-loved corpses are there in the cemetery of her withered amours!

Fréron, for one, lying over there, on the shore of the tropical sea, amid the gigantic vegetation of the charnel-house of the Cape; Fréron, handsome Fréron when the *Muscadins* flourished, and when the Terror was in full swing! Then, too, Leclerc; the husband brought back with honour from the hellish colony, his coffin shielded by the tricolour flag; Leclerc, who sleeps in the marble mausoleum at Montgobert, shadowed by century-old cedars and tall, slender poplars. And Canouville, too, cut down by the Moskowa, beheaded amid the whistle of the bullets and hurled into empurpled snow with his mistress's portrait over his heart; Canouville, who, like Fréron, lies in foreign soil, at peace amidst the enemy. And not so long is it since Septeuil fell from his horse in the Peninsula, and was brought back to Paris on the straw of a baggage-waggon, a living man, thanks to a miraculous chance alone. Tomorrow it may be Duchand's turn, of whom no news comes as yet, save that he is in the thick of the hurly-burly, where the Imperial Eagles are fighting for life.

Altogether this light-o'-love's memory can be serving but to summon up a mournful procession of silhouetted funerals, of tragedy statues draped in shrouds. To that has it come, to memories that people a cemetery, to lovers' stories of a dead, dead past—this seventeen-year long erotic career of Princess Pauline Borghèse.

After the finer months of 1813 she nevertheless regained something of the astonishing vigour that characterizes sufferers from nerves. After a stay at the waters of Gréoulx she returned to Aix, July 12 to August 19. (Frédéric Masson.) Then, as autumn drew near, she went back to Hyères for some months. Early in 1814 she went to Luc, in the Var, taking up her residence at the Villa Charles. "Mme. Borghèse's stay in the Var Department has not influenced ideas at all; she has scarcely been noticed," observes a report dated June 7, 1814, and dating, also, thus early, the waning of her life. Her loyalty to Napoleon, her devotion to her brother, were about to take her out of herself for a while, during the ephemeral reign at Elba.

It was on April 26 that the news of the emperor's overthrow reached Pauline, simultaneously with the announcement that Napoleon was at her door. He soon appeared, attended by the Allies' representatives, on the way to his first exile. A contemporary account (one, however, not above suspicion, it is true), says:

> From that moment, she determined to accompany him to Elba and to remain by his side in future. (Count von Waldburg-Truchsess, commissary nominated by H.M. the King of Prussia to accompany Napoleon.)

Was not now the time for Pauline to show herself as she had ever been? to give full play to that innate kindness, to resume by means of the charm of single-minded affectionateness, what Caroline and Elisa had wrested from her—hard, egotistical, cankered with the disease of politics as they were, during the halcyon days of Imperial splendour—thanks to their acuteness, trickery, and dour scheming. This time 'twas Pauline's turn to reign; a sovereignty of charm, of gossamer grace, of smiles and mirages. Was it not her task at Elba to make the great loser forget the absence of his faithless wife and his ungrateful sisters? To the emperor's veterans, too, was it not likewise her role to personify, in daily contrast with the rough ways of the professed soldier, the essential being of that precious refining recollection of Parisian femininity? Some days subsequently to Napoleon's passage through Luc, she, in her turn, reached the coast. Anglès' report, dated June 7, says:

> On May 19, she put in at Saint-Raphaël with a Neapolitan frigate, on the way to take the waters at Ischia; she has been speaking of landing in Elba. To accommodate her an English frigate hove to at Villefranche to take her across; the captain seemed very much annoyed at not doing so.

She went on to Naples, received a missive from Murat for the emperor, and reached the island on June 1. She only stayed there one night, and then departed. "This interview and the separation seem to have touched Bonaparte deeply," declares the report of June 18, 1814. On September 12 following it explains Pauline's sudden departure as consequent on "her belief that the air would occasion her too much suffering." We are ignorant, then, of the secret reason for the journey. Pauline made a second one in the following October. In spite of the bad state of her health, she decided to embark on the 27th. (Auto-

Elisa Bonaparte, sister of Pauline Bonaparte

graph signed letter from Pauline to Elisa.) Taillade, who was in command of the Elba flotilla, landed her at Porto-Ferrajo on October 31.

Her reign there lasted four months. The record of her stay there is throughout one of gaiety and fascination. With her a vivid ray of hope entered Napoleon's poverty-stricken palace. He received her blithely, and all the islanders rose and cheered at the coming of this radiant guest. Pons says: "Hearts do not pulsate to order; Porto-Ferrajo was ablaze." It was a period, too, of balls and of *fêtes*, of a renascence of youth and cheerfulness, of something of France's charm taking root in rugged Elba. Feminine refinement mitigated the roughness and brutality incidental to a gathering of soldiers.

It was no longer a mere military colony, but a soil ready prepared for the planting of concord and urbanity. It came natural to Pauline to attempt the task, with the help of her seductive powers. She was seen "on very familiar terms with the officers of the guard." Thanks to the emperor she found there an adept dancer for balls. Captain Jules Loubert, who "was considered the Vestris of the guard." Strange to say, he has never been reckoned among Pauline's lovers. The pamphleteers have not invented any anecdotes of the kind in connexion with her stay at Elba, for that which represents the princess as coquetting with General Drouot is only tittle-tattle.

By this period good old Drouot had turned pious, and never dreamt of alternating his hobby of Bible-reading with the practice of earthly and ephemeral pleasures. Nevertheless, the police reports notify us that Pauline had not wholly abandoned her tender ways of bygone days. The "Black Cabinet," it would seem, intercepted letters from her to Duchand, by this time artillery colonel and a baron by virtue of letters patent from Louis XVIII, registered November 25, 1814. Antoine Jean Baptiste Duchand, born at Grénoble, May 11, 1780, seems to have been taken back into favour for the time being. He certainly resumed his correspondence with Pauline after the Hundred Days, inasmuch as she writes to him from Lucca, August 2, 1815, that "his affection has withstood the test of calamity."

Duchand was then a pensioner; at Waterloo he was one of the heroes of the *Immortelle*. Brave as Cambronne, he came to the same end, marrying an English wife, "decidedly pretty and very rich." He waited for the July monarchy to enter active service again. September 4, 1830, he was nominated major-general of artillery and subsequently became the head of the school at Metz, then of the school at Fontainebleau, lieutenant-general, and, finally, inspector-general of artillery. In February, 1848, he was free again, and died at Paris, January 3, 1849. With him must have disappeared one of the last of Pauline's lovers.

As for her, she quitted Porto-Ferrajo March 2, 1815, just when the emperor was beginning the Hundred Days' epic, and landed (April 3) at Viareggio, where, for some reason or other, Borghèse was awaiting her. Sick and bedridden, from that time onwards her decline began. She does not figure at all in the dying agonies of the Empire. Far from the catastrophe, under the surveillance of informers and spies, she resembles a rose in a vase which, slowly, petal by petal, acquiesces in the evanescence of ephemeral queenship. Why should she outlast the splendour of which she was but a ray? The Empire is dead; her day is gone; her death seems near.

And yet it is ten years before it actually comes, and meanwhile she drags out her life in an agony of melancholia. Ah! she is no longer the lively, bright Paulette of the days of old, the "chicken," envied and chaffed by the babblers of the Consulate period, but a poor broken-winged creature, depressed, exhausted, more or less given up by the doctors, an invalid beyond doubt, fluctuating between despondencies and whims, and, at this period of collapse, supervised by Borghèse, who at last begins to have a grievance. ("While really and seriously ill, she, like many neurotic women, indulges in the pre-occupations and the exactions of a sham invalid." L. de Lanzac de Laborie.)

From the year XI to 1814, what has he said, what has he done, in the way of blaming his wife for her carryings-on? What, mocked and deceived, almost held up to ridicule, and aware of everything, has he stood on his wounded and outraged dignity? No; he has done nothing, said nothing, manifested nothing. In a good-tempered way, he has run after unimportant womenfolk, has accepted everything, admitted everything, with eyes shut, conscience easy, and dignity elastic. But now, that is all finished with. As the evening of life draws on, Borghèse finds that he is a gentleman, and has honour and reputation to take thought for; it must be owned that he has plenty of excuse for playing the indignant husband and the frowning tyrant—on a small scale.

The emperor once fallen, he regains an exact sense of duty. Had adultery ever been condoned in his family, a family in which popes, cardinals, and cuckolds may be collected by the bushel? Furthermore, he now discovers that he has nothing in common with the Bonapartes—these Bonapartes, indeed! low-class people, smuggler-princes, little Corsican upstarts. Princess Aldobrandini-Borghèse writes to the Chevalier de Fontenay:

My brother-in-law, my brother-in-law belongs to the Bonaparte family, and, as such, is included in the law which deals with that family; the king is well aware how correct has been his behaviour during the Hundred Days; he is grateful to him for it; he knows that his connexion with the family is a merely nominal one, and he fully realises how wise and prudent his conduct has been.

Even this nominal connexion Borghèse is about to renounce, and from 1815 makes efforts in that direction. Thenceforward it has been his plan to avoid all life in common with the princess, and, to remove temptation to inclination for a better understanding, has had the doors walled up, at the palace at Rome, which communicate with the princess's apartments. This detail has been questioned and formally denied.

It must, however, be conceded, seeing that in a letter of November, 1815, from Louis to Cardinal Cunéo, we read:

After the serious insult to which she (Pauline) has been subjected, after her husband's clear manifestation of his intention not only never to come to an understanding with her, but even never to receive her at his house, there remains no other course for her to adopt than that of any woman who retains any feeling for a wife's dignity.

We can guess what this course is: separation, divorce, which will have to be pleaded before the "*Rota*," the only court whose jurisdiction is admissible. Pauline likewise, on her side, has complaints to make against her husband. She writes to her brother Lucien:

That beast Borghèse, refuses to pay the expenses incurred here on his account. What a frightful thing it is to be perpetually being deluded by men!

Deluded by men! Was she thinking of Forbin? In the end she summarised her grievances, and appealed to her brothers to endorse them. From Albano, June 8, 1816, Louis writes stating that he is willing to sign Pauline's statement. Such was the prelude to the avalanche of memorials and summaries which were going to be issued at Rome by the two parties in order to parade before the eyes of the ecclesiastical tribunal the fragmentary evidence, the naked remnants, of their pitiable love-story.

From 1816 to 1824 occurred a respite in this voluble warfare and the crisis between this married couple seemed to be passing off. The

CAROLINE MURAT, SISTER OF PAULINE BONAPARTE

question of the divorce is relegated to the background, and the separation, though a fact in practice, is not so legally. Had Pauline been appeased? It is said that about 1818, during this period, she became the mistress of a Neapolitan, one Signor Palomba, who, according to his own account, was a *marquis, della Cesa.* (Joseph Turquan,) It may be so, but seems unlikely; we know she was ill at the time, and far from fit for frivolities and gallantry. And, besides, what proof of it have we? Not a letter, not a note, nothing. Some gossip, an anonymous rumour; that is a poor warrant for introducing Palomba and his borrowed title into the paradise of the Imperial Venus.

Subsequently we find her once again busy with the separation question. Here is the evidence of a crisis drawing near again:—

To Monsignor Cunéo, Grand Inquisitor of the Holy Office, Rome.

Porto, May 24, 1824.

My dear Monsignor Cunéo—I have received the letter which you wrote to me through Mme. d'Hautmesnil and I am fully persuaded of all the diligence which you are today bringing to bear to recover all the documents which have been submitted *alla rota* on my behalf. I am in hopes, therefore, that you will have sent some to Cavaliere Gozzani, for I am trusting to his being able to forward them to the prince by tomorrow's courier, who will take my letters to him. I know that my affairs are in good hands; my confidence in yourself is likewise a source of rest and tranquillity to me, I beg you, my dear Mgr. Cunéo, to be so kind as to accept a little souvenir which I send you, and each day, at breakfast, you will think of her who begs you to accept it.

Farewell, my dear Mgr. Cunéo, be assured of my friendly feelings and genuine attachment to you.

Princess Pauline Borghèse.

P.S.—My compliments to the *Cavaliere.* I beg of him to wear this pin in remembrance of me.

Here is no sign of ill-feeling against Borghèse. We may assume that the case was pleaded mildly by Pauline. But what happened then, in the space of the ensuing fortnight? What kind of gratitude has Borghèse shown for her languid, inert forbearance? For we find the Napoleonic characteristics suddenly reawakening in the Cleopatra's heart and a furious note to Mgr. Cunéo giving vent to her wrath. This time she has finished with Borghèse!

Seeing that he is not sensible to the loyalty and submission of my feelings towards himself, and that, on the contrary, he has trifled with me and deluded me horribly, I have resolved to place my case before the *Rota*.

Once more it is nothing but an idle oath, a fruitless promise, as usual. The *Rota* will never have to decide on this case. If the documents are submitted to it, it will not have time to examine them; twelve months later, almost to the day, the princess is dead.

For almost two years she scarcely leaves her sick-bed. Always reclining, she is experiencing the final hours of her silent rest. She writes to Lucien, December 17, 1823;

I suffer a great deal, the cold is very bad for me, and the doctors forbid me to go out in the evening, and even in daytime, unless it is very fine.

Four months earlier she had been transferred to the Villa Paolina, near the Porta Pia, and was now one of those invalids who, guessing that their end is near, lose all faith, all confidence, all hope. In revolt against the remonstrances of "*Madame Mère*," indifferent to what the doctors prescribed, (Baron Larrey), she gives herself up to uninterrupted enjoyment of the heat of the last suns she is to see. At this time, perhaps, during these lonely hours of despondency, re-echo in her memory the echoes of St. Helena.

Across the hostile seas, far away, beyond the equatorial ocean, the imposing, though pitiable, drama is nearing its end. Can she forget that it was to her that the emperor uttered one of his latest cries of distress, one of his final appeals amidst his sufferings. Montholon wrote to her on March 17, 1821, from Longwood:

The emperor counts on Your Highness to bring to the notice of influential people in England the true state of his disease. He is helpless and is dying on this terrible rock. His agony is fearful.

Ill and exhausted as she was, she made a brave response to this cry of anguish and dismay which came from the consecrated island, and, gaining strength from the strength of her loyalty, it is from her hand that issued the last protest of the Napoleonidae against Britain's deicide. For a moment we may digress from the recital of her sentimental-erotic life, the *procès-verbal* of her slow, long-drawn agony, to quote this double appeal to Lord Liverpool in the beautiful letter, written at Rome, July 11, 1821:—

My Lord,

Monsieur l'abbé Bonavito (*i.e.* Bonavita) who left St. Helena March 17 last, and who has just reached Rome, has brought us the most alarming news of the state of the emperor's health. Enclosed I send you copies of letters which will give you full details concerning his physical sufferings. The disease to which he is a victim is fatal at St. Helena, and it is in the name of all the members of the emperor's family that I demand of the English Government a change of climate for him. If so, reasonable a request is met with a refusal it will be equivalent to passing a death sentence, and in this case, I ask leave to set out for St. Helena, to go and rejoin the emperor, in order to minister to him in his last moments.

I beg of you, my lord, that you will be so kind as to apply without delay for this permission from your government, so that I may be free to set out as soon as possible. Since my health will not allow me to travel by land, it is my intention to embark at Civita Vecchia for England, and thence to take the first ship that sails for St. Helena; but I should prefer to be given leave to go to London, to obtain all that is needful for so long a voyage. If your government insists on leaving the emperor to perish on this rock of St. Helena, I appeal to you, my lord, to overcome the obstacles that may be put in the way of my departure, even so far as to ensure that the government at Rome shall not interfere. I know that the emperor's moments are numbered, and I shall never forgive myself if I have not done all that is in me to soothe his last moments and to give proof of my whole-hearted devotion to his august person. Should there be some ships at the port of Leghorn at the date of my departure, I should request a further favour—that one of them should call for me at Città Vecchia to convey me to England.

I implore you, my lord, to acquaint Lady Holland, who has always shown such very great interest in the emperor, with my letter and the copies sent herewith, assuring her of my friendly feelings towards her. Please be assured, yourself, of my deepest respect.

Princess Pauline Borghèse.

Thus, ready was she to go and share in the anguish of the St. Helena agony. But fruitless was the request! vain the prayer!

When she was signing this letter the emperor's corpse had been in its lonely, nameless grave for more than two months. Far away over the water Death had put an end to the epic. The last word had been spoken, and Pauline herself had nothing to do but to wend her way, like a fading rose, along the road of her own agony. Between the emperor's death and her own, four years intervened. Prévost-Paradol said:

> To know how to grow old, is not so easy as people would have us believe, and it is a kind act on Nature's part to many an individual when she spares him that final test.

Such was Pauline's lot; Death came to claim her in the flower of her age, while still young and beautiful. She acquiesces and abdicates. And what, indeed, of the splendours of the past, has she to regret? Emptiness, loneliness, silence, have slowly, insistently woven their web round about her. The beautiful palace of her early married life in the year XI has now been handed over to Charles IV of Spain, and she has left it for the Palazzo Sciarra, a pile of glorious stones, a ruin gilded by the wonderful Roman suns. There she can taste the exquisite bitterness of renunciation of the vanities of grace and charm. She writes, April 29, 1825, to her friend, Mme. d'Hautmesnil:

> I remain alone and lonely; but nothing matters to me now.

She has dismissed her musician Pacini, has sold her horses, has made her peace with Borghèse. Now that he feels she is at the gates of the last farewell, he consents to forgive, to forget. Tomorrow she will be no more. He does not think his honour compromised if he concedes that illusory consolation. And besides, the end is really at hand. White, pallid, thin, almost transparent, reminding those around her of the fairy-like, fascinating slimness of her girlhood days, Pauline has taken to her bed for the last time. The Imperial family are warned, but Jérôme is the only one to arrive in time. (Baron Larrey.)

It is June 7, 1825. All day she has been feeling Death close behind her, and, overcome by the thought of what may happen to her charms and her beauty, she implores them with tears to leave her body untouched. They promise; the post-mortem scalpel shall not cut into that rose-tinted whiteness that the lace on her bed is covering. A *coquette* to death's door! She will disappear arrayed and adorned, with the last recollection of her to be "how pretty she is"; all the more so, if anything, for the marks left by suffering. She will leave them, so to speak, in a halo. But meanwhile. Death comes ever nearer and nearer. All the signs of the final agony make their appearance in turn, and the pallor of Death spreads over that face which once was so charming and so tender. At one moment they thought she had really passed away, but she rallies to utter a final message, a last request—that when she is dead, they will cover her face. They promise her that, amid their sobs. She smiles once more, and resists Death no longer.

Pauline Bonaparte, a Short Biography

Contents

Pauline Bonaparte (Princess Borghèse)

Pauline Bonaparte, a Short Biography

By Joseph Turquan

1

No one could be droller and more amusing than was the Princess Borghèse. Not that she was particularly witty, far from it! but there are some who are amusing from their total lack of wit, and it is rather to this category that the second sister of Napoleon belongs. She was only a little madcap, but a very droll and amusing one—except in the opinion of her husbands and her serious brother, the Emperor of the French, to whom her pranks on more than one occasion caused great annoyance. To draw her portrait is a task that requires a skill which her present biographer admits he is far from possessing, nevertheless some sort of idea of her character may be formed from the manner in which she conducted herself in the following incidents of her life.

If the behaviour of "Paulette" was extravagant, and it was exceedingly so, it is but fair to add that she was also exceedingly pretty. She must indeed have been that to have attracted attention, as she did, from the moment of her arrival at Marseilles. In this a little *coquetry* as well as beauty had its share. At that time, she was as poor and as ill-clad as possible, but her youth and beauty flourished all the same under a dress that proclaimed her poverty and a hat worth some four *sous*.

The little scatterbrain did not find it much to her taste to scrape the earthenware basin out of which the proscribed family ate, or to wash the dirty linen and sweep the humble lodging in which she lived on the top floor of an old house in the old quarter of Marseilles, between the Rue Vacon and the Cannebière. But to wrangle with her sisters, to play tricks on Marianne and enrage Annunziata, no doubt afforded her a little amusement; while it must have been still more exciting to stroll about the town, looking at the fine shops and the fine people and gossiping a little with her friends. For she was not long in making friends, and not insignificant ones either.

Two smart and distinguished young representatives of the people, the Citizens Barras and Fréron, had been sent as Commissioners of the Convention to Marseilles, where they had made the acquaintance of the brothers Bonaparte, who, as political refugees, were not the men to let any opportunity slip of improving their position. They, therefore, introduced the young commissioners to their sisters, and it was through their recommendation that Madame Letizia obtained a pension. The fine fellows, perhaps, rather abused the situation and made the young Citizenesses Bonaparte more frequent visits than was altogether proper. But the latter, out of gratitude, were obliged to submit to their indiscretion, which they did without complaining and without the least unwillingness.

The visits of the representatives of the people were, moreover, anything but disinterested. The young and handsome Fréron was at once smitten with the truly remarkable face of Pauline and paid her assiduous court. It was wrong in Madame Letizia to tolerate this, but she belonged to the age of Louis XV., and the manners of that period were no better than those of the court and even of the family of the *Grand Monarque*, when, as Saint-Simon says in his *Memoirs*:

> The *Dauphiness* (the beautiful and ill-fated Duchess of Burgundy, mother of Louis XV.), used to run about the garden at Marly with all the young people of the court till three or four in the morning.

The son of the celebrated critic and journalist, Fréron belonged to a good middle-class family, and was the godson of King Stanislas, two things of which he scarcely cared to boast at this time. He had also been a school-fellow and personal friend of Maximilian Robespierre, but of this fact he ceased to inform people after the 9th *Thermidor*. He had contributed with considerable zeal to the *Almanach des Muses*; then, becoming a journalist, he had started the *Orateur du Peuple*, which at once gave him a certain notoriety and later on sent him to the Convention.

Young and good-looking, he had acquired a reputation as the handsomest of the *beaux* of the Revolution and the chief of the *jeunesse dorée*. His good manners and his smart clothes obtained him still more notoriety and more success than his articles in the *Orateur du Peuple*, or his speeches in the Convention. Nor were these attributes of his success without their effect on pretty Pauline Bonaparte.

Lucien saw with pleasure the attention his sister received from his friend Fréron, and his ambition leapt at the thought of seeing her married to the fascinating young commissioner. In Lucien's modest circumstances, Fréron appeared an ideal, unhoped-for brother-in-law who could through his influence be useful to him personally. But while waiting for this happy *dénouement* there was no need for Lucien to help to hasten it; the romance required no intervention from without, and the psychological moment for asking her hand in marriage was not likely to be long delayed. For scandal had it that Pauline and Fréron were as good as married already! (Barras *Mémoires*.)

But while these different interests were in suspense the beautiful Paulette had, possibly unknown to herself, though it is scarcely likely, made another conquest.

Owing to the influence of Fréron and Barras, her brother Napoleon, after the taking of Toulon, had been promoted from the rank of major to that of a general of brigade. The good relations that existed between the two members of the Convention and the Bonaparte family perhaps stood the young artillery officer in better stead than his innate genius for war. Immediately after his promotion General Bonaparte had taken as *aide-de-camp* young Junot, who had just been appointed an officer and whom he had remarked for his coolness and spirit at the siege of Toulon.

Junot was passionately devoted to his chief, and on accompanying him to Marseilles he had likewise fallen madly in love with Bonaparte's pretty sister, at whose feet he spent most of his time like a pet dog. Junot, indeed, began to love the entire family of her whom he adored, and his devotion to the general was at first slightly tinged with the love with which he was inspired by the seductive Paulette.

Junot, however, said nothing to him at Marseilles of his feelings, but it was not necessary for Bonaparte to have been gifted with much perspicacity to guess them. Besides, Junot was the last man in the world capable of hiding his feelings. But if the general had divined his *aide-de-camp's* secret, he likewise said nothing, probably thinking that the flame was one which would soon be extinguished. On leaving Marseilles for Paris, whither he was accompanied by Junot, he had perhaps quite ceased to think of the matter, when strolling one evening in the *Jardin des Plantes* with his *aide-de-camp* the latter spoke.

It was the end of spring. The warm air, heavy with the perfume of limes and syringas, had something in it voluptuous and intoxicating

STANISLAS FRERON

which urged one to tender confidences. Junot could no longer contain himself; the balmy spring evening unloosened his tongue, and he confessed to Bonaparte that since the first day he had seen the lovely Pauline at Marseilles he had loved her. He added that though he no longer saw her he loved her each day the more, that he could neither eat nor drink, that he could no longer live in such a state, and he finished by formally demanding of Napoleon as head of the Bonaparte family, in virtue of his position if not of his age, for the hand of his sister.

The general listened without interrupting, and neither refused nor accepted the offer, at the same time leaving it to be inferred that to start housekeeping and to provide for a family something more was necessary than the pay of a lieutenant.

"Paulette is not rich," he said, "and if she is to say 'yes,' it will first be necessary for the family to be assured that you can offer her such an establishment that any children she may have in the future shall not suffer."

Junot, who had already written his father to inform him of his matrimonial intentions, and to inquire how much he could give him on the day of his marriage, had just received a reply. It was not very encouraging. His father said that he could give him nothing at the moment, unless it was his blessing, but that on his death he might count on about 20,000 *francs* as his share.

Junot had this letter in his pocket, and he produced it, saying—

You see that I shall be rich, since with my pay and my expectations I shall have an income of 1,200 *francs*. I implore you, general, to write to your mother, the Citizeness Bonaparte, and tell her that I love her daughter, that I ask for her hand in marriage, and that my father on his side will write and make the formal offer.

Bonaparte listened attentively to the proposal of his *aide-de-camp* as they returned to the centre of Paris. In the perfumed twilight of the *Jardin des Plantes* he, too, had felt the effect of the soft spring atmosphere. Junot's confession had struck a sympathetic chord in him, and he had been on the point of lending a favourable ear to the honest aspirations of the young officer. But the more they became engulfed in the movement and noise of Paris he appeared to regret having almost suffered himself to be influenced by sentiment. The pavements of Paris put an end to romance and brought him back to cold reality. Instead of giving Junot a definite answer, as the latter expected, he held out to him hopes of the future, he said:

I cannot, write my mother and make her this request; for if later you have an income of 1,200 *francs* it will be all right; but you have not got it now. Your father is particularly healthy, and will keep you waiting for it a long time. In fine, you have nothing unless it be your lieutenant's epaulettes; while as for Pauline, she has not even as much. So then, as you have nothing and she has nothing, the total is nothing. You cannot therefore marry at present. Let us wait. Perhaps better days are in store for us, my friend; yes, they will come, even if I am compelled to seek them in another part of the world.

"But, General," pleaded Junot, "think of Paul and Virginia; in their case fortune was preferred to happiness, and what was the result?"

To argue, however, was useless; Bonaparte remained firm. (Duchesse d'Abrantès, *Mémoires*.)

In answering Junot as he did he was not insincere, for he really thought seriously at this time of entering the Turkish service. But in the meanwhile the Revolution proceeded with giant strides, and finding its pace better suited to his size, small though it was, he decided that it was more profitable for him to struggle with fortune in Paris than at Constantinople.

The same year, indeed, he was appointed a general of division, then second in command of the Army of the Interior under the immediate orders of Barras. It is well known what talent he displayed in suppressing the insurrection of the sections on the 13th *Vendémiaire*, as well as the affluence that his sudden rise brought his family. This rise also brought in its train many offers of marriage for his sisters.

Napoleon wrote to his brother Joseph:

A citizen named Billon, who, I understand, is acquainted with you, wishes to marry Paulette. He has, however, no fortune, and I have written mamma that he is not worth considering. I shall try to find out more about him today. . . . (*Correspondance de Napoléon.*)

It would have been more logical, one would think, had he tried "to find out more about him" before writing that he "was not worth considering." But these words clearly show that ambition, natural and justifiable enough, had begun to count with the young general. When

THE 13TH VENDÉMIAIRE AT ST. ROCH.

NAPOLEON'S "WHIFF OF GRAPE-SHOT" WHICH PUT AN END TO THE FRENCH REVOLUTION

it was a question of the marriages of his sisters, he was to prove himself a difficult person to please.

After the 13th *Vendémiaire*, when Bonaparte became Commanders-in-Chief of the Army of the Interior, Fréron, as may be imagined, was by no means anxious to break with the beautiful Paulette. Now more than ever did he court the favour of Lucien, who was his chief supporter in the family. But luck had deserted *le beau* Fréron. He had not been re-elected to the Council of the Five Hundred. To console him, it is true, he was given the post of Commissary at Marseilles, whither he returned. But this was far from the brilliant position he had filled as member of the Convention. At Marseilles he was no longer of any consequence. Of what account is a mere government commissary compared with a popular journalist, an influential deputy, a dazzling dandy, the king of the *jeunesse dorée*, as he had been? So, there was no more talk of poor little Fréron than of one who seeks employment instead of dispensing it. To comfort him and give him fresh courage he had need of all of Pauline's love.

Napoleon, however, whose ambition increased in proportion as one might have expected it to be satisfied, no longer appeared to regard this intimacy favourably. Fréron possessed no fortune, and the extravagant life he had led during the past few years had crippled him with debt. Bonaparte was aware of this. If he hesitated to give his sister to the brave Junot, who had in perspective an income of 1,200 *francs*, it was not in order that she might marry a man who had nothing but debts. Moreover, his ambition increasing on his own account increased also on that of his relations.

"I do not see," he replied to Joseph on January 11, 1796, *à propos* of a fresh offer of marriage Pauline had received, "I do not see any objection to Paulette's marriage, *if he is rich. . . .*"

Fréron, it has been stated, was not rich, he had not been re-elected, and he only held a modest post. So, Bonaparte no longer regarded him, from the matrimonial point of view, as favourably as he had done when he was a member of the Convention, and he, Napoleon, was a mere captain or commander of artillery.

But Pauline, who was still rather young to make all these nice calculations, gave a free rein to the passion with which the fascinating dandy had inspired her. An absolutely perfect intimacy existed between them, and it is curious to note with what complacency the undemonstrative Madame Letizia regarded the close relations the young people had formed. Nevertheless, she does not seem to have desired a marriage between her daughter and Fréron. Her biographer says:

> This alliance, was in nowise pleasing to Madame Mère, who refused her consent in spite of her daughter's entreaties. (Baron Larrey, *Madame Mère*.)

The little romance proceeded all the same at a lively pace, and, to judge from the letters of the two lovers, the justification of their intimacy by marriage was absolutely desirable.

Pauline wrote to Fréron, in February, 1796:

> Yesterday, in the greatest uneasiness on account of your health, my dear friend, I sent . . . but too stupid for words, he returned without finding out how you were feeling. I was in this state when Nonat came, I was not expecting a letter from you; he told me that you had suffered a great deal. Then why did you write me? Since you disobey me, you do not love me anymore. I have not replied to your letter of the day before yesterday, because I wished to talk to you of it. My love is your surety for my answer. Yes, I swear to you, dear Stanislas, never to love anyone but you. No one shares my heart; it is wholly yours. Who could offer opposition to the union of two souls who only seek happiness and find it in loving one another? No, my friend, neither mamma nor anybody can refuse you, my hand.
>
> Nonat told me yesterday that you ought not to go out for a whole week. Well, we must be patient. We will write one another, and that will compensate us for the privation of not meeting. I thank you for your thoughtfulness in sending me your hair. I will likewise send you some of mine, but not like Laura. For Laura and Petrarch, whom you are always talking of, were not as happy as we are. Petrarch was constant, but Laura. . . . No, darling, Paulette will love you as much as Petrarch loved Laura. *Adieu*, Stanislas, dear friend, I embrace you as I love you. (Th. Jung *Didot MSS.*)

For a young girl of sixteen this was not so bad. They corresponded, they *tutoyéd*, they exchanged locks of hair, they embraced, in a word, they played Petrarch and Laura, and all under the complacent eye of the mother, who, while opposed to her daughter's marrying the young man, nevertheless permitted her to love him contrary to all the rules of propriety. What a strange family! More than once, too, Pauline went to consult a woman who had a high reputation in the silly art of fortune-telling to learn if her marriage would shortly take place. (Général de Ricard *Autour des Bonaparte*.)

In the face of such proofs of her love, Fréron could hardly contain himself for joy. For, while loving Pauline, he was at the same time delighted to see, as a *Thermidorian* depreciated in value, that he would find in his future brother-in-law, the general, the assistance he needed to achieve success in the future. So, in his love-dreams, happiness and ambition marched side by side. It was but natural. Was he not young? Had he not filled a high position? Did he not possess a certain ability or tact? And did he not wish to succeed? It was, then, natural enough that he should indulge himself in all the folly of dreams.

So sure, was he of the future—and after the letters he had received from Pauline he had the right to be—that everywhere he spoke of his marriage as very near. Nevertheless, at the same time he was not without a vague uneasiness; Madame Bonaparte raised difficulties, the general dissembled. In love as he was, he suffered much, and could have said with Tasso's *Aminta*, since he composed *madrigals* in Italian with Paulette: "*Piccola si, ma fa pur gravi le ferite.*" ("She is small, but she inflicts cruel wounds.")

In his uncertainty, in his anxiety, he wrote on March 24, 1796, the following letter to General Bonaparte, (Th. Jung):—

You promised me before leaving, my dear Bonaparte, a letter for your wife. We have decided that it will be better for you to inform her of my marriage so that she may not be astonished at the sudden apparition of Paulette when I present her to her. I am sending an orderly to you at Toulon to seek the letter of which I am to be the bearer.

Your mother raises a slight obstacle to my haste. I am sticking to my intention of being married in Marseilles in four or five days, and all the arrangements have been made to this effect, independently of the possession of that hand I burn to unite to mine. It is probable that the Directory will appoint me immediately to some distant post, which will perhaps necessitate a speedy departure. If I were obliged to return here, I should lose precious time, and the Government, which rightly bothers itself very little with affairs of the heart, might find fault at my absence, which would retard the object of the mission confided to me.

So, I implore you to write at once to your mother to remove

every obstacle; tell her to leave me the greatest freedom in de-
termining the date of my good fortune. I have the full consent
of Paulette; why, then, postpone the fastening of those bonds
that the most tender love has already formed? Dear Bonaparte,
assist me to overcome this last obstacle. I count on you.
I embrace you, dear friend, and I am yours and hers for life.
Adieu.

This letter greatly annoyed Napoleon, who no longer wished to
hear the subject of his sister's marriage to Fréron mentioned. He consequently wrote his mother that there could no longer be any question of its taking place. He also wrote to Joseph:

I beg of you to settle this affair of Paulette's. It is not my intention for her to marry Fréron. Tell her so and make her inform
him.

He wrote Lucien to the same effect, and perhaps also to Pauline
herself.

Whilst this correspondence was taking place, the two lovers continued theirs and very likely saw one another. Pauline had actually
packed her things and pretended she would get married in spite of the
wishes of her family. On May 19, 1796, she wrote Fréron as follows:—

I have just received your letter, which has given me the greatest
pleasure, for I was commencing to complain to myself of your
silence; besides, that woman (the fortune-teller?) has considerably upset me. But do not worry yourself, I am only ill of *ennui*
and weariness. . . . Farewell, dear friend, I love you more than
myself. Farewell.
Tell Lucien to write to me; I have already written him twice.
Excuse this scrawl, but in bed one cannot write decently.

It would seem that the obstacles to her marriage raised by her family rendered her, ordinarily so light-hearted and so giddily frivolous,
melancholy, since she wrote Fréron that they took her into the country, where they did their best to provide amusement for her. But she
would not yield without a hard struggle. On July 10, 1796, she again
wrote Fréron:—

Dear friend, everybody unites to oppose us. I see by your letter that your friends are false, even including Napoleon's wife,
whom you believed to be on your side. She has written her

husband that I should demean myself if I married you, and that she hoped to prevent it. What have we done to her? Alas! everything is against us! How unhappy we are!

I advise you to write to Napoleon. I would like to write him myself. What do you think of it? Address your letter to the care of mamma.

Adieu, my friend, for life thy faithful lover.

Amami sempre, anima mia, mio bene, mio tenero amico, non respiro, se non pere ti amo.

Poor Paulette! There was no member of her family, even including her sister-in-law, who had entered the family against the wishes of all, who did not endeavour to prevent her marrying her dear Fréron. But she took good care not to forget this, and to the day of her divorce Josephine was to find in her an implacable enemy.

A few days later, on the 15th of July, she wrote again to Fréron:—

You know my sensibility, and you are not ignorant how I idolise you. No, it is not possible that Paulette can live separated from her darling Stanislas!

Formerly I had the sweet consolation of being able to talk to you and to unbosom myself to Elisa, but this is now denied me. Lucien has shown me your—letter; the situation, I see, continues the same. Ah—how I have kissed that letter! how I have pressed—it against my bosom, against my heart! . . . We are leaving this house. I will send you the new address tomorrow. Farewell, dear friend. Write me often, and pour your heart into that of your tender and constant friend,

P. B.

Ti amo sempre, e passionattissimamente, per sempre amo, sbell'idol mio, set cuore mio, tenero amico, ti amo, amo, amo, amo, st amatissimo amante.

She loved him so much that, as she had told Fréron she would do, she wrote to her brother. But he had now become the glorious Commander-in-Chief of the Army of Italy and decidedly opposed her marriage, which he did in a manner that irrevocably put a stop to the subject. The disagreeable task of setting the seal to the last page of their romance devolved on Lucien. He wrote with much embarrassment to his friend Fréron on January 4, 1797, the following lines:—

My wife sends her regards to you, and mamma charges me

to ask you to what address you wish her to return your correspondence. . . . This detail weighs upon me, my friend; let us have done with it.

Adieu, dear Fréron; the torrent may bring us together again. Whatever may be the whims of the blind goddess, it is sweet to count on a true friend. Count without reserve on your brother. (Th. Jung.)

The "torrent" did, in fact, a little later, bring Fréron and the beautiful Paulette together again, but it was on the ocean during the voyage to Haiti.

2

After missing this marriage, Pauline had need—of distraction. It was given her. The comfortable circumstances in which the family now found themselves assisted not a little to change her thoughts. The poverty of former years would have made her grief more bitter and prolonged it, for one must possess an exceptionally strong character to contend against these two evils united, and not to sink under them. But fortunately for Pauline, her material and pecuniary situation was no longer the same. With the good health she then enjoyed, with her youth and her natural light-heartedness, the inconsolable Paulette speedily found consolation. Moreover, the brilliant victories of her brother in Italy afforded diversion to her amorous regrets.

In the family, as all over the world, nothing else was spoken of but his prodigious successes. And when General Bonaparte, taking advantage of a rather long armistice, invited his mother and sisters to pass some time with him at Milan, Pauline no longer gave a thought to anything but the pleasure of the journey to Italy, of seeing her glorious brother, who in her girlish imagination wore a crown of laurel on his head, and of the desire with which she burned to see reflected on herself some rays of his glory, so resplendent that it already seemed to her like a family heritage of which she was about to obtain her lawful share.

Pauline arrived at Milan with her mother and her sister Annunziata (Caroline) before General Bonaparte had left that city to take up his headquarters at the Château de Monbello. M. and Madame Baciocchi, the Abbé Fesch (Madame Letizia's half-brother), Joseph and Louis had arrived previously. It was the first part of May, and spring, which in Italy is superb, seemed *en fête* to receive fittingly the family of the liberator of Italy. The Italians, with their exuberant and demonstrative temperament always enthusiastic, for their liberators or their oppressors, testified their joy in a manner that was almost delirious.

There were illuminations, fireworks, cheers from the crowd of *"Evviva il liberatore dell'Italia!" "Evviva il General Buonaparte!"* It was more than enough to turn heads stronger than Pauline's, and hers, like her heart, had about as much steadiness as a weathercock. She had scarcely reached the frontier, or, rather, scarcely left Marseilles, before there was no more question of Fréron than if he had never existed. Is not this pretty much the case with all broken loves? At first it seems impossible that one should survive the rupture; there is a sort of bitter pleasure in telling oneself so; one hugs one's grief, so to speak. Then it fades away little by little, until nothing remains but the satisfaction of having broken chains which at first it seemed one could never do without.

Bonaparte received his family with the tenderest affection. He presented to them his wife, than whom no one could have been more gracious. Misunderstandings and coldness disappeared, or seemed to disappear; they kissed one another and seemed to forget their grievances or, at least, agreed not to speak of them. This is what is called "to forgive and forget." Cordiality even would have reigned in the family if those two little pests, Caroline and Pauline, the latter especially, had not taken a wicked pleasure in doing all in their power to disturb it; and one knows what adepts women are at sowing discord in families.

Pauline was one *par excellence*; she seemed, moreover, to cherish a special grudge against her sister-in-law that she wished to satisfy. Though she had quite forgotten Fréron, she had not forgotten the part that Josephine had played in breaking off her marriage with him, and for this she did not forgive her. Josephine, however, had taken pleasure in preparing a charming apartment for her in the Serbelloni palace, where she resided at Milan; but nothing disarms feminine spite. Pauline merely wished to preserve the appearance of cordiality, but that was all.

Time passed quickly at Milan in a succession of *fêtes*, dinners, and receptions, and nearly every day excursions were made into the surrounding country, which was magnificent. At last, when the heat commenced to be disagreeable, they left Milan for the Château de Monbello, a few leagues east of Verona. The poet Arnault, who was at this time at Bonaparte's headquarters at Monbello, has left this charming little sketch of the beautiful Pauline:—

> At dinner, I was placed next Paulette, who, remembering that she had met me at Marseilles, knowing me to be in possession

of her secrets since I was the confidential friend of her future husband, treated me as an old acquaintance. She was a singular combination of the most perfect physical beauty and the most bizarre moral qualities. If she was the most lovely person one could possibly see, she was also the most unreasonable that one could imagine. She behaved like a schoolgirl, speaking at random, laughing at nothing and at everything, making fun of the most serious persons, putting out her tongue at her sister-in-law when she was not looking, nudging my knee when I did not pay sufficient attention to her pranks, and attracting to herself from time to time those terrible glances with which her brother called the most untractable men to order.

But they made hardly any impression on her; the next moment she would begin again, and the authority of the Commander-in-Chief of the Army of Italy fell to pieces before the giddiness of a little girl. Nevertheless, she was a good child by nature rather than from a desire to be such, for she had no principle and was capable of doing good merely from caprice."(Arnault, *Souvenirs d'un Sexagénaire.*)

She was a veritable *enfant terrible*, going into the offices of the general staff, ransacking the papers, listening behind the doors to the conversation of the officers, often permitting herself to be surprised in this pretty occupation, but also on her side surprising others, particularly her sister-in-law, in matters which she never failed to turn to her own advantage. (Comte d'Hérisson, *Le Cabinet Noir.*)

Bonaparte, therefore, desired to find a husband for Paulette. Before he had been appointed to the command of the Army of Italy, he had tried to make up a match between her and M. Permon. This project was most original. The young general offered himself to the widowed Madame Permon, at the same time suggesting to her that her son should marry Pauline and that her little daughter Laura, the future Madame Junot, should marry Louis or Jerome. But the descendant of the *Comneni* only laughed at this proposal, meant in all seriousness though it was, and nothing more came of it. It was at this moment that Bonaparte, who certainly liked widows, fell in love with Madame de Beauharnais, and she decided to accept him as her husband, for lack of a better, in February, 1796.

But to return to Pauline. Bonaparte made Joseph propose her to his *aide-de-camp* Marmont. This officer was very handsome, well born, and distinguished for his fine manners, his education, courage, and military ability. From every point of view, he was a very desirable *parti*. But Marmont had strange ideas; he dreamt of domestic happiness, of love in marriage, of fidelity, and he divined that the beautiful Paulette would bring him just the opposite of all this.

So, while rendering justice to the grace and charms of Mademoiselle Bonaparte, and fully recognising the immense influence such a marriage would bring to bear on his future career, he would not let himself yield to the temptation. The behaviour of this spoilt child had caused him to reflect. So, he declined, and although he did not find the happiness he dreamed of when later he married Mademoiselle Perregaux, the daughter of a rich banker in the Chaussée d'Antin, he never regretted having refused Pauline.

"I have more to congratulate myself upon than to repent of," he said, when writing his *Memoirs*.

But General Leclerc had none of Marmont's apprehensions. He clearly foresaw that a marriage with the sister of his commander-in-chief would not injure his future; the young girl pleased him, and, in spite of reports to the contrary, (Comte d'Hérisson) he proposed for and obtained the hand of Pauline in the most conventional fashion, without the least romance, but also, it is true, without the least delay. In regard to the haste with which Pauline's marriage took place, Arnault remarks, "She was more impatient to become Madame Leclerc than she was afterwards to become Princess Borghèse." (Arnault)

Adjutant-General Leclerc was the son of a rich mill-owner at Pontoise. He had a brother and a sister. Their father had neglected nothing in order to give them a good education, from which they had sufficiently profited. Mademoiselle Leclerc married later Marshal Davoust; her brother was a *prefect* under the Empire. As for the general, he had entered the service as a volunteer, and on October 19, 1791, had been appointed lieutenant in the 2nd Battalion of Seine-et-Oise.

A year afterwards he had become *aide-de-camp* to General Lapoype, and finally had been sent as Adjutant-General to the Army of Italy. He was at the time a young man of twenty-six, gentle and pleasant in appearance, of medium height and a rather delicate constitution. He affected a grave air, which, if it scarcely accorded with the youthfulness of his looks, was nevertheless well suited to the elevated rank he had so rapidly attained. With little money of his own, he was very ambitious, and it was to his marriage alone, says Marmont, that he owed his further rapid advancement in the future.

General Leclerc

The marriage of Pauline Bonaparte to General Leclerc took place at Monbello. At first it was happy enough, though Fouché pretends that Pauline had for nobody so great an aversion as for Leclerc. (Fouché, *Mémoires*.) He did all that his wife desired, and this was no sinecure. Besides, he was very much in love. Pauline, to whom a husband was almost a novelty, and a very droll and amusing one at the start, had the goodness for a few days to suffer herself to be loved.

To quote the poet Arnault again:

I found, General Leclerc in his home intoxicated with happiness. Amorous and ambitious, there was reason for it. His wife seemed to me extremely happy also, not only because she was married to him, but also because she was married. Her new state had not given her as much gravity as her husband, who appeared more serious than ever. As for her, she was always the same giddy creature.

'Is not that a diamond you have there?' she asked me, indicating a very modest one I wore in a pin. 'I think mine is still finer.' And she began to compare with some vanity the two stones, the finer of which was not bigger than a lentil.

I have often laughed at the recollection of this childishness when I have seen her covered with diamonds, among which the finest of ours would not have been perceived. Her jewelcase has filled a bit since that day. . . .

If General Leclerc, as Arnault says, was more serious than ever after his marriage, it was because the various discoveries he made concerning his singular little wife were bound to suggest serious reflections as much as to the past as to the future. Marmont had made them beforehand, and had not married her. He must have congratulated himself more than once on his lucky escape.

As for Pauline, life opened intoxicatingly to her, and adorned with all possible happiness. Each day there were *fêtes*, parties, excursions, and these under the beautiful blue sky of Italy, of an Italy that her brother had just freed from the yoke of the Austrians after a series of victories beside which all the military glories hitherto known to history paled. And she was seventeen! And her husband, who was twenty-six, though somewhat serious, adored her! Was not all this more than sufficient to make one happy? How many women there are to whom but a single day of such an existence would have afforded happiness for the rest of their lives!

But Pauline enjoyed it like a giddy little schoolgirl whose head has been turned, and was merely content to suffer herself to exist, to be spoilt in every possible way, and to be worshipped by everybody, even by her husband, without asking herself if she deserved her happiness, if it would last, or if she knew how to appreciate it at its just value.

In such a whirl of pleasure the time passed quickly. They sometimes spent several days at Milan; once they all went there together in a family party. On this occasion Madame Josephine Bonaparte and the beautiful Madame Leclerc decided to pay a visit to Colonel Junot, Bonaparte's *aide-de-camp*. This brave officer had received several rather serious wounds in one of the last engagements that had preceded the armistice. He was at Milan under the care of the surgeon Ivan, who answered for his recovery, but insisted upon absolute quiet for his patient. These ladies, then, paid him a visit, and Madame Bonaparte was accompanied by her maid Louise.

What is extraordinary in the visit of these three women is that Junot, two years before at Marseilles, had been madly in love with Pauline, who was just married to another; that Josephine had tried to get up a flirtation with Junot, who travelled in the same carriage with her when she went from Paris to Milan to join her husband, but, faithful to the friendship and confidence his general reposed in him, Junot had had the impoliteness to repel these advances, though he did so as politely as possible. To effect this, he decided to conceive a sudden passion for Madame Bonaparte's maid. This was to extricate himself from the situation with spirit and honour.

For Louise, as this girl who was very attractive was called, combined with her duties as maid that of friend to her mistress, who had, in fact, the very singular fancy of making her dress like herself and of having her eat at her table. So Junot— though thoroughly flattered by the court that his general's wife paid him, but too honourable to yield to the caprices of this big doll who was as immoral as she was unscrupulous—had flirted desperately with Mademoiselle Louise, who was luckily at hand as a safety-valve to his twenty-six years, which it amused Josephine to set wildly on fire.

This triple visit must, then, have revived in the young colonel singularly complicated impressions; the pleasure, however, of receiving these ladies dominated every other feeling. He lay stretched on a couch, very pale from the terrible loss of blood that the Austrian sabres had caused, and wrapped in a sort of overcoat or dressing-gown of white *piqué*. They spoke of France, of Italy, of the beautiful women of Milan, of Madame Visconti, and of the passion with which she had first inspired Major-General Berthier, of Madame Ruga, the beauty who was all the rage in Milan, whom Madame Leclerc herself found beautiful, but on condition she suppressed her moustache, "which, she declared, made her look like a drum-major." And she laughed, opening her mouth to show her pretty teeth, an advantage she never neglected to avail herself of, above all when near her sister-in-law, who had deplorable teeth and never permitted herself to smile save with closed lips.

Junot, hearing them speak of the beautiful women of Milan, declared that the most beautiful ones were at that moment beside him. Madame Bonaparte and Madame Leclerc, who, newly married though they were, were not insensible to compliments, especially when they proceeded from other mouths than their husbands', did not attempt to conceal the pleasure the gallantry of the colonel afforded them. The time, therefore, passed very pleasantly for the wounded officer and his pretty guests, when all of a sudden Junot turned deadly white, his head fell back, and his eyes closed.

"Good heavens! Junot, what is the matter with you?" cried Madame Leclerc, rising.

Junot, who had not completely lost consciousness, extended to her his hand, which he had placed on his breast. At the same time a stream of blood ran from underneath his sleeve and covered Madame Leclerc's white dress. The unfortunate man, in the movements he had made to receive the ladies, had displaced the bandages which kept in place the dressing on one of the wounds on his arm; it had opened afresh, and the blood flowed from his sleeve as if from a spout; at the same moment he fainted from weakness.

When he came to, he found himself surrounded with the attentions of his three nurses. One poured water over his face from a full *carafe*, another held a flask tightly glued under his nose and prevented his breathing, while his orderly, having run in on hearing the screams of the ladies, had in the twinkling of an eye stripped him of his dressing-gown and put back in their proper place the dressing and necessary bandages. Junot, later, spoke of that moment as "the sweetest in his existence." (Duchesse d'Abrantès, *Mémoires*.)

As for Pauline, she had been alarmed at having blood on her dress, but after all it was not, she who was wounded, and since she was a kind-hearted girl, her delight had been great when she saw this accident would have no serious result.

3

The *fêtes* and other distractions did not prevent Madame Leclerc from keeping an eye on her sister-in-law Josephine. In spite of the delicate attentions the latter had showered upon her at the time of her arrival in Milan, on the occasion of her marriage, and many times besides, Pauline cordially detested her. Among the conversations of the officers of the staff she had managed to overhear when listening behind doors, were some that dealt with the more than questionable fidelity of Josephine Bonaparte to her husband.

Pauline, who was not easily shocked, had been very much so on hearing that her brother, the glorious conqueror of Beaulieu, of Würmser, of Alvinzi, was reduced by his wife, six years his senior, to the state of one of Molière's husbands. Naturally she could not pardon in her sister-in-law conduct which she herself was soon to imitate. Once married, she had nothing more pressing to do than to seek enlightenment through her husband as to the reports which had come to her ears.

Leclerc did not hide from her that these reports had some foundation, that, in plain terms, Josephine had an "affair," the favourite for the moment being a certain Hippolyte Charles, lieutenant of dragoons, who had just been promoted captain, a good-looking, fastidious young fellow, who only opened his mouth to make puns, and played the buffoon in conversation. These rare qualities had stolen the heart of Josephine, who found her husband, notwithstanding what was said of his genius, a mere greenhorn beside M. Charles.

"Ah! but you know him," said Leclerc; "surely you know my *aide-de-camp*, Charles!"

"Yes, I know him quite well," said Pauline musingly.

She was not alone in her knowledge, which she had gathered from the gossip of officers; it was the common property of the whole Army of Italy. Only General Bonaparte, the husband, as is always the case, knew nothing of it, but he was not to remain long in ignorance. Perhaps it was entirely due to his eagle vision that he acquired the information, or possibly Pauline made it her duty to enlighten him, while giving herself at the same time the malicious pleasure of playing her sister-in-law a bad turn, and thus satisfying the hatred she bore her.

Perhaps there was also in this denunciation another feeling, and a base one at that, a feeling of jealousy, which was on a par with the other two. What right had this Captain Charles to pay attention to any woman other than the wife of the general whose *aide-de-camp* he was?

The Empress Josephine in the park at Malmaison

Be this as it may, one fine day the rumour suddenly ran through the headquarters of the Army of Italy that the commander-in-chief had caused Captain Charles to be arrested, and that the accusations which were brought against this officer were such that he was about to be shot.

General Bonaparte had become aware of the intimate relations existing between his wife and the handsome captain. But if these constituted a fault which a husband could not pardon (he did forgive it, however, and many similar offences), it was not one that came under the military code. This is doubtless just what he told himself, once his first fury had spent itself; for having weighed all considerations, he contented himself with chasing this too enterprising captain from the Army of Italy.

Josephine wept all her spare tears on this occasion, and it is well known she always possessed a goodly store. But Pauline, who had only attained her end very incompletely, gained nothing from her brother's mildness. She, "who, as one knows, was kindness itself," later told her friend Laura Permon, the future Madame Junot:—

> Fancy, Laurette, my sister-in-law very nearly died of grief, and it is certain one does not die of grief on parting with friends. There must on the face of it have been more than mere friendship in question. As for me, I consoled my brother, who was very unhappy. (Duchesse d'Abrantès, *Mémoires*.)

Bonaparte, who adored his wife with all the fire of his genius and his heart, must indeed have been unhappy, to find himself of all men betrayed with such effrontery.

But if Bonaparte, the husband, was deceived, Charles, the lover, was too. "During his early campaigns in Italy," says Sismondi, "Bonaparte dismissed from his headquarters *various* lovers of Josephine." Sismondi, at least, leaves it to be inferred that they were the successors and not the competitors of M. Charles, which, however, was not at all improbable.

As for this Captain Charles, when he became a civilian, Madame Bonaparte continued to extend him her protection, and a little later even continued to grant him her favours during Bonaparte's absence in Egypt. It was owing to her recommendation that he became connected with the provision business of Louis Bodin, and obtained an interest in the concern. From that day dates the fortune of M. Hippolyte Charles, who does not seem to have lost, pecuniarily speaking, through his change of career. If only General Bonaparte had known all this!

However, *fêtes*, love, jealousy, vengeance, everything afforded amusement to young Madame Leclerc. They made excursions in all directions, going even as far as the lakes. In short, time passed very gaily, when one day it was reported that General Bonaparte was about to sign with Austria that peace, since become famous under the name of Campo-Formio.

This was a new *fête* for Madame Leclerc. She would, then, soon be going to Paris! There more court than ever would be paid her; there she would be queen of all the balls, of every *salon*, for who could rival her in beauty? Her sister-in-law? She contemptuously laughed at the idea, calling Josephine merely "a worn-out glove," and as she said it, she shrugged her shoulders with a little disdainful air of pity, so drolly mutinous as to compel one to laugh.

She was not, however, yet to be allowed to go to Paris. General Leclerc was ordered with his brigade, which formed part of the Army of Occupation in Italy, to remain behind in Milan. Furthermore, she was *enceinte*, and the state of her health demanded more care than could be obtained in a travelling carriage between Milan and Paris. She remained, therefore, a few more months in the Cisalpine capital. It was there her son was born, whom she named Dermide, after one of the characters in the poems of Ossian.

It was his godfather, Bonaparte, who chose this strange name for him. La Revellière-Lépeaux did better than this, for he named his son Ossian. Bonaparte was at the time a great admirer of the plaintive and mystical hymns, albeit they sing of courage, of that Scotch bard, to whom, according to Sainte-Beuve, he attributed his genius, and whom, in return, one might add, he made rather famous. But these hymns had appeared more beautiful to him than they really were, because he had read them in the exaltation of his love to his wife Josephine. She, on the contrary, not sharing his fervour, must have found Ossian very boring, and her husband even more so, in making her listen to his reading.

The baptism of the little Dermide took place, without any parade, in a church belonging to the Capuchins, who had not taken the oath to the Constitution. The child was carried there one evening, accompanied by Messieurs Dufresne and de Saint-Léon, who had been chosen as witnesses. The drawing-up of the birth certificate gave occasion for a ceremony, which was celebrated with great *éclat* in the governmental palace. All these matters had been regulated by General Bonaparte, who had sent a formal order from Paris to comply with his instructions. They took care not to disobey him, and everything was done as he had directed.

Shortly afterwards, as soon as Madame Leclerc had regained her strength, she went to Paris, where she took a house in the Rue de la Ville-l'Evéque, and began to cultivate the society of the Corsican colony, if not from choice—this colony, though formed of the richest families of the island, was not composed of millionaires—at least from necessity, for she had no other acquaintances in Paris. Among these various Corsican families, it was the house of Madame Permon that Pauline preferred the most to visit.

Madame Permon has obtained a niche in history without ever having done anything to deserve the honour. The widow of a man who had made a fortune in military supplies during the French expedition in aid of the revolted American colonies, she had a son who, during the Revolution, followed in the footsteps of his father and likewise enriched himself. He was a good son, and gave his mother all she desired, which enabled her to live in a certain style and to keep a very fair establishment. Born a Comnène and descended, as she and her daughter boasted, from the former Emperors of Constantinople, she had known how with this key—which, however, people said was a false key—to open many doors, while her beauty had opened several others for her.

Intriguing, not lacking in a certain push and tact, lively and fond of power, she had succeeded in creating a *salon*, but one met in it more men than women, and, as has been said of that of another woman, Madame de Beauharnais, more men than husbands. For the rest, she had a kind nature, and had known at Ajaccio Letizia Ramolino, the wife of M. Charles de Bonaparte. It was at her house at Montpellier, where her husband had purchased the post of Farmer-General, that Charles de Bonaparte had died.

The Bonapartes did not forget the attention their father when dying had received from the Permons, nor the services they had rendered their family when reduced to poverty. It is, therefore, to her friendship with the Bonapartes that Madame Permon owes her place in history, and also as mother of her daughter Laura, who later married General Junot and wrote the celebrated *memoirs* which bear her name of Duchesse d'Abrantès.

Madame Leclerc went very often, nearly every day, to Madame

Permon's, where she reigned as much by reason of her beauty as owing to the fame of her brother. It was there that she served her apprenticeship as woman of the world. She spared no pains in order to please; she felt vaguely, instinctively, that it was necessary for the sisters of General Bonaparte to appear to advantage in the very few drawing-rooms to which they began to be admitted. But as woman of the world, she was far too much of a spoiled child ever to become more than an apprentice, and not one of the best at that.

It was, also, in Madame Permon's *salon* that she began to lay the foundation of her reputation for beauty. 'To be beautiful was her sole ambition, and she was quite satisfied when she heard herself called the "Queen of Folly." As to her reputation as a good: woman, that is a question which it would be impossible to treat seriously.

Madame Leclerc, then, went every day to visit her mother's old friend, Madame Permon, who loved her as much as if she had been her own child, and even more, for she excused in her a thousand follies which she would never have dreamt of overlooking in her daughter Laura. She would have spoiled her, if that had not already been done. It is difficult to credit the various caprices which at each moment of the day entered Paulette's pretty head; absurdities succeeded one another, each more senseless than the last, not only in words but in deeds. She was so pretty that one pardoned them in her; it was impossible to do otherwise.

Everybody laughed—save General Leclerc, who no longer even smiled. His face, which became each day more serious, not to say sad, contrasted singularly with the frivolous and altogether droll face of his little imp of a wife. The poor man was hardly master in his own house. He had attempted to restrain her follies within reasonable bounds, but at the first advice he offered her, Madame Leclerc assumed a tone, and such a tone that the unfortunate general hastened to refrain from speech and to resign himself to all the whims of his charming wife.

To employ an expression of Brantôme, which will not be out of place here since we are applying it to the wife of a cavalry general, Madame Leclerc was the leader of the squadron of the beautiful women of her time. She maintained the position for many years. Her beauty surpassed all that one can imagine, and suffered little change, in spite of the wear and tear due less to time than to dissipation and maladies, which it amused her to turn into serious illnesses, only to forget all about them on the day of a *fête* or a ball.

It has been said that it was impossible to form any idea of this

LAURE JUNOT (NÉE PERMON), DUCHESSE D'ABRANTÈS

woman, who was truly extraordinary as the perfection of beauty, because she was so little known in the "*Tout Paris*" of the period before her return from Haiti. She was then faded, washed out even, owing to the excess of pleasure, the devastating effects of a climate which swiftly uses up the most robust constitution, and perhaps, also, but this is infinitely less certain, through grief at her husband's death. She still possessed freshness, when she arrived in Paris from Milan, with her "Little Leclerc," as she called the general. But this freshness, as ephemeral as a rose, endured only a day.

After Haiti, she was no longer the Paulette of Milan. A dull tone, resembling an antique cameo, had replaced that phosphorescence, that genius of beauty, which is only met with in the persons of certain privileged mortals—a phosphorescence and genius which intoxicate, possibly, even more those who possess them than those who admire them.

With all this, Madame Leclerc was frank and free and easy and companionable, at once ingenuous and thoroughly self-possessed; in short, the sort of woman men dearly love, but not women. Without any wit, she was no fool; she occasionally had inspirations in conversation, which came from no one knew where, and were altogether funny. At these times she would pronounce her words with a serious and convincing air, which rendered them even more amusing. For at the bottom, they possessed no meaning, and had no bearing on any subject—they had not even the merit of common sense. On the lips of any other woman, they would have been mere folly; with her they were witty. But then she was so pretty!

Yes, she was pretty, but that was all. There was no question of refinement in her tastes, aspirations, or sentiments—"*point d'affaires*," as they said in the seventeenth century; of moral qualities, of virtue, there was still less question. She was able to say, with Mademoiselle de Lespinasse, "Ah, *mon Dieu*, how natural passion is to me, and what a stranger I am to reason!" But passion, with her, was a passion to be beautiful; she loved only herself, nothing else. She had loved Fréron a little, but she was so young then! Perhaps she also loved her husband a little, but it was so little that it is not worth mentioning. He had, however, such a lovely uniform and such a handsome horse! What more did he require in order to be loved?

But of all the lovers she chose during her life, and they numbered quite a few, she chose none because of love, but through mere idleness and caprice; she did not ask to be loved, but to be preferred. In her eyes, her lovers sanctioned and prolonged her reign and her reputation as a beauty. What a poor heart! What a true *"fin de siécle"* woman, as they used to say in 1799.

The life of a woman, so froth-like, could only be a tissue of every kind of extravagance. She made it so, in proportion to the increasing stability of the prodigious fortune of her brother. Chiffons held a larger share in her existence than anything else. Fashion is the one subject on which such foolish little heads are well informed. Madame Leclerc was quite at home here, and on this serious ground rivalled the folly of her frivolous sister-in-law, Josephine.

One day Madame Permon gave a ball in her pretty house in the Rue Sainte-Croix. She had invited all the friends she knew, and had even launched her invitations as far as the Faubourg Saint-Germain. Balls were so rare at this epoch that everybody came. Besides, it had been reported that the Bonaparte family would be present, and the Bonapartes had now become the magnet which drew people to all the evening parties where they were to be met. People, too, went no less to see the Bonapartes than to be seen by them. On this particular evening Madame Permon's *salon* was unusually well composed.

One saw there M. de Trénis, that man of the world who made it his boast to be the best dancer of his time, and who introduced the "subscription dance"; M. Archambault de Périgord, brother of the Bishop of Autun, the illustrious M. de Talleyrand; M. de Montbreton, the assiduous admirer at this period of the beauty of Madame Leclerc, whom later, on becoming Princess Borghèse and Princess of Guastalla, she took as groom-in-waiting; M. de Montrond, a no less enthusiastic admirer of this sister of Napoleon, and whom she was later to enrol in the elegant battalion of her innumerable lovers; the Messieurs Juste and Charles de Noailles, M. Auguste de Montagu, M. de Rastignac, the Messieurs de l'Aigle, M. de Montcalm, the Aussons, M. de la Feuillade, M. de Mondenard, M. de Sainte-Aulaire, finally among the crumbs at the bottom of the basket the youth of Paris, that crowd of idlers who made it their sole occupation to pass all their evenings at balls and *fêtes*, and took good care never to exert themselves otherwise, under the pretext that their precious health was too delicate and that the least work might fatigue their august persons.

Madame Leclerc, who knew in advance from Madame Permon that she was about to receive in her house the *fine fleur* of the youthful aristocracy of Paris, prepared herself for this *soirée* as a general prepares for battle. She dreamt of it, and had a *toilette* made for it which, she said, should immortalise her. When she was asked what this *toilette* was to be, she would reply, "You will see it; I can say no more at present." Madame Germon, a veritable genius of a dressmaker, and Charbonnier, an astonishing artist in the hairdressing line, were obliged to promise on their oaths in no wise to divulge the mysteries of her marvellous invention.

The secret was well kept, even by Paulette. To avoid any possible crushing of her dress or *coiffure* in coming from the Rue Ville l'Évêque to the Rue Sainte-Croix, she asked permission of Madame Permon to have her costume carried direct to her house, together with everything else she needed, and to come there to dress. In this manner she would make an entry without the least danger of crushing her *toilette*.

The reception-rooms were comfortably filled when Madame Leclerc judged the proper moment had arrived to make her appearance. As she valued the success she owed to her beauty, her heart should have expanded under the general murmur of admiration that greeted her dazzling vision, as a rose expands under the kisses of the June sun. She was indeed ravishing. But what eccentricity! Fillets of a very soft fur, spotted like a leopard, were wound round her head, while in her hair and on the fillets were little grapes of gold, without, however, causing her head to appear over-dressed. She had copied the head-dress of a Bacchante in the Louvre. The classical beauty of her face, which breathed youth, sufficiently well sustained the mythological impression, which her dress completed. This was of the finest Indian muslin.—The hem was bordered with gold embroidery, four or five inches broad, representing a garland of vine-leaves.

A Greek tunic moulded itself in a marvellous manner to her graceful figure, and vine-leaves, artistically arranged, set off, without creating any sense of heaviness, this singular costume. She wore clasps of cameos on her shoulders, on her hips, and on her bosom. There were cameos, too, on her sleeves, which were short and loose. Beneath her breasts, white as alabaster, and looking like twin doves ready for flight, was a girdle, a band of burnished gold clasped by a superb stone cut in the antique fashion. She carried her gloves in her hands, which were white and shapely enough to do without them. For the rest, a little air of child-like astonishment and her bosom palpitating beneath the muslin made her strikingly resemble, but for her expression, the picture of the "Young Girl with the Broken Pitcher," by Greuze.

Never did a woman produce a greater sensation upon entering a *salon*. The admiration she excited was enthusiastic and quite spontaneous. Beauty has so wide an empire that prejudices and political hatreds suddenly effaced themselves, and ardent Royalists were seen to applaud the sister of him who had caused so many of their party to be shot on the 18th *Vendémiaire*. The women, however, were by no means disarmed. The beauty of Pauline created the same impression on them as it did on the men, and their silence eloquently attested the fact. But they at once set themselves to search out something to criticise in the *toilette* of Madame Leclerc. Unable to discover anything, they began to attack the woman, but her beauty was unassailable.

This, however, did not hinder them from making unkind remarks. Was she not ashamed, little *parvenue* that she was, who, two or three years back, had not a morsel of bread to put between her teeth, and lived on the charity of the municipality at Marseilles, was she not ashamed to come now and seek to blot out everybody with her brazen luxury? Of a truth there were women who possessed no moral sense! . . . And once started on this subject, and several others, the good tongues wagged on without ceasing.

They were obliged, however, to stop in the long run, for Madame Permon, finding their venomous remarks were being expressed too loud, and fearing they might reach the ears of her darling Paulette, was obliged to use her authority as mistress of the house, and silence the malignant jealousy of her guests. What a singular thing it is that women are not willing to permit one of their sex to exceed all others in beauty!

Among the crowd of envious beholders Madame de Contades, at the moment Madame Leclerc made her sensational appearance, had about her a circle of admirers. As the result of the little revolution effected by the beauty of Pauline, she too looked about her, but in vain, for someone to whom she might give vent to her spite. But her circle of admirers had all suddenly vanished and gone to swell the ranks of Paulette's courtiers. This gave Madame de Contades a fresh grievance against Pauline, and she swore to have her revenge.

"Give me your arm," she said to one of her *cavaliers*, who had so *cavalierly* left her, and who happened just then to pass by her.

And on this arm, which she had gained no less *cavalierly*, she crossed the *salon* and arrived near Madame Leclerc.

The beautiful young woman, who had found the heat too great and was slightly fatigued with dancing, but who in reality preferred to be in another room in order to be admired in comfort, had withdrawn to Madame Permon's charmingly furnished *boudoir*, which adjoined

171

the salon. It was a more suitable frame for her beauty than the bustling ball-room. She had installed herself on a sofa in a manner to display to the best advantage her personal charms and her *toilette*. She was near the fireplace, and the lights in the candelabra lit her up in such a way that one would have sworn it was her face beaming with beauty and happiness that illumined the whole apartment.

Meanwhile, Madame de Contades approached on the arm of her *cavalier*, and no sooner entered the *boudoir* than she proceeded to stare through her lorgnette, in that impertinent little way women have when they wish to be rude, at the beautiful Bacchante of the golden vine-leaves and the antique cameos.

Calm in her triumph, Pauline, who felt happy and took pleasure in her enjoyment, was well disposed towards everybody rather than otherwise, when she suddenly heard Madame de Contades, whom she had supposed in all good faith to be admiring her, utter these venomous words:—

"*Mon Dieu*, what a misfortune! Oh, what a pity! She would be so pretty but for that!"

"But for what?" asked her *cavalier*.

"What! Do you mean to say you do not see? Why, it stares you in the face!"

It was more truly Madame de Contades who was bursting with jealousy; but on hearing her make this declaration of war in a loud voice, everybody turned to gaze on poor Madame Leclerc. She, under the cross-fire of so many glances, not all of which were kindly disposed, thought there must be something out of place in her *coiffure*, and seeing the insistency of those who stared at her, she began to redden and suffocate as if she had been detected in some crime.

"But do you not see what I mean?" persisted Madame de Contades, with the cold cruelty of a jealous woman. "What a pity! Yes, truly, how unfortunate! Such a really pretty head to have such ears! If I had ears like those, I would have them cut off. Yes, positively, they are like those of a pugdog. You who know her, *Monsieur*, advise her to have it done; it would be a charitable act on your part."

It was certainly not one on hers to cause words to be overheard—for she had managed to speak quite loud enough to enable all to have the benefit of her remarks—which were directed with such cruel malignity against a young woman who, when all was said, had done nothing to harm her, and was only guilty of being beautiful, and whom there was no sense in reproaching because she had been born more lovely than Madame de Contades.

The poor creature, blushing in a manner that made her lovelier than ever, rose as if to depart, but tears blinded her eyes, her strength deserted her, and she sank back on her sofa, hiding her face in her hands, and ill in good earnest!

Madame Leclerc's ears were by no means so extraordinary as it had pleased the unpleasant Madame de Contades to proclaim. They were simply too flat, and not chiselled into those little folds that make the ears of certain women so marvellously ravishing, veritable objects of art to be placed under glass. But there was nothing in this on which to base an attack. It was not a failing, if that was all one could charge Pauline with. But, as always happens, when one discovers a fault in a masterpiece, one can see nothing else after the discovery. So, they no longer contemplated the beauty of Madame Leclerc, but only stared at her ears.

To the shame of human nature, it must be owned that the triumph achieved by Madame de Contades through her unkindness was perhaps greater than that won by Madame Leclerc by her beauty. But such gratuitous cruelty so much impressed poor Pauline that after that evening party she almost always dressed her hair so as to conceal the flatness of her ears beneath her hair, or under a sort of bandeau, or *mentonnière*, as may be seen in her portrait by R. Lefevre, which is in the Museum at Versailles.

4

During the winter of 1800 Portugal, supported by England, declared war on Spain. As Spain was on good terms with France, the First Consul determined to come to her aid. Accordingly, he sent a little army of fifteen thousand men to Spain. General Bernadotte was originally chosen to command it, but Napoleon changed his mind and gave the command to General Leclerc.

Finding himself commander-in-chief, he believed that he had as much genius as his brother-in-law, and was even foolish enough to try to resemble him. He was about the same height and equally thin; he imitated his bluntness of speech, copied his attitudes, his gestures, his manners. He even went to the length of wearing over his uniform a grey *redingote* and a hat like Bonaparte's. But he only succeeded in making himself a caricature of his brother-in-law; and the soldiers, quick to detect his ridiculous pretension, nicknamed him "The blond Bonaparte."

The army, moreover, was not pleased that the command of the expedition to Portugal should have been given to a man whose only claim to it was that he had married the sister of the First Consul, when there were so many able and distinguished generals out of employment. Leclerc, too, did not seek to justify the preference shown him. Always short of money, he borrowed from his brother-in-law, Lucien Bonaparte, then Ambassador at Madrid, but since he could not be continually borrowing, he did a little trade in contraband, from which he derived a great deal of money but small consideration. (Thiébault *Mémoires*.)

He, finally, incurred the hatred of the army by the most atrocious crime; for, displeased that Brigadier General Thiébault should have acquitted two soldiers arraigned on a false charge and whom he wished shot all the same "as an example," he said, he caused a soldier of Thiébault's brigade to be arrested and shot immediately. He thus took his revenge by an assassination. This act would be incredible if it were not vouched for by Thiébault himself, who was as reliable as he was brave.

On his return from Portugal, General Leclerc was soon the recipient of a fresh favour as a reward for his services during his first command. Bonaparte was organising an expedition to re-conquer the colony of Haiti (or San Domingo as this island was then still commonly called), of which the slaves, who had revolted in 1792, had ever since been the masters. He took the precaution to gain the consent of England, with whom peace had not yet been concluded, before embarking on this expedition. When the necessary naval and military forces were concentrated at Lorient and Brest, Admiral Villaret-Joyeuse was given the command of the fleet and General Leclerc was appointed commander-in-chief of the whole expedition.

Whilst the troops were preparing for their departure, the First Consul had told his sister that she must accompany her husband to Haiti. This was opposed to the wishes of both. The Duchesse d'Abrantès says:

I believe, that General Leclerc would very willingly have dispensed with this addition to his baggage, for it was a real calamity, after having exhausted the pleasure of regarding her for a quarter of an hour, to have the terrible burden of continually amusing, occupying, and looking after Madame Leclerc.

But the First Consul deemed the departure of his sister necessary to put a stop to the scandal caused by certain excesses in which Madame Leclerc was indulging, and to which Madame de Rémusat alludes without specifying them. (Madame de Rémusat, *Mémoires*.)

Before leaving Paris, Madame Leclerc paid several visits. She was with her friend Madame Junot more than ever, and her bizarre, fantastic character allowed itself full play. At one time she would appear enchanted at the idea of taking part with her "little Leclerc," as she called him, in an expedition which promised so many wonderful adventures, in which she intended to amuse herself enormously. At another time she would be overwhelmed with despair at the bare thought of her departure. She would exclaim:

"How bored I shall be down there, alone with my husband! I cannot bring myself to leave Paris; no, indeed, it is only in Paris that I can live. I cannot understand how my brother can expect a wife to go with her husband! It is ridiculous to the last degree! What difference can it make if I stay and amuse myself in Paris instead of going and boring myself in the society of the general in that barbarous country? Oh, I shall die if I go, I am certain of it! Besides, I am already ill."

And then she would bemoan her unhappy lot, and shed tears over her death as if it were about to occur. She was so overcome at the thought of dying, that she excited the pity of Madame Junot.

"Don't give way like this," said her friend to her one day; "you are making yourself utterly miserable. Just think, you are going to a country where you will be queen. Slaves will carry you in a *palanquin*, beautiful negresses will cradle you in a hammock, under the finest trees in the world, and fan you with immense fans of feathers. It will be an enchanted existence!"

"But the savages? the serpents?"

"Savages! there are no longer any; and besides, you will be surrounded by a whole army of brave men. As for serpents, how could a single one reach Haiti, since it is an island?"

"That is true; you reassure me. Well, I must go and prepare my dresses to turn the heads of the people of the country. Tell me, shall I be sufficiently pretty, do you think, for them, if I wear a *Madras* handkerchief on my head *à la créole*?"

Her friend ordered a Madras handkerchief to be brought, and bound the charming head of Madame Leclerc in its gaudy-coloured folds.

"Yes," she said, "that is not so bad. Oh, I have an idea, Laurette; will you come with me to Haiti? We will give dances, and have parties in the mountains and on the sea; it would be delightful!"

But Madame Junot gently reminded her that she was *enceinte*.

"Ah, true," replied Pauline, "I had not thought of that."

And at the thought of going to Haiti without her friend the tears began to flow again. A moment later all was forgotten. (Duchesse d'Abrantès.)

Madame Leclerc amused herself in preparing for her voyage as if the day of departure would never arrive. She accumulated mountains of costumes, pyramids of hats, piles of useless articles of all descriptions, till it seemed as if it would be impossible to find room in the whole fleet for her luggage. General Leclerc was staggered at the idea of such a convoy, and suggested it should be reduced.

"Then I remain, as I should like to," replied his charming wife; and the general was obliged to yield.

As long as she was at Paris, and afterwards at Brest, everything went well. The preparations and the thought of the voyage distracted her. But when it came to the point of embarking on the *Océan*, which was to carry her to Haiti, it was quite another matter. She wept, she implored, she swore that she would never put her foot on board. . . . However, Fréron, her former lover, was going in the same ship. ("By a malicious intention of her powerful brother she had made this long crossing in the company of her ex-Romeo, the handsome Fréron?" Th. Jung.)

But even this did not comfort her; she did not wish to go further than Brest. As there were no palanquins at Brest, she was put in a carriage and driven to the jetty, where she was deposited by two stalwart sailors in the admiral's launch, and conducted without further delay on board the *Océan*. Her son, little Dermide, went with her. The fleet then weighed anchor, the ships defiled majestically, with all sails set, out of the harbour of Brest, and rapidly vanished beyond the misty horizon.

General Leclerc was not the man to direct so important an expedition, and moreover he knew nothing of colonial affairs. The indecision of his character and his cautious, improvident administration were in a great part the causes of the failure of the campaign and the almost complete loss of the army. On his arrival, he established his headquarters at Cap Haitien. The blacks had set fire to it while the French troops were landing, but the sailors of the fleet succeeded in arresting the progress of the fire before the town had been totally destroyed. Later General Leclerc moved with his wife and staff to Tortuga, a small

AN EPISODE DURING THE ATTEMPT OF THE FRENCH TO
RECONQUER HAITI

island on the Haitian coast, which was safe from the sudden fanatical attacks of the blacks as well as being an agreeable and healthy spot.

In this latter respect unfortunately the same could not be said of the main island. Malaria, yellow fever, cholera, the murder of sentinels, and the massacre of isolated detachments decimated the troops, whose courage was undaunted by misfortune, and rapidly placed the expedition in the most awkward situation, to which the incapacity of the commander-in-chief also contributed its share. By degrees the army was obliged to put itself on the defensive. Cap Haitien was besieged. Leclerc, who had returned there with his wife and child in the hope of repairing the blunders he had made, realising the heavy responsibility that rested on him, commenced to fail in health. All this no doubt prevented him from observing the follies to which his wife abandoned herself in Haiti as she had done in Paris.

Detailed information as to Madame Leclerc's eccentricities in Haiti is lacking, but it is known that she pursued pleasure furiously. The Chancellor Pasquier, a man not given to levity, says (*Mémoires*), that "the tropical sun was astonished at the ardour of her pleasures." It seems, however, that Madame Leclerc displayed at a certain critical juncture extraordinary coolness, which might, perhaps, likewise have astonished the same sun. Constant, the first valet of Napoleon, relates in his *Memoirs* with what *sangfroid* Madame Leclerc behaved during the war in Haiti. He obtained his information, he says, from one who was in her service at the time.

It is not, however, altogether to be trusted, for in the imperial *entourage* one was ever too ready to credit all the members of Napoleon's family with qualities and merits that they hardly if at all possessed. As it was impossible to eulogise Madame Leclerc's private life, while tributes to her beauty had from their frequency become banal, people hoped, no doubt, to flatter Napoleon by relating how heroically his sister, the frivolous Pauline, had behaved. Otherwise, her heroism seems scarcely credible. The following is what was related of it.

About the end of October, 1802, General Leclerc, after having evacuated in succession Fort Dauphin and Port de Paix, withdrew to the north of the island and occupied Cap Haitien. His blunders had now made him ill, and the insurgents, notified by their spies of his illness, wished to profit by this circumstance to attack the whites. On the 28th, Christophe, Clervaux, and Dessalines, at the head of more than twelve thousand blacks, laid siege to Cap Haitien. Before this horde, the French, reduced to about a thousand men, abandoned the advance posts and the surrounding heights, and shut themselves up in the town. The blacks assaulted it vigorously, and were repulsed no less vigorously, with the morose fury of despair. Each knew that in the event of the capture of the town the blacks would give no quarter to the whites. It was an atrocious struggle, a struggle to the death.

General Leclerc, although very ill, directed the defence in person. During this time Madame Leclerc and little Dermide were in the house which the commander-in-chief had chosen as his headquarters. To protect her she had a devoted friend and a half-company of artillery. The house was situated at the foot of the hills that fringed the coast, but fearing lest the blacks should press the attack at this point and not feeling at all confident as to the definite issue of the struggle, Leclerc sent by an *aide-de-camp* an order to his wife to withdraw with her son on board one of the ships of the fleet. Pauline, however, replied that she preferred to remain in the house. The ladies of the town, who, to keep up one another's courage, had gathered around her in this critical situation, implored her to obey her husband's order.

"You can go if you like," she said; "you are not the sister of Bonaparte."

General Leclerc, on being informed of her decision, sent the *aide-de-camp* again to his wife with the order to tie her into a chair, if necessary, for on board he was determined she should go, either of her own accord or by force. Pauline, persisting in her refusal to quit the house, was consequently tied fast to a chair as her husband had ordered, and conducted, under an escort of artillerymen, to the pier, where a boat was waiting to take her on board. A soldier, carrying Dermide in his arms, walked at her side, while the women of the town followed, to seek also a refuge on the French ships. But on arriving at the pier an *aide-de-camp* came to announce the end of the battle and the flight of the blacks.

"Now you see," said Pauline, " whether I was right or not in refusing to inconvenience myself."

Seeing the last assault repulsed and the enemy routed, Leclerc collapsed. He died of cholera a few nights later, on November 1, 1802.

Madame Leclerc was capable of any and every whim. In these trying circumstances she proved herself a devoted wife, and during the short illness of her husband she did not leave his bed, nursing him, in spite of the danger of infection, with tender care.

She also was ill; not from cholera—but the zest with which she had pursued pleasure since her arrival in Haiti. She returned to France with her little son, Dermide, on the *Swiftsure*, taking with her the body of her unfortunate husband. After his death she displayed her devotion to him—which, hitherto, unless it was during the last three days of his life, he had never experienced—by placing him in a superb coffin of cedar-wood. Further, finding that her hair was falling from ill-health and being advised by the doctors to cut it, she did so, declaring with a sigh that "she offered it as a sacrifice to the shade of the dead."

Pauline, whom flattery at this time compared to Artemis, arrived at Toulon in the month of January, 1803, and went immediately to Paris, where she made a theatrical display of her grief. Fouché declares that she was overjoyed to find herself free. It is not unlikely, but if she rejoiced, she did not forget she was ill. Madame de Rémusat asserts (*Mémoires*), that she was "ever after subject to attacks of the malady with which she was at this time first afflicted." And Madame d'Abrantès says (*Mémoires*), "that she had for some time a sore in her hand, which to the despair of the doctors was no sooner cured than it reappeared."

Fouché is a little more explicit on the subject of this mysterious illness. He says, (*Mémoires*), it was the result of dissipation, and that "she had recourse to all the treasures of Aesculapius before she was cured." He adds:

"A remarkable thing, about this wonderful cure was that her beauty, far from being impaired, was more brilliant than ever, like that of those curious flowers that require to be fertilised before they open."

The praise that Fouché bestowed on her beauty was echoed by Madame de Rémusat, who declared that "although ailing and dressed in deepest mourning, Madame Leclerc seemed to me the most charming person I had ever seen."

5

On her return to Paris the First Consul insisted that she should give him her word of honour as a guarantee of her future good behaviour. To please him she gave it to him, without any intention of being bound by it. But Bonaparte, who had very limited faith in his sister's promises, knowing that neither marriage nor widowhood had sobered her, commissioned his brother Joseph and his wife, Julie, to watch her conduct. He wished her period of mourning to be passed in the conventional fashion, resolving to find another husband for her as soon as it was over. Madame Leclerc, accordingly, took up her abode with Joseph in the splendid *Hôtel Marboeuf* in the Rue du Faubourg Saint-Honoré, which was later given as a wedding present to the wife of Marshal Suchet.

The body of General Leclerc was buried in the Panthéon, in state, like that of a commander-in-chief who had been killed in action.

The death of his brother-in-law gave rise to a little incident that, to close observers, indicated the monarchical tendency which was becoming more and more marked in the daily habits of the first magistrate of the Republic. General Bonaparte had naturally gone into mourning for Leclerc, and as a mark of respect his household, from the palace officials and attendants on Madame Bonaparte down to the grooms and scullery-maids, had followed his example. This was quite natural, but it was remarked the diplomatic corps also wore black when they paid their official visits of condolence to the First Consul and his wife. This was due to a suggestion that had been previously circulated, to the effect that it would be etiquette to wear black; and as the ambassadors had no time to refer the matter to their courts, this opinion had prevailed, and the ambassadors paid their visits in state. 'They could not have done more had he been a sovereign.

Madame Leclerc, however, was soon bored to death. Incapable of finding any occupation, never opening a book, never singing or playing, and as little able to use a pencil or a pen as she was to use a needle, it seemed to her that the days were endless.

"Oh," she would sigh a hundred times a day, "I am so bored that I shall die; and if my brother continues to prevent me from seeing people, I shall kill myself!"

In the meantime, while waiting to put this threat into execution, she sought to kill time, and when the weather was fine, she had herself carried about in a litter, as the means of taking the air best suited to her delicate health. She would, too, frequently interpret the promise she had made her brother in a very liberal sense, and receive visitors. There was no great harm in this, and those who visited her at first were only old friends, the Permons, General and Madame Junot, and some others. She soon, however, took advantage of their coming to invite others.

One in particular, whom she sent for more than once, was a fortune-teller, whom she had formerly consulted in Marseilles, where she was celebrated in the days when General Bonaparte was not. She had a weakness, in common with her sister-in-law, Josephine, for consulting prophetesses, sorcerers, and other persons of the same stamp, and like Josephine, too, she believed in their predictions more than she believed in God.

Nothing was more grotesque than to see this fortune-teller solemnly seated at a table in a superb *boudoir* filled with the choicest works of art, while the beautiful widow contemplated her with the closest attention. "She was a little woman, with a wrinkled face and meanly clad, but not lacking in cunning, and her eyes, though very small, were piercing." (Général de Ricard.) What the fortune-teller predicted is not known, but there is considerable information as to what Pauline did, in spite of the orders of the First Consul and the surveillance under which she lived while at her brother Joseph's. This princess, "a glutton in pleasure," to employ a phrase of Madame de Motteville, sought consolation, or rather distraction, and her amusements were not of the sort that conform either with morality or conventionality.

Her conduct was light to a degree. She had several liaisons, which she did not attempt to hide, one especially, that was the talk of Paris, being with Lafon, an actor of the *Théâtre Français*. Her fancy for this comedian had begun before her departure for Haiti, and was, perhaps, its cause. The First Consul had found it an excellent opportunity to nip this *liaison* in the bud. But the voyage to Haiti was only an *entr'acte*; on her return Pauline recommenced her little comedy with the comedian. From all accounts Lafon was madly in love with her. When it was reported at the *Théâtre Français* that Madame Leclerc would accompany her husband on the distant expedition he was to command, Mademoiselle Duchesnois exclaimed, "Lafon will never get over it; it is certain to kill him!"

The fresh gallantries of the incorrigible Pauline soon reached the ears of Napoleon. He was very annoyed, but he could do nothing. To shut her up in a convent was out of the question. A husband, however, he thought might keep her quiet.

Pauline had at this time taken a fancy to Prince Camille Borghèse, who had recently arrived in Paris from Rome. The fact, however, that he possessed an income of two million *francs*, joined to looks of a type scarcely likely to attract Pauline, would lead one to suppose that there was more calculation than love in her fancy for Prince Borghèse. At any rate, the *liaison* had hardly become public before the First Consul interfered and resolved to render it respectable by marriage. The prince was induced to believe he was in love with Pauline, and consented to marry her. Both acted foolishly in this matter, but did so with their eyes open.

Camille Borghèse was a Roman prince, who had served in the

Prince Camille Borghèse

ranks of the French Army during its first campaign in Italy. Although he belonged to one of the most distinguished and richest families in Rome, although he was the great-nephew of the Pope Paul V., he had been, says Méneval, one of the first in Italy to accept the principles of the French Revolution. For this he was much praised in France, but when one knows his motive, the praise was scarcely deserved. For Camille Borghèse had a brother, Prince Aldobrandini, and in order to save the immense fortune of the family during the events that were revolutionising Italy, one of the brothers joined the French party and the other the Papal. Thus, in the event of the success of the French the fact that one of the brothers could prove he belonged to the patriotic party would cause the Borghèse estates to be respected, while in case of defeat he who belonged to the Papal party would likewise serve to protect them.

Prince Borghèse was not altogether devoid of good looks; with his black whiskers and curly hair, he had a certain air of distinction, spoilt, however, by the grotesque manner in which he carried himself, that made him look like a clown dressed *à la mode*. On coming to Paris, he lived in the same splendid and luxurious state as that to which he had been accustomed in Rome. The *Hôtel d'Ogny* that he rented in the Rue Grande-Batelière was superb. He loved horses, and his equipages were soon cited as the equal of those of Prince de Fuentès-Pignatelli and Prince Demidof, who at that time were the standard by which Paris judged smartness. But if no one could drive a coach and four better than he, no one was less able to carry on a conversation.

An excellent coachman, a perfect horseman, he was nothing out of a saddle or off the box-seat of a carriage.

His intelligence, moreover, was limited, though he possessed enough to prove his mediocrity. As a boy his education had been neglected, and he had picked up all he knew as he best could, for his father. was of the opinion that his children would always know enough for the subjects of the Pope. When he arrived in Paris, finding the conversation of his *concierge*, whom he thought *distingué*, suited to his taste, he passed his evenings with him and his wife. But with his name and his fortune he soon received invitations and made friends. He was in demand everywhere, and acquired a reputation as a good dancer and a good fellow. In a word, he was as good-natured as he was stupid.

Marriage between such a man and Pauline would be incomprehensible if vanity had not been the motive of both. She wished to be a princess, and the prince was flattered at the idea of becoming brother-in-law of the First Consul of the Republic. It was, too, a step in the direction of monarchy, and this union insensibly prepared opinion. If Pauline and the Bonapartes were flattered at this union, or rather with the alliance with this Roman prince, the Italians on their side were equally pleased.

★★★★★★★★★★

"My origin," Napoleon himself said, "has caused me to be regarded by all Italians as a compatriot. When my sister Pauline married Prince Borghèse there was only one opinion in Rome and in Tuscany in the family of the latter and all its branches: 'It is not a *mésalliance*, they said; 'she belongs to one of our old families'" (*Mémorial*, August 6, 1816).

★★★★★★★★★★

The same, however, can scarcely be said of the Faubourg Saint-Germain, which, on the creation of the Empire, observed, with as much jealousy as irony, "that there was at least a *real* princess in the Bonaparte family."

As *dot*, Napoleon gave his sister 500,000 *francs*. Pauline brought her husband besides the estate of Montgobert, not far from Paris and at about the same distance from Mortefontaine, the seat of her brother Joseph, and from Plessis-Chamant, that of Lucien. Prince Borghèse had a fortune of which the income was two millions, a gallery of pictures and sculptures that was considered one of the finest in Europe, and a collection of diamonds the bare thought of which intoxicated with joy his frivolous *fiancée*.

The First Consul was at the camp of Boulogne when the marriage took place. It was solemnised at Joseph's superb place at Mortefontaine, and the couple shortly afterwards left for Rome. Prince Borghèse appeared devoted to his wife; her affection for him, however, seemed to have exhausted itself before marriage, and as always in such cases, there was none left for her husband.

Borghèse would have liked to lead a quiet *bourgeois* existence, but his wife would not hear of it. Certain social functions were obligatory, particularly the customary calls on the different members of the family. Of these, the visit to be paid to Madame Bonaparte was the most important. What a pleasure, what a revenge, for Pauline to call as a princess on her sister-in-law, whom she hated, and who was only Madame Bonaparte *tout court!* This visit was a great event in her life. She wished to crush Josephine with her splendour, who in this respect feared no rival. The colour, the material, and the style of her dress were matters of too great importance to be settled in a moment.

After having taken various opinions, discussed the matter in detail and cautioned secrecy, she declared that she would wear a costume of green velvet and all the Borghèse diamonds. She spent the whole day in dressing, assisted by a regular staff of maids. When ready to set out she was dazzling in her glittering shell of diamonds. Not only were her dress and head covered with them, but her neck, her arms, her hands; she was like a river of fire. On looking at herself for the last time in a mirror before getting into the carriage, she was so delighted at the dazzling reflection that her joy scarcely permitted her to speak.

Josephine was staying at this time at St. Cloud. On the way thither Pauline had time to compose herself and accustom herself to the happiness of being so beautiful. The thought of the rage of her sister-in-law when she beheld her gave her exquisite pleasure. Never woman was happier—if vanity, doubled by a little jealousy and a dash of wickedness, is happiness—than Pauline when driving from Paris to St. Cloud.

On her side, too, Madame Bonaparte had prepared for battle. She had been informed of all the details of her sister-in-law's *toilette*, and knowing that she would wear green velvet, she thought that the effect of this colour might be considerably diminished by a background entirely in blue. Inspired by this charitable idea, she had the *salon* in which she proposed to receive Princess Borghèse entirely upholstered in blue. In seeking to counteract as far as possible her sister-in-law's triumph, she neglected nothing to increase her own. Pauline would be covered in diamonds, Josephine affected the greatest simplicity.

The arrival of the Princess Borghèse in the courtyard of the Château of St. Cloud caused great excitement. It was nine o'clock at night. The carriage, richly decorated with the Borghèse arms, was drawn by six horses. A piqueur preceded and another followed on horseback, each having a torch. All the windows of the *château* were filled with people, curious to behold a sight to which they had not been accustomed since the commencement of the Revolution.

Pauline thoroughly enjoyed all the noise and light, but her heart opened like a rose at the first kiss of the morning sun when she heard the usher, on opening the door of the *salon*, announce:—

"Monseigneur le Prince and Madame la Princesse Borghèse."

These words produced a magical effect Everybody rose, Madame Bonaparte like the others, and waited with a gracious smile while her sister-in-law approached. To Pauline, intoxicated by the general murmur of admiration as she crossed the room, it seemed as if she walked in a ray of sunshine. If ever the word "dazzling," applied to a woman, was deserved, it will describe Pauline at this moment. Her beauty really sparkled in the flame of the flashing jewels she wore. The effect she produced was, no doubt, loud and vulgar, but it was prodigious. Pauline's conviction, however, of her success was so serious as to be droll.

The visit passed off well, Josephine was exceedingly gracious, and had the kindness to compliment the princess, with a slightly mocking smile, on her dress. Pauline no less graciously accepted the compliment; and the visit finished, the sisters-in-law kissed one another with an amiable smile, as if they had not detested one another for years.

On returning to Paris Princess Borghèse invited Madame Junot, whom she met at Josephine's, to accompany her. Madame Junot at first discreetly refused.

"I do not like," she said, "to interrupt a *tête-à-tête* with the prince. You are in the middle of your honeymoon, you know—and——"

"A honeymoon with that fool!" cried Pauline. "How absurd to think such a thing!" (Duchesse d'Abrantès)

In reality Madame Junot did not think it, and seeing from Pauline's reply that there was no reason why she should not accept her invitation, she went back to Paris by the light of the princess's torches. On the way Pauline, who, because she was a princess, believed she had no need to be polite and had entered her carriage before her friend, made the following reflections:—

"Did you see, Laurette, how all those women were dying of jealousy? I came late on purpose. I knew my brother would have left, but that was nothing. If I did not see him, the others saw me! But did you notice how jealous *she* was? Her face had an expression that spoke volumes. Well, I am delighted. She thought to play me a mean trick by making me cross the room alone, but she little knew in acting thus all the pleasure she gave me, for it enabled me to display my beauty and my dress to the best advantage. I produced the effect I desired. But what an idiotic idea to receive in a blue *salon!* It was very ugly; blue goes with nothing—and yet they say she has taste!" (Duchesse d'Abrantès)

6

Some days after this the young couple left for Italy. Scarcely had she arrived at Rome when the Princess Borghèse, who had now quite ceased to love her husband, though he was, however, still very smitten with her, became involved in intrigues even in his very palace.

Everybody knows the beautiful Palazzo Borghèse, that is called in Rome the *Piano Borghèse*, because in form it resembles that instrument. The memory, however, of Pope Paul V., who built it, did not succeed in instilling gravity to the light character of the new inmate of this celebrated mansion. But then Paul V. himself, Pope though he was, had not been free from vanity, or rather from the deadly sin of pride, when he had inscribed above the lofty pillars of the grand central portico of this too splendid palace: *"Paulus V., Burghesius Romanus."*

The strange manner in which Pauline interpreted her duty as a wife was hardly affected by the death of her son, little Dermide Leclerc, the godson of Napoleon. 'The princess, however, according to certain historians, displayed heroic courage in the face of this misfortune, and insisted on preparing her child for burial with her own hands. It may be true. Fantastic women, whose hearts are as light as their heads, often act as if they were good. Unfortunately, with them their actions are only whims, and the good ones are rare.

As for the prince, he suffered much at first from his wife's indifference, and still more from her infidelity. In Italy, however, where such things were excused by the customs of the period, and where even the name of the lover of the bride appeared in the marriage contract as part of her *dot*, this was not of much consequence. But in France, in spite of the great laxity of morals that prevailed at this time, it gave occasion for scandal.

Prince Borghèse, who might have expected such treatment from his wife, but who doubtless did not expect it so soon, should have armed himself with philosophy, and, like many another husband, endured his wife and his misfortune patiently. He had a thought of divorcing her, but his powerful brother-in-law, now become Emperor, would not hear the word "divorce" mentioned in his family. He did not yet foresee that after having failed to divorce Josephine on his return from Egypt for the most serious offence, he would some years later have recourse to divorce when he could allege no other motive but his own pleasure, or rather his convenience and that of his dynasty, which is the same thing.

There was, then, no judicial separation between the prince and princess, but they no longer lived together. As a consolation the First Consul appointed his brother-in-law lieutenant-colonel in one of the cavalry regiments in the Consular Guard. But later, for sake of appearances, the emperor insisted on a reconciliation between the husband

and wife. This took place at Nice in 1807, after the Peace of Tilsit, but it did not last long.

When the First Consul was proclaimed Emperor of the French, the whole Imperial family (save Madame Letizia, known henceforth as Madame — Mere, and Lucien) came to Paris for the coronation. Napoleon had quarrelled with Lucien for having married, against his express command, a certain Madame Jouberthon, a divorced woman who had been his mistress, after having been that of many others, and who completely ruled him. He had gone to settle in Rome and his mother had followed him there. Madame Mère figures, however, in David's great picture of the coronation which is now in the Louvre. It was by the emperor's order that she was included in this picture, for the imperious character of Napoleon was as capable of constraining history to obey him as everything else.

The coronation was, of course, an immense event in the Bonaparte family. But the sight of the Pope coming to Paris to consecrate one of its members lawful sovereign of France in the face of Europe and its representatives fired all sorts of ambitions among the brothers and sisters of the emperor, and awoke jealousy and hatred. The elevation of Elisa to the rank of sovereign princess of Piombino was one of the causes of the family broils. Pauline and Caroline pestered their brother in their turn to do something for them too. The emperor finally consented.

On March 30, 1806, a series of decrees was sent to the Senate which created as profound an impression in France as in Europe. Cambacérès read them to the Senate. The first regulated everything which concerned the Imperial household and fixed the duties of the princes and princesses to the emperor; another made Prince Murat sovereign ruler of the Duchies of Berg and Cleves; while another granted the little territory of Guastalla, raised to the dignity of a principality, to the Princess Borghèse. In virtue of this decree her husband bore the title of Prince of Guastalla; and if they had no children the emperor could dispose of this principality as he liked.

Pauline was intoxicated with joy on learning that she had become a reigning princess. But since her education had been much neglected and she had not deemed it necessary after her rise in the world to make up for lost time, she still remained very ignorant.

"What is Guastalla, *fratello caro?*" she asked the emperor. "It is a city, I suppose, and I shall have a fine palace, subjects, and an army with fine regiments and handsome officers."

THE EMPEROR NAPOLEON

"Guastalla is a village," replied Napoleon, in amazement, "in the States of Parma and Placentia."

"Only a village!" exclaimed the capricious princess. "I should not have believed it, the name is so pretty. You are fooling me. What do you think I can do with a village?"

"Do what you please with it."

"What I please? I repeat, of what use do you suppose a village is to me? You have made Annunziata Grand Duchess of Berg and Cleves, and you have given her a State, a real State with ministers and an army; while to me, who am older than she, you only give a miserable village and a few pigs running about it. Good God!"

And she began to weep.

As the emperor impatiently left her, she said to him—

"My very dear brother, I warn you that I shall scratch out your eyes if you do not give me a State to govern a little bigger than a pocket-handkerchief, with subjects who have not four feet and a twisted tail. I need it for myself and for my husband. . . ."

"He is a fool."

"Nobody knows that better than I; but what, pray, has that got to do with governing a country?"

Pretty Pauline, so happy on learning that she was a reigning princess, was now as unhappy to know that Guastalla was only a village. (Comte d'Hérisson *Le Cabinet Noir.*) But her tears were not without effect. The emperor, by a decree of the Senate, later satisfied her by creating for her husband a new and great Imperial dignity. He made him Governor-General of the Provinces beyond the Alps.

On September 21, 1807, Napoleon went with the empress to Fontainebleau, and never was his court more brilliant than during the two month she remained there.

Among those invited to accompany the sovereigns were Hortense, Queen of Holland; Caroline, Grand Duchess of Berg and Cleves; Madame Mére; the Grand Duke and Grand Duchess of Baden; the Prince Primate; the Grand Duke of Würtzburg; the two Princes of Mecklenburg; the Prince of Saxe-Coburg; the Ministers of the Empire and those of Italy; the Prince of Benevento and the Prince of Neufchâtel, each of whom had a household, as well as the great officers of the Imperial household and a number of others. Princess Pauline was necessarily of the party.

Among all the pretty women at Fontainebleau she was the most remarked. At night, seen in the blaze of a thousand candles, or in the day, her beautiful eyes and her creamy complexion were equally dazzling. The emperor desired that the ladies of his court should join him when he hunted in the forest, as he frequently did in the fine, sunny autumn weather. He organised even the women. A council, presided over by the empress, assisted by Leroy, the chief milliner then in vogue, designed their habit.

"It was," says Madame de Rémusat, "a kind of tunic or *redingote* in velvet, short, with a skirt of embroidered white satin. The boots as well as the hat were of velvet to match the skirt, and there was a white scarf."

The empress had chosen for herself a purple habit with gold embroidery, and a hat of the same colour, also embroidered with gold. All her household naturally adopted her colour. On the other hand, Queen Hortense chose blue and silver; while the Princess Borghèse, after a great deal of hesitation, decided upon lilac and silver embroidery. This habit suited her wonderfully, for nothing could have harmonised better with her complexion, always a trifle pale, than lilac.

It would have been difficult to behold a more pleasing sight than this squadron of women habited for the chase, although it was somewhat suggestive of a cavalcade of circus-riders, as they plunged into the sombre forest, flecked with gold by the rays of the sun and the autumn-tinted leaves. The tails of the horses, the laughter, the ostrich plumes, the cracking of the whips, mingled in the air with the tinkling of bells and the heavy beat of the galloping horses. . . . Then the vision disappeared in the foliage of the forest trees, while there resounded afar the brazen sound of the horns calling the hunters to assemble.

History has abstained from chronicling the pranks of the Princess Pauline during her stay at Fontainebleau. Her state of health, over which she worried herself less, however, than she worried her entourage, was perhaps the cause; while the discipline which the emperor maintained in his court was certainly another. But although Lord Holland writes that "if the court of Napoleon was not the most polished and delightful, it was the least dissipated and immoral of any France had had for three centuries," it would be difficult to find a gathering of women more corrupt, with certain rare exceptions, than that which formed the Imperial court. How could it be otherwise, when the empress, her daughter, and her sisters-in-law were the first to set a vicious example? (Lord Holland, *Souvenirs des Cours de France, &.*)

It was during this year 1807 that Pauline, bored as usual, took it into her head to learn music. There was at the time in Paris an Italian composer named Blangini, whose graceful melodies and songs, which he sung himself in drawing-rooms, were much in vogue. So, Pauline sent for Blangini and ordered him to teach her to sing. He accordingly obeyed—so well, in fact, that after having taken up music the princess took up the musician, and after a few days made him musical director of her household. This had occurred before the departure of the court for Fontainebleau. On returning from Fontainebleau, the Empress Josephine, who, if she piqued herself on knowing music and protecting artists, did not pique herself on seeking to please her sisters-in-law, particularly Pauline, took it into her head to give Blangini the same post in her own household.

On hearing this Blangini went to Pauline and told her.

"Ah," she said, "that is so like the empress. Till I noticed you she never gave you a thought, but now she wants to deprive me of your services by acquiring them for herself. My dear Blangini, it is for you to choose between her and me."

Blangini protested that his choice was irretrievably made, and that he could desire no greater happiness than to be allowed to devote his existence to her whose favour he had first won.

A smile was the reward of this flattering response; but his constancy was later to receive from this inconstant fair other and more material benefits.

Doting for the moment on harmony, the princess took to writing songs, which she got Blangini to set to music for her. One, of which the words were by her and the music by Blangini, had immense success, and she was so delighted that she sent her collaborator, as a means of thanking him, a splendid jewel. One must admit that if Pauline was often inclined to avarice—as she was to all the other deadly sins—she had still more often bursts of generosity.

When she had artists to sing at her receptions, she knew how to recompense them in a manner worthy of their talent. Thus, she gave Garat a valuable scarf-pin as a souvenir of the first time he sang for her. Crescentini, who was a Knight of the Iron Crown, received a diamond cross; and Madame Grassini a superb ornament. It is only fair to say that never was a reigning house so generous to artists as Napoleon and the princes and princesses of his family.

The following is an example of their generosity, which, in this instance, was excessive:—

Princess Pauline, who was one evening entertaining her brother Louis, King of Holland, requested Blangini to sing. He, unfortunately, had a cold and was unable to sing a note.

"Where in the name of the devil did you pick up such a cold?" asked the King of Holland.

"Yesterday, sire, while walking in the rain."

"Princess Pauline," said the king at once, turning to his sister, "how can you let your musical director walk? You should give him a carriage. Promise Blangini that he shall have from tonight what I ask for him."

"I promise," said Pauline.

And this is how Blangini came to have his *coupé*, two horses, and the money necessary to keep them and a coachman into the bargain. (Blangini, *Souvenirs*.)

7

Towards the end of 1808 the Princess Borghèse went to Nice for her health. She had previously taken the thermal baths at Gréoulx, in Provence. All the bathers who have taken this cure are familiar with the little Château de Laval, to which Pauline often drove, and also the old oak that is still called the Princess's Oak, under which she would pass the whole day.

At Nice she resided in a charming house belonging to a M. Vinaille, which she had rented for the season. It was beautifully situated, with a garden filled with orange-trees and sweet-smelling flowers that extended to the sea. (Later a convalescent home for naval and military officers.)

The princess had left etiquette behind her in Paris. The regulation of etiquette, at the time the Empire was proclaimed, had at first greatly amused her, and, like her sisters, she was pitiless in exacting all the honours due to her rank. The emperor had even been annoyed by the refusal of these recently created princesses to abate a little of their pride. But with etiquette, as with everything else, Pauline had ended by being bored; and at Nice there was not a suspicion of it. In the mornings the princess breakfasted alone in her room, and in the evenings dined with her whole household.

This little court was composed of Madame de Chambaudoin, Madame de Barral, Mademoiselle Millot, her reader, and Mademoiselle Faivre, her maid of honour; while Dr. Peyre was responsible not only for the health of the princess and her ladies, but for the general management of the household. Soon, the walks in the beautiful garden, the drives, and excursions by sea ceased to distract the beautiful, bored

Louis Bonaparte, King of Holland

princess. It was useless to suggest reading or fancy-work. She took a fancy, however, for music, and recollecting that she had a director of music, she sent to Paris for him, and after this there were concerts at her little court. These only took place at night, for after breakfast everybody assembled in the *salon*, where the princess would amuse herself with relating all sorts of anecdotes, more or less *risqué*, of the Imperial court. She spared none of the members of her family, and in moments of excitement related even the most private affairs.

The monotony of the life she led at Nice would have bored others besides Pauline, and she sought to amuse herself in a manner that was not altogether innocent. Dreaming one day, probably of Rosina and Lindor, and perhaps too of Julie and St. Preux, while singing with Blangini she fell suddenly and sympathetically into his arms. From that day the princess manifested a passion for music, or rather, as no one in the little court doubted, for the musician. She was, indeed, so wrapped up in him as to become jealous to the point of refusing to allow him to go out without her permission, and even then, obliging him to say where he was going.

Her permission, moreover, was not always granted. One day the musician informed her that he was engaged to dine in the evening at the *prefect's*.

"Blangini," replied the princess, "this evening you are dining with me."

There were other objections to the position of favourite. It was necessary to guard against the personal jealousy of the little court; there was everything to fear from the emperor, who was sure to be informed of this new caprice of his sister; and there might perhaps also be reason to dread the rage of the offended husband, though this was infinitely less probable. Blangini, who was by nature anything but quarrelsome, had finally worked himself into a state bordering on distraction, when one day his princess invited him to go for a drive with her in her carriage.

At the idea of the unexpected honour paid him he turned pale. It was to announce publicly her *liaison*. What would the emperor say? He who knew so well how to remove their lovers from his sisters by sending them to gallop over Spain and Portugal, where the guerillas disembarrassed him in his turn of them. He feared lest he should be sent by the next mail a subaltern's commission, with the command to carry post a dispatch to Lisbon. And then he would make the acquaintance of bullets and cannon! If this music pleased Charles XII1., who, the first time he heard it, declared he never wished to hear any other, and if it delighted thousands of soldiers in the French Army, it was far from being to the taste of this musician. At the thought the unhappy fellow broke into a cold sweat. Fear, however, gave him courage, and he dared to say—

"Go for a drive with your Imperial Highness! To be compromised in that way! What would the emperor say?"

"I command you to accompany me," replied Pauline, who laughed at everything—at the emperor, at what people would say, and at her lover into the bargain.

This adventure terminated for the pusillanimous musician in a manner that wounded his *amour propre*. Some days later the Princess Pauline told him that the emperor had been informed that she had been for a drive with a "*monsieur,*" but that when he learnt "this *monsieur*" was only her musical director he had said nothing. Blangini was then completely reassured, but he could not at the same time prevent himself from feeling annoyed that the emperor should consider him, after the danger he had run, as a man of no importance. (Blangini, *Souvenirs.*) If it had been Crescentini, *par exemple,* but he...!

One day the Princess Pauline took it into her head to go to Antibes. She wished to revisit the house known as Château-Sallé, where she had lived with her mother and sisters at a time when none of them dreamt of the immense fortune in store for them. As the journey was to be made by water a large barge was engaged. It was gaily decked with flags and festooned with flowers. In the centre of the boat a sort of *howdah* had been erected of glass, with red silk curtains, for the sister of the *puissant* Emperor of the French, along each side of which a double row of rowers, clothed in white with blue facings, ran like a garland. Flattery, of course, did not fail to inform the gracious princess that 'her galley recalled that of Cleopatra when going to meet Antony. Pauline was not quite sure who these personages were, but she acknowledged the comparison as the most delicate of compliments, and her smile testified her pleasure.

This excursion was not made *incognito*. The commandant of Antibes had been notified of the visit of Her Imperial Highness, and he awaited her on the quay, while the whole population lined the banks, less to render homage to the august visitor than to satisfy a very natural curiosity. Scarcely had Pauline set her foot on shore than she was saluted by the cannon which protected Antibes, and conducted to the commandant's house, where every preparation had been made to receive her befittingly. A banquet was given in her honour, after which there was a reception and ball. The following day the visit was made to the house that was the object of the excursion.

On finding herself once more in it, Pauline pretended she was fifteen again; not that she was once more a child—she had never ceased to be one—but playful and gay as a little girl. She ran from room to room, relating prettily her impressions to the official people who followed her.

"That," she said, "was my mother's room. I slept in that little closet next her; my sisters were on the other side of the house. My brother, Napoleon, used to occupy this room when he paid us a surprise visit for a couple of days. Ah, how fond he was of us!"

Indeed, Napoleon proved himself to be the most affectionate and devoted of brothers, but except from Pauline he was destined to receive nothing but ingratitude and treachery!

It was a sensible idea that the frivolous Pauline had conceived in wishing to revisit a spot where she had passed so many happy days as a girl, and it proves that her heart at all events was not completely stifled by the brambles and weeds of her passions, caprices, and vanity. But she should not have revisited Château-Sallé with the pomp she did. It is only in solitude that one can enjoy the reflection of tender memories. The least display, the presence even of a stranger, prevents them from returning to the soul that has experienced them, as a crowd in a flowery mead chases away the butterflies and makes the birds silent.

Not only was Pauline accompanied in state by a train of military and civil functionaries, but she even brought with her her lover, Blangini! What reflections, had she been less frivolous, her soul might have made on the contrast between the innocence of her youth and the moral ruin of her brilliant existence!

On the following day Pauline, enchanted with her excursion, returned to Nice in her galley decked with its multi-coloured flags. The morrow of a *fête* is not often gay. Scarcely had she returned to Nice when a messenger in the emperor's livery brought a dispatch for her Imperial Highness. She no sooner opened it than her face immediately assumed a sullen expression. Someone asked what had happened.

"*Pardi*, it's my husband; who else do you suppose it could be? Yes, the prince is coming tomorrow. The emperor has appointed him something or other in Italy. He is to pass through Nice on his way to Turin, and take me along with him. Could anything be more ridiculous?"

And thereupon the princess, who expressed herself in regard to her husband with the utmost freedom, fell into a rage, in which she said a number of bitter. things, and with a surprising volubility that only women when angry are capable of, the upshot of which was that she would have preferred to remain the widow of General Leclerc, with only twenty thousand *francs* a year, rather than to be the wife of——. (Blangini, *Souvenirs.*) But respect for the reader will not permit the word the princess employed, in the hearing of her whole court, to be repeated.

Prince Borghèse did, indeed, arrive at Nice. Before leaving for Bayonne when he embarked in that unjust and disastrous Spanish War, Napoleon had appointed his brother-in-law Governor-General of the Provinces beyond the Alps. This high post, after having been held by Marshal Jourdan, was then filled by General Menou, he who when in Egypt had become a Mahometan, changed his name to Abdallah, and married an Egyptian woman. All this, however, had not given him talent, and it was owing to his incapacity that Egypt was lost. But Abdallah-Menou, *ci-devant* Marquis de Menou before the Revolution, was seventy, and Napoleon deemed it time for him to retire and to give him a successor. This latter was Prince Borghèse, who received orders to assume the duties of his post at Turin immediately. He had at the same time received a magnificent diploma, illuminated on parchment, which contained the decree of the Senate of 2nd February, creating the Governor-General of the Provinces beyond the Alps a Prince of the Empire.

Commanded by the emperor to go to Turin, to pick up his wife *en route* and carry her with him to the seat of his government, the prince quitted the splendid *Hôtel Borghèse*—formerly the *Hôtel de Choiseul-Charost*, and now the British Embassy in the Rue du Faubourg Saint-Honoré—on April 4, 1808, accompanied by Colonel Curto, his principal *aide-de-camp*. His household followed three days later.

Before leaving Paris, the emperor took a mean advantage of Borghèse. He had done the same once before in the time of the Consulate, when he made him marry his frivolous sister. This time he bought his gallery of sculptures. This collection, unrivalled in Europe, was not for sale. But Napoleon, chatting one morning with his brother-in-law, said—

"*À propos*, Camille, I forgot to tell you that I am buying your statues."

It was in vain that the prince replied that they were not for sale, being heirlooms of his house, which he had not the right to dispose of.

"I did not ask you if you wished to sell them," replied Napoleon, "I said that I would buy them. Name your price."

"Sire," returned Borghèse, "my father refused twenty-five millions that an English company offered him."

"Twenty-five millions! It is too much; I will give you eighteen."

The prince was obliged to submit to his despotic brother-in-law, who was besides equally unscrupulous in paying, for Borghèse was far from getting the eighteen millions he was promised. Accordingly, the unlucky prince was in no very pleasant humour when he went to take up the reins of government at Turin. Nor did the necessity of resuming possession of his wife at Nice tend to restore his good nature. Tricked by his brother-in-law and deceived by his wife, his character began to be embittered. Of a truth there was reason.

His arrival threw the little court at Nice into a state of consternation. Etiquette, or rather constraint, arrived with him. The couple, however, resumed their conjugal yoke as if they had never been estranged. It is true they did not meet at meals, and others were always present to save them from a *tête-à-tête* that they avoided as sedulously as other couples seek it.

The prince only stayed a few days at Nice, merely time enough to allow the necessary preparations to be made for the journey to Turin. He then set out with his wife and suite. The baggage filled seven wagons. They travelled slowly on account of the delicate health of the princess. Delicate, so she said, for her health was good or bad, according to circumstances, like the princess herself. She travelled in a *berline* that had been made expressly for her by the best coachbuilder in Paris; the springs were so elastic and the cushions so soft that it was almost impossible to feel the least jolt.

But this did not prevent the princess from using a sedan-chair as well. Uphill or down, that is to say at every moment, she would quit the *berline* for the sedan. Then a few minutes later she would declare that the motion was insupportable, and that she would be much less fatigued if she went on foot. Alighting, she would proceed to walk like a mere ordinary mortal. But this caprice did not last any longer than the others. She would suddenly recollect she was an invalid and was on the point of dropping from exhaustion. Then she would painfully get into her carriage again, groaning and sighing over the hardships of the journey and the cruelty of her brother who compelled her to undertake it.

But he who had the most reason to complain was poor Prince Borghèse, forced as he was to endure the grievances and caprices of his charming wife. He consequently sought to avoid them as far as possible, getting out of the carriage when she got in, and getting in again when she got out—in short, he made the greater part of the journey on foot. He preferred this, as one can easily understand, to putting up with a *tête-à-tête*. But women, like children, are pitiless. Pauline, as much of a child as a woman, had less pity than any other. Scarcely would the prince seat himself beside her in the *berline* than she would begin to torment him. Her favourite method was by declaring that his Roman title was nothing in comparison with his French one that he owed to his marriage; and she would expatiate on this subject with a complacency and tediousness that was distracting.

"We shall receive addresses in the towns through which we pass," she said, "to which it is my duty rather than yours to reply. I will prove to you that I am right. By the decree of the Senate of February 2nd it was settled that the French princes should take precedence of you. It is true you are also a French prince, though solely by virtue of having married me, and consequently I take precedence of you. That is clear, is it not? Therefore, if you please, I shall reply to the addresses." (Blangini, *Souvenirs*.)

Prince Camille might argue the subject as he liked, he only wasted his eloquence; and in order to preserve what patience he still possessed he would make a numbness in his legs the pretext for getting out of the carriage and walking several miles to calm himself. As for the members of the court, they were obliged, by their position and by respect for etiquette, to endure all the caprices of their sovereign. They had not, like the prince, the resource of dismounting from the carriage to stretch their legs and fortify their patience.

This pretension of Pauline's gave rise to an unpleasant incident on their arrival at the first village under the prince's jurisdiction. The mayor, surrounded with all his subordinates and their families, was waiting on the road outside the village to welcome the Governor-General and his august consort. He delivered his little speech gracefully enough, and stood hat in hand waiting for the reply.

Then occurred a grotesque, absurd scene. The prince was on the point of replying to the mayor, without knowing what he was going to say, when his wife, who for her part certainly knew still less, prevented him from speaking. She told the mayor that it was she who was to reply to official addresses, that it was her duty as well as her honour, and that she would always know how to perform the one and safeguard the other. Then, in conclusion, turning to her husband, she asked if it had not been agreed between them that she would reply to addresses of welcome.

Borghèse impatiently made signs to his wife to be silent; while the mayor, astonished by a discussion which seemed about to degenerate into a quarrel, continued to await his reply, secretly thinking that the prince and princess would have done better to argue in private instead of in the exercise of their official functions. At last, fearing to be indiscreet, he withdrew to the side of the road, followed by his peasants, while Their Highnesses, without replying, but still quarrelling, remounted their carriage and left an unpleasant impression of their passage in the village.

M. de Clermont-Tonnerre hereupon took it upon himself to warn this spoilt child, whose chamberlain he was, of the consequences this little scene might have for her should it reach the ears of the emperor. It was always necessary to threaten her when one wished to make her listen to reason. Pauline was afraid of her brother, and she abandoned her pretensions, swearing, however, that she would have her revenge.

At Coni everything passed off well. Their Highnesses were lodged at the *Prefecture*. The bishop sent them the same evening the address which he was to make to them the following day. The chamberlain spent the night preparing a reply, which the prince repeated the next day without changing countenance. He and the princess had a great reception in this town. Everyone lauded his wit, his tact, and his eloquence, and opinion was unanimous as to the grace and goodness of his distinguished wife. The common people went into raptures over her.

The next day they left Coni at an early hour and proceeded to Racconiggi, the former country residence of the princes of the house of Savoy-Carignan, which has a fine park designed by Le Nôtre. A day later, April 22, 1808, the Governor-General and Princess Borghèse entered Turin. A guard of honour escorted their carriage, *vivats* rent the air, the bells were rung, cannon were fired as if for a victory, and the heart of Pauline beat with joy at the thought that all this fuss was made for her.

They established themselves in the wing of the castle that was known as the Palais Chablais. The princess chose for her apartments those nearest the *Place Impériale*, while her husband was free to make himself at home in the other extremity. M. de Susiano, the *prefect* of the palace, had prepared apartments not only for Their Imperial Highnesses, but also for the members of their suite.

The city of Turin gave them a splendid *fête* at the theatre.

8

The court of Turin was composed almost entirely of the same
persons who formerly made that of the King of Sardinia. (Stanislas Girardin, *Journal et Souvenirs.*) It was extremely brilliant. As to the
household of Princess Borghèse, she had in reality two—one at Turin
and another in Paris. If she took with her to Italy some gentlemen and
ladies-in-waiting from Paris, she brought a little later some Italians to
France. But the two households, although often mingled, remained
very distinct and were never confused.

Mention has already been made of M. de Clermont-Tonnerre. He
possessed certain serious qualities which passed unperceived in the
frivolous world in which he lived. But he had flippant ones too, which
were highly appreciated. He had a gift for making puns, which he did
constantly, and which, in a court that in conversation did not observe
the traditions of *le grand siècle,* earned him a serious reputation as a wit.

M. de Montbreton, another gentleman-in-waiting, had come to
Turin at the same time as M. de Clermont-Tonnerre. He was a thoroughly "good sort." Good husband, good father, good citizen, he had
also been a *bon vivant*, and possessed all the qualities that as a rule are
only accorded to the dead—he was like a good epitaph. His excellent
character and his anxiety to please permitted him to sojourn, without
being the worse for it, in a world that was scarcely exemplary. Indeed,
had he not been, before M. de Forbin, in the highest favour with his
charming mistress?

M. de Forbin was likewise a gentleman-in-waiting, and as distinguished in his appearance and his manner as he was noted for his wit
and his artistic tastes. At once poet, painter, and novelist, it would have
been hard to find a mortal endowed with so many of the attributes
of genius. Being, moreover, as rich as he was intellectual, one might
have wondered how he came to accept the post of mere gentleman-
in-waiting, had it not been the fashion for every well-born man to
dance attendance on one of the Imperial princesses. There was, however, another reason. A lover of the beautiful, he naturally admired a
beautiful woman, and was not the Princess Borghèse beautiful beyond
compare?

At least it pleased M. de Forbin to tell her so in verse and prose, and it pleased Pauline to be praised in any and every manner. M. de Forbin painted her portrait, full face, profile, three-quarters. Pauline, who also loved the beautiful, regarded these pictures with admiration, but above all him who painted them. Believing it her duty to encourage art, she thought she could not do better than encourage artists; and she encouraged M. de Forbin so well that she ended by making him her lover. This idyl, however, attracted the notice of the emperor to the happy gentleman-in-waiting, and was the cause, it is said, of his subsequent banishment.

M. Alfieri de Sostegno, the grand master of the ceremonies, the director-general of etiquette, was a nullity and a bore. He was also a widower. One pretended that his wife had died solely of the *ennui* that emanated from him. The gravity, however, which he feigned concealed his insignificance so cleverly that fools, that is to say the majority, regarded him as profound, for who ought to be bored in a court where all found amusement?

Nor should history forget to mention one who filled the modest position of scullion. He had formerly been a king—of the Congo, it is true, but still a king. This dethroned sovereign, brought from Africa on a slave ship, and sold as a slave. The princess had given him, doubtless out of irony, the name of Don Juan. Before having been relegated to the kitchen Don Juan had been appointed "superintendent-general of the bath of the princess." (Blangini, *Souvenirs.*)

But he had been so penetrated with the importance of his duties, and performed them with so much majesty, that, having no regard for *les convenances*—which at a European court, even though it was that of the Princess Pauline, were not those of the Congo—he had more than once crossed the *salon* during an official reception carrying in his hands the articles that proclaimed his office. As he could never understand that such behaviour was not only not sanctioned by etiquette, but was absolutely incongruous, his mistress had finally lost patience with him and provided him with other employment in the kitchen. Don Juan was a gourmand, so in default of a throne the post of scullion was one which suited him the best.

The household of the princess was not so well furnished with ladies as with gentlemen. Madame de Chambaudoin, however, was conspicuous for her intimacy with her beautiful mistress. Madame de Champagny, whose husband later became Duc de Cadore and Minister of Foreign Affairs, was also a member of Pauline's household. Proper, dignified, and always appearing to be slightly bored, one wondered how she came to be there. Scandal charitably pretended that she was too ugly, too foolish, and too badly dressed not to be virtuous.

Madame de Barral was the favourite of the Princess Pauline. She was as tall as a drum-major, and had a charming, tiny head, full of wit. One could not help asking oneself how so small a head could contain so much wit. It was probably because it found the place in which it lodged so confined that it was always seeking to escape. No one at court dressed better than she.

Madame la Marquise de Bréhan also was charming, with her blond hair rippling in fluffy curls behind her ears. She had great eyes, very small hands and feet, and teeth as white as her skin. Her temperament was as lively as her tongue was caustic, but she was popular and a very devoted friend.

Mademoiselle Millot was a very important personage, though so small herself. She was the princess's reader. The post was a veritable sinecure. So not knowing how to occupy her time, and being constantly in a state of restlessness, Mademoiselle Millot gave free rein to her original turn of mind, which not being restrained by a calm reserve, frequently conceived ideas of which the extravagance was only equalled by the actions of her mistress. There was a romance in her life which finally brought her to her grave.

There were various other ladies, whose names are, however, not worth repeating, unless it be that of Madame Hamelin, the princess's maid. She was the widow of a naval officer, who had been obliged to accept this post, so little in accord with her character, or her station, as a means of educating her children.

Among all these women there were, doubtless, many worthy of respect, but "public opinion held in light esteem those who were in attendance on the Princess Borghèse, for her behaviour was, unfortunately, reflected on the young and pretty women who composed her court." (Madame de Rémusat, *Mémoires*.) It was, too, not every woman whom Pauline would have liked to have had in her household that would accept the honour. It was flatly refused by Madame de Lostanges, among others.

There is no royal establishment without its chaplain. This one possessed two, but never, it must be admitted, had a court greater need of their services. They were the Abbé de Sambussy and the Abbé de Bombelles. The care of the souls of the household was, however, beyond their capacity. In such an atmosphere perhaps even, the chaplains were in need of salvation. Never was *abbé* more singular than the Abbé de Bombelles. He had been a major-general in his youth, in the days when a few privileged persons came into the world with a colonel's *aigrette* on their heads. Later he became a priest, when so many others, like Talleyrand and Fouché, gave up the calling.

So, the *cavalier* manners of the court of the Princess Pauline did not shock this former *cavalier*. At the Restoration, appointed Bishop of Amiens, he preserved, among other habits formed at court or in the barracks, that of dancing, in spite of his violet cassock. He also made a collection, consisting of eighty-four volumes in manuscript, of stories which were more or less edifying. It was Bombelles who, to recall the fact that he had been a major-general, attached two silver stars to his mitre, emblems of his former rank!

Princess Pauline had hardly been a fortnight at Turin when she received a letter from her brother Lucien, informing her that he was coming to visit her. As Lucien was not on good terms with Napoleon, Pauline dared not risk the chance of displeasing the emperor by receiving him at Turin.

She would have preferred to have written her brother not to come on some pretext or other, but Lucien followed in a few hours the letter that he had sent her. She therefore decided to go to Stupinigi, a villa outside Turin, where she intended to spend the summer, and where her brother's visit would not attract attention.

Lucien's visit was the beginning of a series of other visits. 'There were so many that the Chablais Palace was called at this epoch the "Imperial Tavern." The kings and princes coming and going between Italy and France never failed to stop in the Piedmontese capital. Prince Aldobrandini, brother of Prince Borghèse, King Joseph leaving Naples to rule in Spain, King Murat going to Naples to replace him—all stopped at the Chablais and gave an air of great gaiety to Turin.

There were large receptions, dinners, balls, and suppers, but in spite of all Prince Borghèse was bored. He did not know how to kill time any better than his wife. The only paper he read was the *Journal des Modes*, and he was constantly regretting the society of his old friends in Paris, the *concierge* and his family of the *Hôtel d'Ogny*, when, without wife and free from care, he saw the future open before him bright and beautiful.

His wife was not much happier. She, too, frequently yawned. The aversion she had for her husband extended likewise to the nine departments he governed. She wrote letter upon letter to the emperor beseeching him for permission to leave Piedmont, which was not granted. Her fury was far from being dumb.

"I am," she would complain, "a French citizen, and no one has the right to keep me out of my country against my will. Is it because I am Princess Borghèse? A fine excuse! I did not wish the title. I was content to be the widow of General Leclerc, with my twenty thousand *francs* a year. For God's sake why can't I be free to do as I please instead of being tyrannised over in this manner? In truth, if they wished to kill me, they could not find better means. Yes, I am sure they wish to kill me. *Pardi!* this damned climate and the *ennui* which oozes out of this palace will soon do it. They will bury me within three months if I remain here. I am much more ill than any one has any idea of." (Mademoiselle Avrillon, *Mémoires*.)

And in the belief that she was ill, or rather to make others believe it, "she drugged herself and affected to suffer in a manner compatible with her imaginary disorder." (*Ibid.*) She took all sorts of medicine without procuring any benefit. One night at Stupinigi her whole household was roused; the princess declared she was horribly ill and the doctor was sent for. She had convulsions, syncopes, in a word, "all that she had wished to have."

The doctor, who had at first believed that it was merely one of the nervous attacks to which she was subject, was this time really alarmed. He now agreed that a change of air was necessary, and wrote to this effect to the emperor, who finally permitted her to take the cure at Aix, after which she managed to visit Paris.

Napoleon, whom she had exasperated by her previous conduct, lectured her very seriously and made her give him her word that she would behave herself for the future. She promised all he asked—and resumed as before her usual manner of life.

★★★★★★★★★★

Her beauty gave her so much pleasure that not wishing to deprive her *entourage* of the pleasure of admiring her beautiful form, she had Canova execute her statue—the famous *Vénus Victorieuse*. À *propos* of this statue, it is said that the princess, seeing Canova hesitate when she proposed that she should herself pose for him, cried, "Why not? What are you afraid of?"

"Of falling in love with my statue," was the reply.

"You're a silly flatterer, Canova," she laughed.

Later, a lady asking her how she could have brought herself to pose quite naked, Pauline replied, "Oh, there was a fire in the studio!"

★★★★★★★★★★

Berthier, Prince of Neufchatel and of Wagram

As the emperor wished that the members of his family should keep up their position in a suitable manner, Pauline received once a week. But she did not know how to receive; of the three sisters of Napoleon, she was the worst in this respect. Yet how could it be otherwise? Thinking only of herself, her beauty, and her own amusement, she neglected her guests, especially the ladies; and being ignorant, she had no conversation, an occasional *bon mot*, a lively retort, some affected efforts to please, and that was all. However, her *salon*, by reason of the people she entertained rather than owing to her amiability, was not a disagreeable rendezvous.

She gave some very brilliant balls in Paris. The dancers were principally officers of the general staff and of the Imperial Guard. Among those who especially attracted the notice of the princess was M. Jules de Canouville, "one of the *beaux* of the army," (Général de Marbot, *Mémoires*), attached to the staff of Marshal Berthier. At this epoch one lived so fast and the officers passed so little of their time far from the battlefield that no time was wasted in commencing an intrigue.

This new *liaison* of the Princess Pauline was of all—and she had many—the one that lasted the longest. (Thiébault, *Mémoires*.) She was so destitute of the moral sense that she did not even seek to hide her weakness. Her lover was equally indiscreet. Both of them talked openly of their passion, and *tout* Paris soon followed their example. Each day some new scandal was reported of the beautiful sinner, and the one that was the most *risqué* was, as ever is the case, the one most appreciated. The following had an immense success.

Bousquet, the fashionable dentist, was sent for by the princess to examine her teeth. He hastened to obey her summons, and on arriving was shown into a room where he found Pauline in a charming dressing-gown, while a handsome young man, lazily stretched on a sofa, was contemplating her with a languishing air. Her Highness explained to the dentist, who listened to her respectfully, the nature of her dental ailment, and was opening her pretty mouth, which did not seem to require the least service of the practitioner, when the young man on the sofa let fall these words:—

"Pray take care, *monsieur*, what you are about. I am extremely fond of my Paulette's teeth, and I shall hold you responsible for any accident to them."

"Make yourself easy, sir," replied the dentist; "I can assure Your Imperial Highness that everything will be all right."

And he set himself to his task. Whilst he scraped the princess's teeth with a care that was almost religious, the young man made his observations in a tone of the utmost solicitude. The dentist continued to reassure him to the best of his ability, and having finished his work withdrew. As he crossed one of the antechambers, some of the ladies-in-waiting asked him how Her Highness had borne the operation.

"Her Imperial Highness supported it excellently," he replied, "and she should be very proud of the devotion of her august husband, who has just manifested it to me in the most touching fashion. In truth, it is a pleasure to see a home so united and great folk set an example not only of beautiful teeth but of conjugal virtue. Fancy, His Imperial Highness was so anxious about the princess's teeth that he never ceased to make all sorts of observations to me. No, truly, I am touched, deeply touched, and I shall make a point of letting everybody know what a tender scene of domestic attachment I have just assisted at." (Duchesse d'Abrantès.)

No one had the heart to deceive the excellent dentist and tell him that Prince Borghèse was at Turin, and that the young man whose conjugal anxiety was so edifying was Captain de Canouville. But the same evening *tout* Paris was convulsed by the recital of the adventure.

Napoleon did not look with a favourable eye on the young officers on the staff of the Prince of Neufchatel, whom he knew were likewise on that of the Princess Borghèse. (Thiébault.) Besides Captain Jules de Canouville, there were M. Achille de Septeuil, M. Sopranzi, M. de Flahaut, M. Fritz de Pourtalès, M. Alexandre de Girardin, &c. The emperor, who was not certain which of them was the special favourite of Pauline, was informed by the following incident.

During the festivities to celebrate the famous interview at Erfurth between the Emperor Alexander and Napoleon, the latter had given His Russian Majesty a superb silver-gilt dressing-case, a compliment which Alexander repaid by sending the French Emperor three fur cloaks of inestimable value, for it was impossible to procure the sables of which they were made at any price, since they were a tribute of the Samoyedes to the *Czar* that they had not the right to sell. Napoleon, in his turn, had himself made a present of one of these furs to his sister Pauline, who appeared to him capable of appreciating it. The second he gave to Madame Bernadotte, Princess of Ponte-Corvo, and he kept the third himself.

But one day Canouville, after having recited some pretty verses to his mistress which he had composed, and which alma had taught him to declaim properly, happened to mention that he had got a new hussar's uniform, when Pauline exclaimed—

"I have an idea! You shall have the Emperor Alexander's sable. It's the very thing for your *pelisse!*"

Canouville protested, but consented in the end. The fur was immediately cut into strips and sent to the tailor.

A few days later the emperor held a great review in the court of the Tuileries. Captain Canouville wore his new uniform, and looked very handsome in his *pelisse* trimmed with the precious fur and its diamond buttons, which were also a present from Pauline. He rode a very fine but restive English horse. At a certain moment, when the emperor was surrounded by his staff, Canouville's horse began to back till, in spite of all the rider could do, it backed into the Imperial *entourage*. Canouville could have killed it on the spot, as Marshal Oudinot did his one day at a similar review; but this would only have attracted Napoleon's attention to him the more, which was what he wished above everything to avoid. So, he continued to struggle with the cursed beast, till it finally backed into the horse of the emperor himself!

"Who is that officer?" cried Napoleon furiously.

Whilst Berthier advanced to reply, the emperor with his eagle eye noticed the sable that he had given to Pauline—there was none other like it in Paris—and the diamond buttons that he had also given his sister in Italy. After the review he took the Prince of Neufchâtel aside.

"What are all these giddy fellows that you are surrounded with doing here?" he said. "Why are they not at the front? What does this idleness mean when somewhere or other cannon are always rumbling? I can't understand you, Berthier. You always have to be told a thing before you perceive it."

Berthier bit his nails and said nothing.

"Well," continued the emperor, "let M. de Canouville leave this evening for Spain. There should be some dispatches for the Prince of Essling; it is he who shall take them."

The journey to Spain became from this moment "a sort of ostracism inflicted on gallants when the intrigues of the virtuous princesses of the blood and the great ladies of the court made too much noise." (Duc de Broglie, *Souvenirs.*)

During Canouville's absence, which was not so very long, the Princess Borghèse being bored as usual, sought other distractions. Scarcely had her lover departed than she wanted another. So, she gave a hint to Captain Achille de Septeuil, a young, good-looking fellow, that she liked him. It is certainly flattering to be noticed by the prettiest woman of her day, particularly when she is a princess, and vanity takes as much pleasure in such a thought as in any other. Pauline, who till now had ever been victorious in her affairs of the heart, never imagined she could suffer defeat. This, however, now happened to her. M. de Septeuil's heart was not free; he was in love with someone else. He did not consider an infidelity with the same tranquillity as women in general and the Princess Pauline in particular. To her intense astonishment, then, he let her understand as respectfully as possible that she could flutter elsewhere.

At the same time Canouville returned to Paris, but scarcely had he arrived at the War Office than he was given fresh dispatches for the Prince of Essling. So, he was obliged to mount his horse again and return at once to Spain. But this time he did not travel alone. For companion he had poor Septeuil. Strange irony of fate! The one was exiled for having responded to the advances of Her Imperial Highness, the other for having refused to respond to them. (Duchesse d'Abrantès.)

This campaign was destined to be unfortunate for Septeuil. At the Battle of Fuentes d'Oñoro his leg was broken by a cannon-ball. "It was necessary," said General de Marbot, (*Mémoires*.) "to amputate it on the field of battle. He endured this terrible operation with courage, and is still living."

As for Canouville, after having made the disciplinary journey to Spain four times he was sent to Russia, and had his head blown off by a cannon-ball at the battle of Smolensk, according to the Duchesse d'Abrantès, or at the Battle of Moscow according to Marbot. Constant declares (*Mémoires*), that this brave officer was killed by a ball from a French cannon that was fired after an action in which he had displayed the most brilliant courage.

10

The bath was regarded by the Princess Borghèse as an institution of great importance. She was in the habit of taking the cure at one of the fashionable *villes d'eaux* every year, and she always had her bath every day. On passing through Bar-sur-Ornain, the principal place in the Department of the Meuse, on her way to Aix-la-Chapelle, Her Imperial Highness sent a messenger in her livery to inform the *prefect* of her arrival. The *prefect* was M. Leclerc, a brother of the princess's first husband, General Leclerc. The messenger having delivered his message, added that he had been ordered by Her Highness to request the *prefect* to have a bath of milk and a *douche* of the same liquid ready, so that the princess might take it as soon as she arrived, before breakfasting. A strange manner, one would think, of getting up an appetite!

The *prefect*, who was on the most friendly terms with his sister-in-law, at once had all the cows in the department milked. When the cracking of whips and tinkling of bells announced the arrival of the pretty, capricious, spoilt child, the *prefect* hastened to help her alight.

"Carry me, as you used to do, dear brother; I can't possibly walk by myself," said Pauline coaxingly.

The *prefect* did not wait to be asked twice, and taking her in his arms, carried her up the stairs and placed her on a sofa in the best room of the *prefecture*.

"And now my bath," she prattled, "is it ready? And my *douche*?"

"Ah," he replied, "the latter is another matter, there is no apparatus."

"On the contrary, it is quite simple," she rejoined. 'Have a hole pierced in the ceiling above the bath in this very room, which will be just as convenient for me as another, and from the floor above I can have my *douche*. I am afraid I am causing you a lot of trouble, dear brother, but it is necessary for my health."

One would have thought that she had completely forgotten the time when she lived on the charity of the municipality of Marseilles.

The *prefect*, however, surpassed himself in his zeal to satisfy the bizarre caprice of his former sister-in-law. The smiles of the princess were his thanks; but imagine the confusion into which the quiet *prefecture* was thrown by the milky freaks of the lovely traveller! And what a big hole in the ceiling! "As a result," says the Maréchale Oudinot, who relates this episode, "numerous splashes of milk curdled on the furniture and for a long time made the room smell like a badly kept dairy." (Duchesse de Reggio, *Récits de guerre et de foyer*.)

A few months later, after her return from Aix-la-Chapelle, the Princess Borghèse had one of the greatest pleasures of her life. This was to see the emperor finally decide to *unmarry* himself. She had always urged him to get divorced, and now it took place. She was so happy on the day of this ceremony that she was less remarked for the beauty of her dress than for the little care she took to control her feelings.

A triumphant joy was painted all over her face in a manner that contrasted with the gravity of the great historical event that was taking place. But Pauline only saw the fall and effacement of her whom she had hated since 1797. She was radiant, and she wished Josephine to know it!

During the marriage ceremony of the Emperor and the Archduchess Marie Louise all the members of the Imperial Family had a role to fill. That of Pauline consisted in carrying, with her sisters and sisters-in-law, the Queens of Westphalia and Holland, the train of the new Empress. Pauline also gave a superb *fête* at her seat at Neuilly in honour of the marriage. She was then in all the *éclat* of her beauty; there was only one voice as to it, and that was a cry of admiration. Rarely was she so delighted with her success and the praise she heard on all sides. But Stanislas Girardin, who was present, could not help making the following grave and just reflections:—

> This *fête*, where money was of so little account, was very unpopular, and one cannot prevent oneself from reflecting sadly when one thinks that the yearly revenue of several provinces was wasted in a few hours. Such extravagance is the tribute the court levies on its vanity and is a step towards ruin. Experience teaches but never corrects.

The excessive splendour of this entertainment also caused Napoleon to reflect. Perceiving that the effect on the people of Paris would not be good, he thought to make it so, says Girardin, by ordering Pauline to give another *fête* two days later, when five thousand people of all ranks should be invited. The invitations were distributed by the municipality, which caused the *bourgeois* to say, "The court has sent us the leavings." For this Tivoli where one entered free had no success, as might have been expected. The private apartments of the palace were closed and everything seemed to say, as before the Revolution, "It is good enough for the *canaille*." (*Journal de Maréchal de Castellane*.)

The scandalous conduct of his sisters, particularly of Pauline, was one of the causes, and far more powerful than one thinks, of the disaffection of the masses for Napoleon. The people are honest and indignant at weaknesses at which the world only smiles, and which certain historians pass over complacently in silence when they do not cite them as traits.

The winter of 1811-12 was not as brilliant at Paris as previous ones. The harvests had been bad, and the political horizon was darkened by threatening clouds. The war with Spain, which devoured men by thousands, was a terrible sore in the nation's side and a heavy chain on Napoleon's feet. A general uneasiness was apparent, which the excessive luxury of the court and the high civil and military authorities scarcely concealed. These symptoms, however, of an approaching crisis did not disturb Pauline. Taken up, as ever, with her medicines and her follies, she did not notice them. At a ball she gave on January 17, 1811, dress-coats were seen in Paris for the first time.

With the year 1814 the Empire began to go to pieces.

Pauline, who had passed the winter partly at Nice and partly at Hyères, was living, in the month of April, in a villa situated at Luc. She was only acquainted with a few of the great events that had just taken place; even the abdication of the emperor was unknown to her, when on the 26th April a messenger arrived, about two in the afternoon, to tell her that he would soon pass through Luc. In fact, a carriage shortly afterwards stopped at her door; it was the carriage of the Commissioners of the Allies, who informed the princess of the events which had just overwhelmed France and hurled Napoleon from the throne.

Pauline could not believe what she was told; at last, when it was impossible to continue to doubt, she fancied that her brother had been killed in the midst of these disturbances and that the news was being kept from her, or that she was being prepared to receive it.

"If the Empire is no more," she said, "my brother, then, is dead!"

They tried to convince her of the contrary, and the unhappy woman, in a transport of anguish, exclaimed:—

"But how could he survive it all?"

Then the tears began to flow, and the excitement brought on a fainting attack. When she recovered, she heard the cries of hate and fury of a ferocious mob under her windows!

It was in the midst of these cries of "Down with the tyrant!" "Down with Nicolas!" which she heard as she lay in her bed with only Madame de Saluces and M. de Montbreton for protection, that Napoleon alighted from his carriage at the door of the princess.

★★★★★★★★★★

At the time a pamphlet was being sold all over France, entitled *Histoire véritable et lamentable de Nicolas Bonaparte, Corse de naissance, dit Napoléon le Grand,* and the name of Nicolas had become very popular with the enemies of the emperor, who no longer called him anything else,

★★★★★★★★★★

The news she had just heard had been a terrible blow to Pauline, and she had taken to her bed. She wished to rise to receive her brother, but her strength was unequal to the effort, so M. de Montbreton received him for her. The chamberlain did not recognise him at first. The emperor was wearing an Austrian uniform to escape the fury of the people, who had at last risen against him.

"The wretches would like to kill me," he said, "I have been obliged to assume this disguise to escape them."

The chamberlain ushered him into Pauline's room, who, recognising the voice of her brother, stretched out her arms to him. But noticing the Austrian uniform, she dropped them.

"I cannot kiss you in that," she said; then added in a heartbroken voice, "Oh, Napoleon, what have you done?"

The emperor withdrew into an adjoining room, and having changed into other clothes, came back to his sister. In the meantime, Pauline had risen, and she greeted Napoleon tenderly and tearfully. The emperor was also moved, and those who witnessed this interview were deeply touched by it.

Pauline kept the emperor a day and a half at her villa, and when the hour came for the "Man of Destiny" to go into exile, she proposed to accompany him, declaring that she was ready to depart instantly for Elba.

She went the same night to Muy, in order to have only a few leagues to travel the next day in going to Fréjus. But she did not accompany the Emperor to Elba; he would not hear of it. She went there once, however, on the 1st June, to carry him an urgent dispatch from Murat, but only stayed a day in the island. She returned again two months later. Her mother had been for some time living with Napoleon. Pauline occupied a house on a cliff overlooking the little town of Porto-Ferrajo.

After Napoleon's departure from Elba, Pauline set out for Rome, but she stopped at Viareggio, between Pisa and Lucca, where she rented a house in the suburbs. She wished to remain there in order to take the baths at Lucca, as she had done for several seasons with beneficial results. But finding herself recognised and watched, she quickly escaped this espionage and came to Paris,

In the straits in which Napoleon found himself the princess, giddy and frivolous though she was, nevertheless proved that she was not altogether devoid of heart. To assist her brother, she placed at his disposal a part of her fortune and her diamonds. It was but a natural act that has been lauded too much, but history should all the same record it to her credit; for kindness, generosity, gratitude are so rare in this world that one should not miss the pleasure of acknowledging them when met with. In thus assisting Napoleon with her resources, in despoiling herself of her diamonds for him—she who loved them so much!—Pauline did her duty.

It is, perhaps, the sole time she ever did it, but once again, we repeat, it was to her credit, and her conduct during this unhappy period almost makes one forget her misconduct during her years of prosperity. What a difference in this respect between her and Elisa and Caroline! Napoleon accepted Pauline's sacrifice, but the carriage which contained her diamonds was captured by the English after the Battle of Waterloo, and these jewels were exposed in London to the curiosity of the public.

11

When the news of the defeat of Waterloo reached Paris, Cardinal Fesch, foreseeing difficulties without number which the fallen family of Bonaparte would have to face, wrote to his niece Pauline to urge her to face the situation bravely and to avoid foolish expenditure.

"You should," he wrote to her, "practise the greatest economy. In the situation in which we now find ourselves we are all poor, even with what remains from last year." Lucien, he added, was of the opinion that the whole family should cross the ocean with Napoleon and settle in the United States. This resolution he did, in fact, take, as the following letter to Pauline proves:—

Neuilly, June 26, 1815.

You must have heard of the new misfortune of the emperor, who has just abdicated in favour of his son. He is going to the United States, where we shall all join him. He is calm and full of courage. I shall try to join my family in Rome, in order to take them to America. If your health permits, we shall meet there. *Adieu*, dear sister. Mamma, Joseph, Jerome and I all send you love.

Your affectionate brother,

Lucien.

(*Mémoires de la Générale Duran.*)

He did not, however, act on this resolution, and Joseph alone went to America.

Cardinal Fesch returned to Rome, where he rented the Palazzo Falconieri for his sister, Madame Mére, who shortly afterwards went to reside there. This palace, situated in the Via Julia, at the junction of

CARDINAL FESCH

the Corso and the Piazza Venezia, contained two suites of apartments. The cardinal reserved the second floor for himself, while the mother of Napoleon occupied the first and gave a home in it to her daughter Pauline, whose health was shattered by these last disasters.

Prince Borghèse withdrew to Florence.

It had finished, then, the dream in which Pauline had lived for twenty years. The unfortunate creature fell seriously ill, and to her great distress she could not even think of going to Saint Helena to mitigate by her presence the captivity of her brother. Besides, the English would not have given her permission. But "she endeavoured to sell everything she possessed of value in order to send the money to the great exile." (*Rapport de M. de Blacas*, April 1, 1817.)

When Napoleon, writing to his mother, begged her to find a cook who would be willing to go to Saint Helena, Pauline undertook the commission, and was not long in discovering a man named Chandelier, who accepted with joy the mission of going to cook for Napoleon. Pauline likewise wrote the following letter to Lord Liverpool, when early in July, 1821, the Abbé Buonavita, a Corsican priest returning from Saint Helena, came to Rome to inform Madame Mere of the desperate state of health of her illustrious son:—

Rome, July 11, 1821.

My Lord,

The Abbé Buonavita, arrived from the island of Saint Helena, which he left the 17th March last, has brought us the most alarming news of my brother's health. I enclose a copy of some letters which will give you the details of his physical suffering. His disease is fatal at Saint Helena. In the name of all the members of the family I implore that he may be allowed a change of climate. If our prayer is refused it will be his death sentence. . . . . (Héreau, *Napoléon a Sainte-Hélène.*)

Alas! it was too late; the fatal news was already on the way.

Dr. Antommarchi, having left Saint Helena after the emperor's death, went, as is well known, to deliver his last message to his wife, Marie Louise. He found her at the theatre. She had already forgotten and replaced her husband.

He then went to Rome and called on Louis, ex-King of Holland. He, it can scarcely be credited, would not receive him, giving as his excuse that he was too ill!

But Pauline, who was quite as ill as Louis, did not hesitate to receive the worthy Antommarchi when he called. She asked him a thousand questions about her brother, his sufferings, his last moments, and was so deeply affected by what Antommarchi told her of that long agony that her grief aggravated the bad state of her health.

Pauline was not without sensibility; unfortunately, she had not received any kind of moral training, and the germs of goodness that are observable in her had never been developed. Moreover, though she knew her "*Petrarch*" slightly, she had almost no education at all. It is to this lack of moral and intellectual culture that the countless inconsistencies that signalised her passage through life must be attributed. Her responsibility is, therefore, less great than that of Elisa, who was brought up at Saint-Cyr, or that of Caroline, who was a pupil of Madame Campan.

It seems that Madame Mère was more responsible than one has imagined, or has cared to say, for the frivolity of her daughters. She did not know how to instil into their minds the precepts of virtue, but left them to rush, like wild horses, across the pleasures and frivolities of life, without requiring of them any duty, or without teaching them respect for themselves and for the dignity of life. Although she has been greatly belauded, she was really unequal to the task of performing the duties of a mother. Did she ever encourage morality in her family? Did her children ever consult her in the great crises of their lives? Never, and they married without even consulting her. In such things is not a mother always more culpable than her children?

In the month of September, 1823, the Princess Pauline's health being worse, the doctors declared that the air of Rome was not good for her. She was removed, then, very carefully to her beautiful Villa Paolina, near the Porta Pia. But it was still Rome; the air of the open country or the sea would have been preferable.

A while later, when her health permitted, she was taken to Florence. There she languished between ups and downs, when a singular event gave her her death-blow. Some brigands, under a redoubtable chief named Decesaris, broke one night into the house of the Prince of Canino (Lucien Bonaparte) and carried off his old friend, the Comte de Chatillon, who had linked his fortune to his for twenty-five years. The brigands immediately sent to inform the prince that his friend would be at his disposal on the payment of a ransom. This Lucien paid, and Chatillon was restored to him.

This incident, which in the days of her prosperity would have diverted her, gave Pauline a severe nervous shock. From this time her health became worse daily, and on June 9, 1825, she who had been the "Queen of Folly" under the Consulate and the Empire, expired at Florence.

Prince Borghèse, at the request of Pope Leo XIL., whom Madame Mère had begged to intercede, decided to carry the poor sinner the pardon for her sins.

Pauline, however, feeling that the "hour of God," as Bossuet says, had struck, had a mirror brought to her and, like Nero, who when dying exclaimed "*Qualis artifex pereo!*" (What an artist the world loses in me!), said, looking at herself in the glass for the last time, she could die in peace, for she was still beautiful.

This was her consolation.

She entered eternity with a smile on her lips and a mirror in her hand!

![LEONAUR]

ALSO FROM LEONAUR
AVAILABLE IN SOFTCOVER OR HARDCOVER WITH DUST JACKET

THE WOMAN IN BATTLE by Loreta Janeta Velazquez—Soldier, Spy and Secret Service Agent for the Confederacy During the American Civil War.

BOOTS AND SADDLES by Elizabeth B. Custer—The experiences of General Custer's Wife on the Western Plains.

FANNIE BEERS' CIVIL WAR by Fannie A. Beers—A Confederate Lady's Experiences of Nursing During the Campaigns & Battles of the American Civil War.

LADY SALE'S AFGHANISTAN by Florentia Sale—An Indomitable Victorian Lady's Account of the Retreat from Kabul During the First Afghan War.

THE TWO WARS OF MRS DUBERLY by Frances Isabella Duberly—An Intrepid Victorian Lady's Experience of the Crimea and Indian Mutiny.

THE REBELLIOUS DUCHESS by Paul F. S. Dermoncourt—The Adventures of the Duchess of Berri and Her Attempt to Overthrow French Monarchy.

LADIES OF WATERLOO by Charlotte A. Eaton, Magdalene de Lancey & Juana Smith—The Experiences of Three Women During the Campaign of 1815: Waterloo Days by Charlotte A. Eaton, A Week at Waterloo by Magdalene de Lancey & Juana's Story by Juana Smith.

NURSE AND SPY IN THE UNION ARMY by Sarah Emma Evelyn Edmonds—During the American Civil War

WIFE NO. 19 by Ann Eliza Young—The Life & Ordeals of a Mormon Woman During the 19th Century

DIARY OF A NURSE IN SOUTH AFRICA by Alice Bron—With the Dutch-Belgian Red Cross During the Boer War

MARIE ANTOINETTE AND THE DOWNFALL OF ROYALTY by Imbert de Saint-Amand—The Queen of France and the French Revolution

THE MEMSAHIB & THE MUTINY by R. M. Coopland—An English lady's ordeals in Gwalior and Agra duringthe Indian Mutiny 1857

MY CAPTIVITY AMONG THE SIOUX INDIANS by Fanny Kelly—The ordeal of a pioneer woman crossing the Western Plains in 1864

WITH MAXIMILIAN IN MEXICO by Sara Yorke Stevenson—A Lady's experience of the French Adventure

.